THE WORK AND LIVES OF TEACHERS

The Work and Lives of Teachers offers a simple but original argument: that the cultural attitudes toward the teaching profession measurably influence how students perform. Cohen uses both ethnographic portraits and personal accounts from thirteen teachers – from Finland, Taiwan, Greece, Azerbaijan, France, Chile, South Africa, Siberia, Brazil, Romania, Philippines, Norway, and the United States – to explore the meaning and value of teaching worldwide. This study includes the ways in which teachers in these countries are educated, recruited, compensated, and perceived by parents, students, administrators, and the culture at large. Teachers' voices, so rarely heard in international educational studies, are front and center here, highlighting the daily work in the classroom and the pleasures and struggles of engaging in the teaching profession in 2016. The lesson, briefly stated, is that societies are only as good as the people who teach in them.

Rosetta Marantz Cohen is a professor in the Department of Education and Child Study at Smith College, where she holds the Sylvia Dluglasch Bauman Chair in American Studies. She serves as Director of the Kahn Liberal Arts Institute at Smith and Director of the Smith College Internship Program at the Smithsonian Museum.

The Work and Lives of Teachers

A GLOBAL PERSPECTIVE

Rosetta Marantz Cohen

Smith College

CAMBRIDGE
UNIVERSITY PRESS

CAMBRIDGE
UNIVERSITY PRESS

One Liberty Plaza, 20th Floor, New York, NY 10006, USA

Cambridge University Press is part of the University of Cambridge.

It furthers the University's mission by disseminating knowledge in the pursuit of education, learning, and research at the highest international levels of excellence.

www.cambridge.org
Information on this title: www.cambridge.org/9781316501634

© Rosetta Marantz Cohen 2017

First published 2017

Printed in the United Kingdom by Clays, St Ives plc

A catalogue record for this publication is available from the British Library.

Library of Congress Cataloging-in-Publication Data
NAMES: Cohen, Rosetta Marantz, author.
TITLE: The work and lives of teachers : a global perspective / Rosetta Marantz Cohen.
DESCRIPTION: New York, NY : Cambridge University Press, 2017. | Includes bibliographical references and index.
IDENTIFIERS: LCCN 2016035550| ISBN 9781107135741 (hardback) | ISBN 9781316501634 (paperback)
SUBJECTS: LCSH: Teachers–Cross-cultural studies. | Teaching–Cross-cultural studies. | BISAC: PSYCHOLOGY / General.
CLASSIFICATION: LCC LB1775 .C723 2017 | DDC 371.102–DC23 LC record available at https://lccn.loc.gov/2016035550

ISBN 978-1-107-13574-1 Hardback
ISBN 978-1-316-50163-4 Paperback

For Ruth, Samuel and Elizabeth
Great teachers: past, present, and future

Contents

Acknowledgments .... *page* ix

Introduction: The Work and Lives of Teachers 1

1 Finland: Autonomy and Respect 17

2 Taiwan: Tradition and Change 40

3 Greece: A Week of Austerity 57

4 Azerbaijan: Teaching in the Shadow of War 75

5 France: Defending Rigor 97

6 Chile: Revolution and Resignation 122

7 The United States: Diversity and a Passion for Leadership 141

8 Conclusion: The Teacher in Comparative Perspective 163

9 Teachers in Their Own Words 188

Notes 217

Index 227

Acknowledgments

I am indebted to many people in helping me develop and shape these portraits. Colleagues, family, and friends read or heard presentations on these chapters, offering advice and encouragement. Thank you especially to Carrie McGee, Craig Murphy, Nate Berry, Patti Lessard, Christie George, Sujane Wu, Janie Vanpee, Carl Geupal, Sam Intrator, Aachal Khanna, Ahalya Raman, Fran Fahey, Ann Cleaveland, Paula Marantz Cohen, and to the editorial and production staff, David Repetto, Ezhilmaran Sugumaran, and Stephanie Sakson. I am also deeply grateful to Smith College for providing research funds and for nurturing my development as a scholar and teacher for more than twenty-five years.

The book would not have been possible without the assistance of the Institute for Training and Development in Amherst, Massachusetts, and especially its wonderful co-executive director, Julie Hooks, who first introduced me to several of these teachers and who accompanied me on my trip to Azerbaijan. I am indebted to Julie for her unflagging support throughout the project and for the friendship that has emerged from it.

Sam Scheer, husband and teacher extraordinaire, is at the heart of this book. Sam's insights about teachers and teaching formed the basis for the book's thesis. Indeed, everything I have ever written about education has been improved and sharpened by his keen editorial eye and his ability to wisely reflect on the profession and his own work in the classroom.

Finally, and most of all, I am grateful to the teachers profiled here. I am thankful to them for letting me into their classrooms and their private lives, for tolerating, at every turn, my e-mails and requests. In every case, the subjects of these chapters co-developed their profiles alongside me, reading and critiquing first the transcripts of their lengthy interviews and, second, the first drafts of my portraits. Portraiture is a wonderful but tricky enterprise. The portraitist sees things necessarily through the filter of her

own life and experience, and the subject – if she is to be involved throughout the process – must ultimately accept that subjectivity, correcting
blatant misapprehension while tolerating the ethnographer's idiosyncratic
eye. I am deeply grateful to Annukka, Feng-juan, Vasso, Gulnaz, Laurence,
Mauricio, and Bonnie for their time, enthusiasm, and generosity throughout this process.

Introduction: The Work and Lives of Teachers

One teacher works with 40 students a day, another with 150. One stands austerely on a raised platform in an unadorned cinderblock room. Another weaves around a brightly decorated classroom, laughing and chatting with small clusters of students. One teacher saves up her meager salary for months to replace a broken washing machine. Another spends weekends in her second home and collects shoes. Across the globe, being a teacher means very different things: poverty or affluence, low status or prestige.

At the same time that these vast differences exist, rhetoric about education and reform, in the United States and around the world, hardly takes the working and living conditions of teachers into account. Policy-makers, corporations, politicians, and curriculum reformers focus on everything but how the reforms they propose will affect the viability of the profession, its appeal to the best and brightest. Today, charter schools, standardized testing, and accountability are the catch-phrases for reform. Thirty years ago, it was site-based management and essential skills. In the neo-progressive 1970s, the answer to failing schools meant an open curriculum and elective choice for students. Two decades before that, it meant back-to-basics and intelligence testing. In whatever era one looks, the one variable that would make the most difference is the one that is consistently overlooked: the teacher, her attitudes about herself, and her place in the larger culture.

Some years ago, I collaborated with my husband, Sam, a veteran urban high school teacher, on a book about school reform entitled *Teacher-Centered Schools: Reimagining Educational Reform in the 21st Century.*[1] The book was predicated on a commonsense thesis: if America is really interested in reforming and improving its schools, it needs to attract a talented workforce and, even more important, retain those teachers over the course of a career. There is an extraordinary body of evidence, both qualitative and quantitative, showing that great teachers change lives. Even accounting for parental income and differences in cultural privilege, the number one factor in improving student achievement on any measure of success – including standardized test scores – has been continuously shown to be the intellectual skill and preparation of the teacher.[2] In that earlier study, we argued that to truly transform society, America needs to make the work of teaching so desirable that every brilliant, creative, and idealistic young person graduating from college will automatically gravitate to that profession, considering teaching as a first choice – not a last-ditch fallback when other options fail. And in order to attract the very best and brightest into the field, and retain them over time, schools need to rethink their priorities, to focus their energies and support not only on the students but on the teachers. If we could build a system that afforded professional prestige and prioritized the needs of teachers – many of whom, if we are lucky, will remain in that system for thirty years or more – we will have found the most effective way for saving failing schools.

This book tests that theory in a global and comparative way. For the last three years, I have been looking at how teachers around the world perceive their profession and their place in the culture. What is the state of teacher prestige internationally? Do teachers around the globe see themselves as American teachers do? Are their complaints the same? Are their views about the meaning and value of their work the same? And what are the implications of those teacher attitudes for the twenty-first century world? I try to answer those questions here by tracing the experience of teaching in seven different cultures, documenting that work through the eyes and words of individual practitioners.

A HISTORY OF SECOND-CLASS STATUS

To understand the changes that are taking place in the profession around the world, it is useful to begin at home. The history of the teaching profession in the United States offers interesting parallels to evolving attitudes in other countries. Teaching in America is not a high-status occupation, and it has never been one. Since the very first years of European presence in the New World, the teacher's place in the community was always secondary at best. Historians have ample, concrete evidence of this. We know, for example, that teachers in the seventeenth century were assigned the duty of sitting up with the dead, sweeping out the church, and other tasks that were eschewed by clergy. Records show that early teachers were often paid in grain or, if a community decided they were dissatisfied with the outcomes of their children's education, they were simply not paid at all.

In the earliest years of the Republic, when grammar school teachers were mostly men, popular stereotypes emerged of teachers as brutal and incompetent, effete or effeminate. Depictions found in the memoirs of people such as Bronson Alcott and in short stories by Washington Irving and Philip Freneau show teachers as superstitious, dim-witted, and obsessed with their meager salaries. Sadistic and bullying, these characters are often depicted as having entered the profession under duress, remaining in it on sufferance and exiting as soon as something better came along. One particularly vivid example of this vision can be found in the work of the eighteenth-century scholar and poet John Trumbull, who documents the making of a new teacher in a poetic satire aptly entitled, "The Rare Adventures of Tom Brainless." After charting the progress of his moronic teacher protagonist through Harvard, where he sleeps and cheats his way to a diploma, Trumbull presents us with a portrait of the teaching candidate:

> Few months now past, he sees with pain
> His purse as empty as his brain
> His father leaves him then to fate
> And throws him off as useless weight:
> But gives him good advice: TO TEACH
> A school at first ... and then to preach.[3]

Teaching, in short, was depicted as the default profession for fools and scoundrels. Indeed, for ordinary Americans in the early nineteenth century – farmers and cattle-rangers, millworkers and miners – deep biases existed against those who did not engage in manual labor. Teachers were seen as idlers, individuals who were too frightened or lazy to engage with the "real world."

This stereotype of the disengaged teacher changed with the feminization of the profession, a shift that began with the rise of the common schools in the early nineteenth century, and then quickly became endemic by the 1870s. An exploding population, combined with new mandates for universal public education, created massive teacher shortages. In an effort to fill classrooms, reformers such as Horace Mann and James Carter argued to initially resistant communities that women were actually superior candidates for teaching positions. Unlike men, women were naturally modest, self-sacrificing, and subordinate. Women could be paid little without complaint. Women's piety and self-abnegation, they argued, would serve a Christian nation in ways that could only be healthful to the moral development of children. The feminization campaign was presented as a win-win prospect: hire women for the moral uplift of your community and save money in the process. Mann and Carter proved to be fantastically successful: at the start of the nineteenth century, roughly one in ten teachers was a woman. By the first decade of the twentieth century, almost 90 percent were women.[4] Teaching became a "calling" – a term not found in eighteenth-century descriptions of the profession but pervasive in popular magazines, newspapers, and novels by the second decade of the nineteenth century.

This yoking of teaching with self-effacement and service can be found in the earliest writings addressed to female teachers, often, ironically, from other women. It reaches its nineteenth-century apotheosis in Catherine Beecher's famous 1846 injunction to educated women to abandon the idleness of class privilege and devote themselves to the service of children. In her address entitled "Evils Suffered by American Women and American Children: The Causes and the Remedy," Beecher lays out a scenario for the feminization of the American teaching force that formally cast the work in explicitly religious terms:

> The plan is to take women already qualified intellectually to teach, and possessed of missionary zeal and benevolence, and to send them to the most ignorant portions of our land, to raise up schools, to instruct in morals and piety, and to teach the domestic arts and virtues . . .

Beecher had an almost messianic view of the profession. She goes on to imagine the teacher in her Western home as follows:

> If our success equals out hope, soon in all parts of our country . . . the Christian female teacher will quietly take her station, collecting the ignorant children around her, teaching them habits of neatness, order and thrift, opening the book of knowledge, inspiring the principles of morality, and awakening the hope of immortality. Soon her influence in the village will create a demand for new landowners, and then she will summon from among her friends at home, the nurse, the seamstress, and these will prove her auxiliaries in the good moral influences, and in Sabbath school training.[5]

Feminization, then, allowed for service and sacrifice to become the prevailing metaphor of the work, and by the early twentieth century, the cult of service was deeply embedded in public consciousness about the profession. Indeed, the earliest comprehensive sociology of the profession, published in 1932 by Barnard professor Willard Waller, shows how successful that campaign had become by the twentieth century. In this early ethnography of teaching, Waller described a job where the concept of professional service has devolved into servitude or even slavery. A teacher's contract, reproduced in Waller's volume, documents a level of community control that is almost impossible to believe:

> I promise to take a vital interest in all phases of Sunday-school work, donating of my time, service, and money without stint for the uplift and benefit of the community.
>
> I promise to abstain from all dancing, immodest dressing, and any other conduct unbecoming a teacher and a lady.
>
> I promise not to go out with any young men except in so far as it may be necessary to stimulate Sunday-school work.
>
> I promise not to fall in love, to become engaged or secretly married.
>
> I promise not to encourage or tolerate the least familiarity on the part of any of my boy pupils.
>
> I promise to sleep at least eight hours a night, to eat carefully, and to take every precaution to keep in the best of health and spirits, in order that I may be better able to render efficient service to my pupils.
>
> I promise to remember that I own a duty to the townspeople who are paying me my wages, that I owe respect to the school board and superintendent that hired me, and that I shall consider myself at all times the willing servant of the school board and townspeople.[6]

"Women teachers," Waller concluded, "are our Vestal Virgins."

A GLOBAL PERSPECTIVE ON THE PROFESSION

In considering the history of the profession outside the United States, however, the story is very different. Globally, the work of teaching has been historically both prestigious and desirable. In Europe, Asia, and the Middle East, teachers were traditionally drawn from the educated elite, a status that drew veneration, not contempt. Countries such as China and Japan are built on cultural norms that venerate teachers and see their role as crucial to civilized order. A Chinese friend told me that from early childhood, he heard repeated the ancient mantra: "A teacher for a day is a father for a lifetime." China's most famous professional teacher was Confucius, the first to call for the education of the masses, to focus his teaching on "how to be good," on self-improvement and ethical living. Chinese still point to Confucius as a symbol of the profession and its link to ethical and spiritual principles. In the Islamic world, teaching has its own extraordinary history, a celebration of secular wisdom that dates back to the ninth century where teachers in the House of Wisdom in Baghdad taught subjects ranging from agriculture to medicine, philosophy to mathematics. Even in Europe, where the earliest teachers were linked to the Church, the profession was held in the highest of repute. Literacy and scholarship were seen as precious currency. Again, while teachers were not wealthy, they were among the most respected people in society. Teachers were among the elite, an attitude about the profession that persisted in many European countries throughout much of the twentieth century. In Soviet Bloc countries such as Poland and Romania, the rise of Communism did not dampen that historical respect; rather, it served to nurture it. As the instrument for socialization and indoctrination, the role of the teacher in Communist countries was critically important, carrying a kind of immovable authority. Impoverished countries in Africa turned to their teachers as symbols of hope. Any chance of future prosperity resided in the teacher and the tangible value of knowledge so closely associated with teachers.

Starting in the late twentieth century, that sense of the specialness of the teacher seems to have quickly eroded, spurred on by economic changes, globalization, and the Americanization of international cultures. As a researcher, I had begun to see evidence of this change by chance, through an earlier comparative project. In 2006, I began gathering classroom teacher narratives – lengthy personal stories – from veteran high school teachers all over the world. I was teaching a course on qualitative research in education and had gone looking for cases and examples beyond the American-based materials I had on hand. A local nongovernmental organization (NGO), the Institute for Training and Development (ITD), offered an ideal cohort for collecting and developing those materials. Each year, ITD had been bringing twenty to thirty English teachers from around the world to participate in a six-week summer program, where they learned about American culture through lectures and discussions, and then embarked on a mind-bending trip through the American West. Articulate and deeply engaged in their profession, the teachers who participated in these summer programs came from developed Western countries such as France and Germany, but also from some of the most remote places on earth. I began to gather personal essays from anyone in the groups who cared to participate, asking these international teachers to simply document their daily experiences in the classroom and to speak about how their work had changed over time. I was astounded by the descriptions that emerged. A teacher from Togo, in the South Pacific, described his community as so destitute that students took their lessons sitting in trees. A teacher from Tipo Tipo in the Philippines said that constant tribal warfare posed a daily threat to her life. There were also teachers from

Eastern Europe who had lived through the dramatic cultural transformations of the last generation, describing their impact on schools in a way
that was fascinating and sad at the same time. Teachers from Ghana,
Nigeria, and other African countries described how their careers have
spanned extraordinary economic and political changes. Indeed, virtually
all the teachers who contributed narratives to the project had seen the
nature of their work dramatically change. The general consensus was that
teaching had become an increasingly undesirable profession. The basis of
the status shift seems to derive from different sources, but for those
teachers working in emerging or developing countries, the change was
universally perceived as a transition to Western values – values that are
defined as "anti-intellectual" and "relativist." There were dozens of
examples of this perspective in the essays. Anya, an English teacher from
Poland for example, wrote bitterly:

> The reverence for learning has been replaced with the West's obsession
> with a quick buck. While it is still true, according to the Polish values,
> that one should not consider the financial aspect of a [career], this is
> changed in practice now after the communist system collapsed. Bright
> and resourceful teachers, once quite certain about their teaching voca-
> tion, leave schools after a couple of years, seizing the opportunity for . . .
> a better life. Schools attract those who have been losing everywhere else.

In most every narrative, the same complaints emerged again and again.
Jeanette, a black teacher from South Africa whose essay is included in the
volume, sees the shift in status happening – ironically – after apartheid. As
a young teacher in an all-black school in 1991, Jeanette remembers feeling
as if she was a respected professional. Though pay was low, teachers were
venerated as examples of those who had "made it" in a segregated society
where poverty was the norm. Now, as an administrator charged with
developing curriculum in an integrated system, she sees the erosion of
status among both black and white teachers. Alphonse, a teacher from the
Democratic Republic of Congo (DRC), wrote about his experiences over
the course of a thirty-year career. His powerful description of life in the
classroom presents a dark picture of the profession that has less to do with
inadequate resources and more to do with shifting attitudes:

> It is important to note that from the 1960s to the 1980s, the teaching
> profession was characterized by social, cultural, and intellectual prestige
> in the DRC. An English teacher was well paid. The work was a high-
> status occupation in a country where few were educated. Teaching a
> foreign and international language like English was considered to be an

extraordinary accomplishment for a person in a country where the rate of illiteracy was higher than 70 percent. English teachers could easily travel to English speaking countries on diplomatic and cultural/educational missions.

Starting in the early eighties, however, the conditions of teaching began to deteriorate along with the social status afforded to teachers. This occurred because of growing corruption, immorality, and general ill-governance on the part of those charged with managing the educational system. As foreigners left, conditions worsened, resources were worn out and not replaced, and curricula languished. Sadly, but unsurprisingly, the systematic deterioration of the schools has left its mark on those who remained in the field.

Today, the Congolese teacher's attitude toward his profession is generally that of dread, deceit, and shame. Although the teacher training period ranges from three to five years in a higher education institution, a trained teacher's salary is generally extremely low. For this reason, the teacher's social status has plummeted. Many are now as poor as those who are altogether illiterate. Indeed, English teachers in the Congo must often supplement their meager salaries by tutoring illiterate people in their own homes.

Daily work in schools is marked by deprivation: most teachers teach in overcrowded classrooms with insufficient resources, no benches, desks, or air conditioners. Typically, where desks or benches are available, pupils sit four or more to a single desk. It should be noted that all the teachers, male and female, receive the same treatment in the DRC. The poor treatment is meted out equally across genders

There is no social security for Congolese teachers. The Congolese teacher has never benefited from the national health insurance. A sick or dying teacher is bound to rely on his colleagues or relatives for social or financial assistance. There is no retirement policy. Since retired teachers are left alone without any financial or social assistance, they often die shortly after they retire.

In a country where teachers' living and working conditions are deteriorating every day and where there is little to no professional development, it is hard to imagine that many will devote their careers to the work.

What has become increasingly clear to me through the course of collecting these narratives is that we in the United States are no longer alone in this dilemma of undervaluing our teachers. Just as America's best and brightest began choosing other work when it became available to them, so have those in the rest of the world. As economies grow, as expanding wealth creates an acquisitive middle class, potential teachers will continue to be wooed into higher-paying and more attractive work. And with the teaching profession yoked as it is to the idea of service and sacrifice, the cachet of the work diminishes. The moral of the exercise seemed disturbingly clear: unless we listen to teachers' voices, worldwide, unless we heed their complaints, it will become increasingly difficult to fill the classrooms of the world with committed, intelligent teachers.

METHODOLOGY

The seven teachers in this study are presented through the methodological lens of *ethnographic portraiture*, an approach to qualitative research that has a distinguished history in the work of twentieth-century scholars. The phrase itself – ethnographic portraiture – requires parsing, since each term carries with it certain distinct resonances. It is a kind of scholarship that moves between art and science, between the objective and the subjective, in ways that require explanation.

As an ethnography of the lives of seven teachers, my research represents an attempt to enter into the world of my subjects using the anthropologist's tool of participant observation. Unlike quantitative researchers, ethnographers are not concerned with forming generalizations or with parsing cause and effect. Their goal is simply to create a window into real-life experience. It is in this sense that my profiles are ethnographic. In developing these portraits, I spent my days immersed in the lives of my subjects. We shared meals and sometimes living space; we engaged in ongoing, open-ended conversations. I met friends and colleagues. I also supplemented my understanding of the work lives of these teachers by gathering artifacts that impacted their daily lives: schedules and curricula, government mandates, and school memos. This kind of triangulation – using the voices of subjects, my own first-hand experiences, and the material data available through institutions and archives – affords a rich mine of material for understanding a life.

I also refer to these chapters as *portraits*, something drawn or composed with an organizing aesthetic in mind. The notion of seeing ethnography as an art form dates back at least to the early 1970s in the work of seminal researchers and theorists such as Clifford Geertz (*The Interpretation of Culture*, 1973) and John Berger (*Ways of Seeing*, 1972). Both of these scholars laid the groundwork for a form of interdisciplinary thinking and cross-field methodology that is fundamental to twenty-first-century research. In *The Interpretation of Culture*, Geertz speaks about the highly interpretive nature of ethnographic work, even as the researcher works to remain true to the details and intentions of the social reality she is documenting. What I am calling portraiture, Geertz called "thick description," a phrase that evokes the multilayered nature of the process, the building up of a realistic image through layers of metaphorical paint.[7]

Emerging more recently from this tradition is the work of Harvard anthropologist Sara Lightfoot, whose body of research walks the delicate line between art and scholarship. Lightfoot defends the portraitist's stance in ethnography by analyzing the nature of artistic sight: "Portraits make subjects feel 'seen' in a way they have never felt seen before," she writes, "fully attended to, wrapped up in an empathetic gaze."[8] As a research strategy, portraits are designed to capture the richness and complexity of human experience in social and cultural contexts, honoring the perspectives and the voices of the people who are negotiating those experiences, blurring the boundaries between aesthetics and empiricism.

Qualitative research of this kind never pretends to be completely free from bias. Indeed, it seems inherent in the nature of the methodology that the researcher's voice and vision should make themselves manifest to some extent. This is particularly true in research efforts that span cultures. By definition, the researcher is an outsider looking in. Adding a different nationality to that outsider status necessarily makes the work even more challenging. No matter how much research I do in preparation for my work, I will never be Taiwanese or Azeri. I can only bring my own empathetic gaze to what I see. Addressing the problem of objectivity and subjectivity, Geertz likens the work of ethnography to the playing of a Beethoven quartet where interpretation is inevitable, but the score is Beethoven's. Berger, though writing specifically about visual art, also reinforces the profound impact of subjectivity on all human creative work. "The way we see," he writes, "is affected by what we know and what we believe."[9] One image, one action, one statement can be read differently depending on who is looking, when, and why. As Lightfoot and others have contended, the subjectivity that is inevitably present in ethnography can be seen in positive terms, as an enriching factor rather than a negative one. In order to successfully identify with another person's perspective, Lightfoot contends, one must be able to experience and reflect on one's own.

This subjectivity also operates on the level of the teachers profiled here. My intention, in this book, is not to develop portraits of the education systems in seven countries but to profile the way seven teachers experience their work. Those are two very different endeavors. It is relatively easy to find factual material about class size, licensure laws, pay scales, and other information documenting the structures and regulations of international education systems. Here, however, the focus is primarily on what teachers tell me about those rules and structures, and their statements are not always corroborated by the latest statistics or government reports. I see this occasional discrepancy as a vital part of what I am trying to achieve in my research, exploring the disconnection between mandate and practice or between what statistics claim and what teachers actually experience.

In American and British educational scholarship, a suspicion of numbers has long served as a quiet corrective to the empirical research that dominated the field in the first half of the twentieth century. The "process-product" research of the 1970s – a bottom-line form of teacher assessment that reduced classroom practice to a series of scripted behaviors – inspired a furious backlash that opened the way to ethnography, portraiture, and the privileging of teacher's voices, both in policy making and in setting the research agenda for scholars. During the 1970s and 1980s, many qualitative educational studies, newly interesting to mainstream audiences, made their way into popular literature. Jonathan Kozol, Greg Michie, Samuel Freedman, and others showed us that portraiture had the power to spur political change in a way that statistics did not.[10] Ethnography and case studies became central tools in teacher education programs, and doctoral students (including myself) were encouraged to listen to teachers' voices and to pitch our narratives to a popular audience. That interest in a teacher-focused approach to research has abated considerably in the last decades, especially in the wake of "No Child Left Behind" and the renewed concern for a concrete bottom line of educational outcomes. It is harder to find ethnographic studies in major educational journals; they are replaced more frequently by efficacy studies of high-stakes testing and descriptions of new digital technologies.

One of the factors that makes this work useful and timely, then, is that it reasserts the value and currency of understanding a teacher's lived experiences. If American teachers' voices have been heard less in the last decades, international teachers have been heard almost not at all, neither in English-language journals nor in journals in their own countries.

SUBJECTS

The countries I have chosen to write about are profoundly varied: wealthy and poor, first world and third world, secular and religious. In choosing which teachers to profile, I looked for a way to document as wide a range of experiences as possible. One source for selecting countries to study was the international Programme for International Student Assessment (PISA) test, the common examination sponsored by the Organisation for Economic Co-operation and Development (OECD) and given to fifteen-year-olds in seventy-five countries around the world. Because the test is so inclusive and so politically powerful, it seemed sensible to use it as one factor in determining where to focus my attention. Given my initial hypothesis, that there is, within a culture, a correlation between the success of students and the prestige of teaching, it made sense to select countries that seemed to perform at the top and bottom of the PISA assessment rankings. Included here, then, are some of the world's highest-scoring countries (Finland, Taiwan) and lowest-scoring ones (Chile, Azerbaijan, Greece). There are also countries that score in the middle of the pack – highly developed countries such as the United States and France – that express confusion and consternation over their lagging performance. Together, their placement on the PISA scoreboard is one more piece of information useful in considering how and why respect for teachers matters in attracting and retaining teachers.

I came to select the individual teachers in this study based on a number of factors. The first and most crucial was their willingness to participate in the research and their ability to articulate what they do and why, how they feel about their work and their lives, and what the future of teaching looks like in their country. All seven of the teachers profiled here are at the top of their fields: two have won national teaching awards, and all are both talented and experienced. Their skill and their veteran status make listening to these teachers all the more important; their years in the field offer perspective; and their concerns carry weight. Four of the seven teachers were participants in the summer program at the ITD in Amherst, and so they had already been vetted by both the State Department and by the Fulbright Foundation, which helped sponsor that program. The other three were found through colleagues, through word of mouth, and after ongoing email conversations across the span of a year. Because I knew the individual portraits would ultimately invite comparisons across countries, I selected only high school teachers in public schools. Beyond this shared trait, the teachers profiled in this book differ a good deal. They are male and female, married and single. They represent a range of races and ethnicities, are gay and straight, Christian, Jewish, Muslim, and Buddhist.

The book begins with a consideration of teaching in Finland, the country that has made headlines in the last few years for its remarkable educational transformation and its astounding ascent on international measures of student performance. In Chapter 1, I describe the work and life of Annukka Suonio, an eighteen-year veteran English teacher in Tampere, Finland's second-largest city, located north of Helsinki. Annukka is in many ways the embodiment of Finland's new educational system, embracing technology and thriving in the newly informal and collaborative system of schooling established less than three decades ago. Annukka, like all teachers in Finland, develops her own curriculum and works collaboratively with colleagues in a school structure that is at once child-centered and adult-centered. Her enthusiasm for teaching and her belief in the methods she employs was unparalleled among all the teachers I studied. Some of Annukka's colleagues, however, offered a more subdued assessment of present-day Finnish schools, and their voices, too, are included in this chapter.

The freedom and creativity in evidence in Annukka's classroom were hardly visible in the Taipei classroom of Fen-juan Kuo, the subject of Chapter 2. Feng-juan is also an eighteen-year veteran, but she is a teacher of literature (Chinese) and an artist with a very different sensibility from Annukka's. This chapter documents her more modest lifestyle, her solitary and focused work life, and her more traditional attitudes about teaching and learning. Where Annukka moves around her classroom encouraging collaboration, creativity, and open-ended talk, Feng-juan stands on a platform, lecturing to rows of uniformed students. That two countries as dissimilar as Finland and Taiwan could score in the top five on PISA tests is a curious fact that I will discuss at some length in the Conclusion of this book.

Chapter 3 describes the work of Vassiliki Michailodou, a teacher of English at an alternative public high school in Athens. Vasso, as she is called, has lived through the brutal deprivations brought on by austerity measures in Greece, having seen her salary cut by 50 percent over the course of a year, and her school stripped of all staff support. Teachers carry a heavy teaching load while rotating into the newly vacant jobs of secretaries and janitors. For Vasso, teaching cannot be separated from the political environment in which she is working, and her attitudes toward her students and her work mirror in conscious and unconscious ways her liberal values and progressive ideals.

Gulnaz Haciyeva, the subject of Chapter 4, is an award-winning teacher from Mingechevir, Azerbaijan. Azerbaijan and Greece share the dubious status of falling low on the PISA scale, and even a glimpse at the conditions of teaching in both countries is enough to explain why. Gulnaz's school is bereft of resources, and her own work as a teacher is insufficient for earning a living wage. This chapter considers the transformation for Azerbaijani teachers between a Soviet past, when teaching carried status, and an independent present, where top students opt for more glamorous and high-paying professions. Gulnaz finds resources for her classes wherever she can, having become skilled at networking, applying for grants, and tapping into funds that others have not found. Still, her life as a teacher is very difficult, requiring her to work three jobs and travel from site to site in order to earn a decent wage.

Chapter 5 considers the life of Laurence Manfrini, a French teacher working in the diverse *banlieue* of Paris, the area made infamous after the Charlie Hebdo attacks and the terrorism of 2015. Laurence teaches in a school with a large immigrant population. Her own classes, however, are less integrated than others in the school. She is a teacher of the *classes preparatoires*, a long-standing program designed for the most intellectually elite students in France. Conversations with Laurence and her colleagues underscore the dramatic challenges faced by France as it strives to balance an ideal of rigor and a commitment to democracy with the changing reality of its schools and students. For French teachers, concerns about falling standards and the future of French culture invariably bump up against concerns about access and equality.

Chapter 6 describes the working life of a teacher in Santiago, Chile, where again, politics, class, and a long history of oppression color the work of the teacher. The profile of Mauricio Ramirez, an English teacher in a public girls' school in central Santiago, addresses all the injustices and aspirational reforms that have impacted Chilean schools in the past twenty years. Mauricio has lived through the abuses of Pinochet and the hopeful years that followed. But strikes and protests continue to interrupt the school year, and drastic differences remain between affluent and poor schools. Mauricio's down-to-earth perspective on teaching and school reform in Chile reinforces the sense that change is more complex and elusive than politicians would like to admit.

I end this exploration of teachers' lives with a chapter about Bonnie Fineman, a high school English teacher in Windsor, Connecticut. As I discuss in Chapter 7, Bonnie's school is in many ways representative of many American public schools: north of Hartford, Connecticut, the population of Windsor High School is wholly diverse, and its sprawling campus embodies the postwar ideal of social mixing, a shopping mall array of courses and tracks. Bonnie and her colleagues teach students who read five or six grades below level, as well as brilliant students headed for the Ivy League. She herself is exceptionally gifted at reaching every student, regardless of background or skill level. Her observations about what works and what doesn't, what needs to happen to support and attract great teachers into her school, is particularly interesting in light of the teachers' voices that preceded hers.

Chapter 8 seeks to draw connections across these portraits, to highlight what is the same and what is different and, more important, to consider why those similarities and differences exist. Much has been written in the last decade about the difficulty of transferring best practices across various cultures. Whenever I champion certain practices in Finland, for example, colleagues and friends invariably say, "But isn't that a much less diverse country?" The assumption, I suppose, is that diversity (and here, I believe, most people mean racial diversity) creates inevitable and stubborn barriers to the fair treatment of teachers – an absurd notion. Economic diversity is certainly a factor in the quality of schooling, but a country such as Taiwan, which performs at the top of the PISA list, is highly diverse in terms of social class. Others point to limits in district spending as if this were an immovable barrier to student success. A close, comparative look at where money is spent within school districts around the world shows dramatic differences in priorities. In the United States, accountability measures, administrative salaries, and standardized testing drain huge percentages of school budgets. In countries such as Finland, with the very best education systems, the cost per pupil is less than in America, even though the teachers are better paid relative to the cost of living. They are not spending more money, it seems; they are simply spending money differently. In the last chapter of this book, I address this issue of "transfer," looking closely at how countries "sell" the profession of teaching, and how teachers see themselves in the larger context of their societies. Ultimately, I argue that comparing the working lives of teachers internationally is an important step in understanding how to improve education everywhere and that focusing on the appeal of the profession to the world's best and brightest should be a global priority in the twenty-first century.

The final chapter presents excerpts from the personal narratives of other teachers around the globe. These are the voices of those teachers I came to know through my work with the ITD. Though I could not visit their classrooms, I have included excerpts from their stories, written in their own words (mostly unedited, and with minimal grammar changes), which provide a rich and vivid addition to the portraits that precede them. Some of these teachers write about dramatic moments in their teaching lives; others simply describe, in their own words, how they earned their positions, how they feel about their work, or what their daily experiences are like in the classroom. Whether their stories are dramatic or quotidian, they are interesting, shedding a light on lives that would otherwise be invisible to the world.

1

Finland: Autonomy and Respect

Annukka Suonio, eighteen-year veteran teacher at Tampere Classical High School in Tampere, Finland, smiles at the classroom of bent heads leaning over their notebooks and laptops. She is forty-four, with the broad face of a Russian nesting doll and a slim, athletic body. She is dressed in jeans, a peasant blouse, and brown cowboy boots. Her long, auburn hair is loose on her shoulders. It is a Wednesday afternoon in May, during the last term of the school year, and this is Annukka's first class of the day, a sophomore English class. There are twenty-eight students in the room, a large airy space with whitewashed walls covered in posters, pictures, and bookcases filled with books. There is a picture of the Globe Theatre, a map of the world, a map of England. There are postcards from Sonoma, California; Wales; Australia. There is an American flag and a large poster of Alcatraz prison.

Triangular desks have been arranged in groups of four and five, with students facing inward toward one another in intimate clusters. A large screen in front of the classroom projects the assignment – a word game composed by Annukka for testing vocabulary. Students work alone or sometimes bend over to consult the notebooks of those next to them. Annukka flashes a new list of English vocabulary words up on the screen.

"Next up, ladies and gents," she says, "Please translate these into Finnish, or you can make a game of it by providing clues in English."

Students listen compliantly, then turn back to their work groups. Near me, in a desk group composed of four girls and a boy, a girl with white-blond hair takes the lead.

"Let's do a word game," she says, turning to her textbook and reading the prompt: "A person is really annoying when ... "

"Arrogant," interrupts the boy before she can finish. All five laugh.

"When you come to a right place at the right time . . . " says the girl next to her, moving to the next sentence.

"Punctual," says her deskmate. And so it proceeds.

"Ladies and gents, sorry to interrupt," Annukka says, after a short interlude. She has been moving around the room, listening in on the conversations and adding a comment here and there in a friendly, low-key way. "Any questions or problems? Did everyone understand?"

"We understood enough," says a boy in the corner, and everyone laughs again.

"You understood enough," Annukka repeats. "What more can you ask in life?"

***

Teaching at Tampere Classical High School, as in many upper-secondary schools in Finland, requires stamina and flexibility. Annukka's year is composed of six separate terms, each offering students a range of required and elective courses. With each new six-week "period," teachers assume a new schedule. Classes can be larger or smaller depending on the popularity of the subject, with each class meeting three times a week. The complicated system allows for a great deal of choice on the part of students, and much variation for teachers, who are free to develop new classes and pitch them as electives. Altogether, Annukka teaches sixteen classes a year. Home-rooms and other kinds of duties count as classes and relieve teachers from one or two of their academic requirements. Because of the flexible and changing system, teachers' schedules can vary drastically from term to term; some terms, Annukka can have as many as six classes; in others, she can have as few as two. This term, Annukka has no classes on Fridays. Tuesdays, she works steadily from 8 to 4, including time spent teaching an online course.

As international researchers have noted, Finnish teachers spend less time in their classrooms doing actual teaching than most other teachers around the world. When Annukka is not engaged in actual classroom instruction, however, she is immersed in other work-related activities: meeting one-on-one with students, developing curriculum and lesson plans, composing online materials for her students, meeting with colleagues, and reading. One of the most striking differences for a visitor accustomed to American schools is the leisurely pace of life in Tampere Classical High School. There are no bells to signal the start and end of periods, and no mass movements from one room to another. The day unfolds at a genteel pace; teachers come and go from the building whenever they must, with no rules governing midday sign-outs or prohibitions regarding the "performing of personal business" during school hours. As I move through the school, the sense of autonomy among both students and teachers is almost palpable.

That autonomy and lack of hierarchy is immediately evident in the school's teachers' room. The lounge is messy and full of easy activity – printers grinding away, teachers grading papers. Young teachers and older ones talk cordially with one another. No one seems tired or disaffected. Ann Lieberman, the American scholar of school reform, has noted that conversation in the American teachers' lounge is often characterized by "jousting or griping": cynical jokes or complaints. Here, I witness neither, just subject-based conversations, talk about students, and friendly banter about the upcoming weekend.[1] On my first morning in the school, Kari, the principal, or "head teacher," joins us for coffee. He is a tall man in his early fifties, with a self-effacing manner and a shy smile. Kari was trained as a mathematics teacher and (like all Finnish school administrators) still teaches two classes a year. The assistant principal, Mirkka, a woman in her mid-forties, teaches twelve classes a year, six fewer than Annukka. She wanders in soon after and sits down at our table. "Here we are with the King and Queen," Annukka says with a gently ironic tone that produces a sheepish smile from both administrators. "No king and queen here," says Mirkka. Also sitting with us this morning is Tuija, a teacher of English, Italian, French, and Latin, and Annukka's closest colleague in the school. She is older than Annukka, a serious, energetic blond woman in her fifties, whose English, like Annukka's, is so impeccable as to make her seem wholly bilingual. Another colleague named Kari, a history teacher close to retirement, also joins us midway through the period, and then Hannu, a young math teacher, who has been listening in near the Xerox machine and whom Annukka coaxes over after he has proffered several comments from across the room. We speak about school reform and America's struggle to address the needs of its hugely diverse school population. The challenges of working in a diverse system, I suggest, are very different from those faced by Finnish teachers, where virtually the entire population is Northern European Anglo. Annukka immediately corrects me: there have been recent demographic changes in Finland as well, she says. More immigrants are coming into the country. Schools have begun to feel the press of their needs. Change is imminent, though no one knows what it will be or when it will come. The conversation turns to other subjects: the defection of Crimea and Ukraine's ongoing battle with Russia. The situation in Ukraine feels urgent and intimate; Tampere Classical still retains its large Cold War–era bomb shelter, which a visitor passes en route to classrooms in the basement of the school. Fears of Russian aggression, fears about extremism, fears about change: all of this is discussed over coffee. I am struck throughout our talk by the absolute lack of hierarchy among the assembled group, the ease with which people disagree, and the intelligence of the participants. It is the kind of conversation one might have at a dinner party, among close friends.

THE FINNISH "MIRACLE"

In both the popular press and in academic journals, the "Finnish miracle" – the brilliant metamorphosis of a national education system from mediocrity to excellence – has been analyzed and parsed. Cover stories in the *New York Times* magazine and *Time* present the thrilling story of Cinderella-like transformation where shared purpose and galvanized brainpower move students to the top in international measures of success. This success is a new phenomenon. Education in Finland was, through the 1960s, elitist and inefficient, following a model of frontal instruction and traditional testing that had been borrowed decades before from its Northern European and Soviet neighbors. As Pasi Sahlberg and others have recounted, the onslaught of a major recession at the start of the 1980s led to a period of national soul-searching; schools and teaching became a central focus.[2] Vilho Hirvi, then director general of the Finnish National Board of Education, looked not to outside policy experts for advice on reform but to teachers and students, a decision that would be key to the philosophy of reform that still undergirds the Finnish education system. Teachers at the time called for more flexibility and creativity, more freedom. The rigid links between state mandates and local schools needed to be loosened. Teachers needed to wield more direct control over their working lives, to feel more personally invested in the daily activity of teaching. As successful corporations came to realize in the early 1980s, institutional health is predicated on the attitudes of those who work within those institutions. The new system was built around the promotion of "self-efficacy" in teachers and confidence in the good sense of gifted and committed professionals. Identify the country's best and brightest, the policy went, and then entrust that talented pool of teachers with the freedom to design curricula, work collaboratively, and make their own decisions about what and how to teach.

These two driving forces of reform, trust and collaboration, inform every aspect of Annukka's work. As a teacher, she is charged with designing her own approach to the material she teaches, and that trust yields huge payback. She spends inordinate amounts of time preparing lessons and composing developmentally appropriate games and exercises for her students – work of which she is justifiably proud. It is *hers*, and that sense of ownership fuels an energy and investment that would be difficult to inspire in someone who was teaching ready-made materials. There is a craftsman's pride in what she does, a kind of process-oriented focus that makes her both invested and critical. When a lesson is less than successful, she considers how to change it without blaming the textbook or the state frameworks. "When I enter a classroom, I say to myself, what do I want to accomplish here?" she says. "When I leave, I think, did I accomplish my goals?"

***

Annukka Suonio was born in Kangasala, a small suburb of Tampere, into a middle-class family of professionals. Her father, a technical manager, worked his way up the ladder to the position of head foreman in a local factory that manufactured corrugated board. Her childhood, Annukka remembers, was dominated by the presence of her mother, a teacher of English and Swedish in the lower comprehensive school in her town. Annukka was born with a heart problem and, at eight months, was taken to Helsinki for a rare surgical procedure that left the family vaguely traumatized long afterward. Annukka's brother was not born until thirteen years later, when it was clear that the family's first child was wholly out of danger. Both before and after the birth of her brother, Annukka remembers her home life as loving and active – filled with family ski trips and summers spent at the family's cottage "in the country," a small second house where Annukka's father could gather berries and mushrooms and where she and her brother could wander in the cool woods.

Like many Finnish children, Annukka did not start school until seven. When she did, Annukka can still remember the difficulty of the transition. This was the period before Finland's educational transformation, and schools still resembled those of their Soviet neighbors. After seven years of childhood freedom, elementary school seemed "constricting and oppressive" to Annukka. Middle school was no better; it was full of strict rules and rowdiness, bad food, and bad odors. For Annukka, the highlight of this uncomfortable period in her life came during one summer in her early teens when she went to live with an American family and their teenage daughter in Florida. The trip was arranged through a children's exchange program advertised in her school. The following summer, the Florida teen came and stayed with Annukka's family. Again, the experience was a great success. By high school, Annukka says, she longed for a more extended and immersive experience with English. Through an organization called "Youth for Understanding," Annukka spent a full year of high school living with an American family in Mansfield, Massachusetts. "My mom never had the financial opportunity to do this kind of thing," Annukka explains, "so she was the one who really encouraged me." The year was the best of her life, she says, a time when her ambitions for the future became solidified.

After returning from America, Annukka resumed her high school studies for two more years. During these last years of comprehensive school, the system had begun to change. Annukka's high school English teacher Maija-Leena Kallela became a role model and mentor. "She wrote the book we used in our English class," Annukka says, "and continues – even now in her seventies – to translate Latin into Finnish, things that have never been translated before." Annukka says she remembers her teacher's ability to combine rigor with huge enthusiasm, and her memory of Kallela still sets a standard for practice in her own classroom.

Despite her love of English and her success at it, Annukka's initial ambition was not to teach. Her mother, like many teachers, feared that a teaching career would be too stressful and time-consuming and encouraged Annukka to go into physical therapy – a field that paid well but would make fewer demands on her daughter. What's more, the English department at Tampere University – the first step toward a teaching license – was newly competitive. The program took only fifty students per year, so competition, even at that early point in Annukka's career, seemed daunting. Still, according to Annukka, she had long suspected that teaching was her destined profession: "I suppose that all kids who have parents as teachers do this: helping Mum mark multiple-choice quizzes, watching her read and prepare. I remember the pleasure of sitting cross-legged on the floor, helping my mother put papers in alphabetical order; at six or seven, adding up points for her ... "

As it turned out, and despite her mother's concerns, Annukka performed extraordinarily well on her matriculation exam. Though the system has now been changed to require a set range of test subjects, at the time that Annukka took her exam, students were allowed to choose to be tested on any six subjects in which they excelled. "I was good in languages, and so I chose English, Finnish, Swedish, German, and Latin ... and then psychology. No math. Just words, people, and languages." Her overall scores gave her access to the top slot in the university's English department, and she arrived at college with the clear ambition to teach.

Teacher preparation in Finland is highly rigorous. It begins with three years of intensive subject study for a bachelor's degree in the subject the candidates hopes to teach. That is followed by a two-year master's program for teacher licensure, a degree that is required for all teaching positions in the country. After a year of theory and pedagogy courses (her fourth at the university), Annukka began a year-long internship in the university's high school laboratory school where, in her words, "the best teachers teach you how to teach." In Finland, all teacher education programs control the sites at which students engage in practice teaching. Unlike in the United States, where teachers-in-training often find internship placements with teachers who can vary dramatically in their skills and methodological preferences, Finland's system seems to ensure that models of teaching will be consistently strong. University faculty control the hiring of mentor teachers and can thus control the quality and the philosophical approach of those charged with modeling pedagogy for new teachers. Annukka's internship year was composed of a combination of practice teaching and observing; she was grouped with three other student teachers, working collaboratively on their pedagogic skills. As novice teachers, they would observe classes together and then discuss what they saw; one would teach a class, and the others would give feedback. Periodically, the groups would return to the university classrooms for lectures or directed group discussions. Key to this approach, says Annukka again, was the uniform excellence of the teachers they observed.

Throughout her year of intern teaching, Annukka compiled a portfolio composed of lesson plans, self-evaluations, and writing that charted her growth as a teacher. Though self-reflection was a core part of her preparation, it was rigorous scholarly research writing that formed the cornerstone of the program. Finland's goal for teachers is to form "research practitioners," educators who understand how to problematize classroom experiences and then systematically find answers to those problems. This research orientation culminates, for all Finnish teachers, in a master's thesis based on a topic of the students' choice. For Annukka, whose love of English had taken a turn toward linguistics, that topic was an in-depth analysis of English popular science writing. Having taken a class with a professor whose own work was in this area, Annukka spent the next year extending his research with her own sophisticated grammatical analysis, focusing on the use of adjectives and their cultural context and significance in popular prose.

Before Annukka could complete her thesis, she was notified by her former mentor, Maija-Leena Kallela, that a teaching position was available at Tampere Classical High School. Without the completed master's degree, however, Annukka was qualified only as a full-time substitute, paid an hourly wage. Still, she took the job and loved the work from the start. By the end of her first year at the school, Annukka's supervisor gave her a reality check: "She told me the students loved me and wanted me to continue next year, but that in order to do that, I'd have to finish my masters immediately. 'As of now,' she said, 'you're not qualified.'" The possibility of the job gave Annukka the incentive she needed to finish the last of her graduate work. "Christmas break came, and I worked night and day," she remembers. "I got in touch with my supervisor [at the university], and we decided I should do whatever it took to finish. I even did one of the required thesis exams in a broom closet because all the classrooms were in use. To his credit, my advisor made it happen. And then I was done."

Annukka began teaching full time the following fall, and received tenure soon after. In the United States, tenure is granted after a three-year probationary period. In Finland, it happens almost immediately. Once a candidate is deemed worthy of being hired, the assumption is that everything must be done to persuade the candidate to stay. The offer of tenure, after six months, is one mechanism for retaining these talented and rigorously vetted new teachers. "Tenure becomes an incentive for getting the very best person for the job," Annukka's colleague explains, "and given how many people apply and the quality of the pool, it is not very risky to offer tenure from the start. You want people to stay, to be committed to one place for the course of a career."

Since she began teaching, professional development has been an integrative part of the daily work of Annukka and her colleagues. Teachers are required to engage in three days of formal professional development work each year, work that can be completed in a wide variety of ways. Annukka chooses to complete her professional development through lectures and workshops offered at the central office in Helsinki, welcome breaks from routine that are paid for by the school system. Other colleagues take their professional development at the local university, building on coursework toward their PhDs. Annukka explains that in Finland, teachers who have completed their master's degrees have automatic acceptance into PhD programs, an incentive to continue studying. Two of the thirty-five teachers in Annukka's school have PhDs, and others are in the process of completing them. The additional degree translates into a modest salary increase.

For Annukka, the most potent form of professional development is the active creation of curricular materials for her own classes and the writing of textbooks used by teachers around the country. All Finnish teachers create their curricular materials, and textbooks are composed by teams of practicing teachers, selected by textbook companies. Annukka was selected ten years ago and has already authored two books. The writing process, she says, "is fantastic," especially because it means working "with teachers as motivated as you are" and because it allows her to move back and forth between theory and practice: the team comes up with ideas, and then they test them out in their own classrooms. Working like this, with a gifted team of fellow teachers, Annukka feels that the textbooks gain a kind of integrity that is often missing when nonteachers create classroom materials. Annukka's first and second textbooks, completed during the summers, were composed with a strong team of veterans: a bilingual International Baccalaureate teacher, also from Tampere; two teachers from Turku, and two from Helsinki. "The work is so creative and intellectually stimulating," she says, "and it allows me to meet teachers outside my own small community." She is currently working on her third textbook with new team members from Helsinki, Seinäjoki, Vaasa, and Hämeenlinna.

***

Two hours by car from Helsinki, Tampere is the second-largest city in Finland, with a population of approximately 220,000. Poised between two large lakes, the city has a long industrial history dating back to the early nineteenth century and the beginnings of Finland's period of modernization. The first electric light bulb in Europe was manufactured in Tampere. Textile mills dot the landscape of the city, as do massive red brick factories, many built for Findlayson, a cloth manufacturer whose expansion drove early industrial development in Tampere. Many of these buildings have been converted into apartments and condos, with restaurants and retail shops – like firm material anchors – installed on the bottom floors. Tampere has been called the "Manchester, England, of Finland," but the city is more varied and homey in its architecture. Traditional square factory buildings are offset by smaller structures with art nouveau motifs and buildings that suggest the charmed fairytales of the Finnish past. Residential areas are characterized by pitch-roofed houses with vertical boards, many with scrolled lattice decorations over the doors and windows.

There is throughout Tampere – as in much of Finland – a tension between opposites: the playful and the somber, the decorative and the subdued. Finland's national aesthetic is typified by the design of the Marimekko company. Bright geometric designs appear everywhere – a kind of national signature printed on everything from Finnair paper napkins to tampon boxes. Their bright colors seem like a conscious antidote to the pervasive gray of the sky in the long winter, and a cheerful nod to the colors of Finnish summers: green, blue, yellow; trees, sky, sun.

Another striking feature of this country for a visitor from America is the unerring and pervasive quiet of public spaces. In restaurants and stores, airports and schools, people walk together in silence, or speak in low voices that cannot be easily overheard. As one who is accustomed to the rowdy chaos of American schools and the noise and hubbub on American streets, this quiet is surprising and even unnerving. Arriving in Helsinki airport, I noticed the cultural difference immediately: men and women walked together throughout the airport like cats, padding silently to their gates, silent children in tow. A popular travel book warns its readers, "Finns only speak when they have something to say," and, as a people, they "don't go in for small talk." Still, I had not imagined how this trait would translate into the "feel" and ethos of the country and, particularly, of the schools.

Just off the main thoroughfare in downtown Tampere is the Lenin Museum, which boasts itself to be the only museum outside Russia devoted solely to the Russian revolutionary. The museum is appropriately situated on floor 2½ of a musty, multipurposed building near the center of the city, the original site of the first meeting between Lenin and Stalin in 1905, when both were in exile in Finland. In the two cramped rooms of the museum, amid dust motes and slanting sun, is correspondence between Lenin and his revolutionary comrades back in St. Petersburg and Moscow. In one corner there is a reconstruction of the table and chairs where Lenin and Stalin sat, drinking tea and talking revolution. Also displayed are several statues of Lenin, a heroic bust, photos of Lenin as a boy, and photos of his wife – first young and beautiful, and then plump and withered like a typical Russian babushka. As I read through the exhibit (on a stained, Xeroxed handout that must be returned after use), it seems to become clear why Finland owed a debt to Lenin. According to the literature, Lenin protected Finland from Russian domination. When I tell this to Annukka, however, she says this is Russian propaganda, advanced by Communists in the 1970s. "Many Finns would be insulted," she says, "were this stated as a fact."

A second cultural claim to fame for Tampere is as the home of Tove Jansson Museum, the cartoonist and children's book illustrator who invented the character of Moomin, a charming white hippopotamus with big eyes and no mouth – the national mascot. Like Marimekko, Moomin appears everywhere: on mugs and tee shirts, stationery, magnets, bookbags.

The Moomin museum is situated in the basement galleries of the Tampere Art Museum, and it is the only place in the city that is noisy. School groups move from exhibit to exhibit (drawings, paintings, a doll house filled with Moomin creatures and furniture, vitrines with Moomin characters posed in various dramatic poses). Lenin and Moomin, in a strange way, serve as appropriate symbols for the Finnish national character. In the revolutionary, one sees the Finnish idealism, reformist sensibility, and egalitarianism; in the cartoon character, the silence (Moomin has no mouth!) and the gently ironic stance toward the world.

One afternoon after school, Annukka takes me on a tour of the city. We begin at Pyynikki Ridge, the highest gravel ridge in Finland, formed during the ice age. A vast lake stands on either side where huge ice age boulders receded, leaving a green ridge in between. Covered with neat wooden structures, a network of former factory worker housing, it is now transformed into private residences. The "castle," the original home of the Finlayson family, sits perched on a hill above them. There is also a Finlayson church, an understated brick structure with small, hexagon-shaped stained glass windows. Churches dot the landscape, reminding a visitor that there is no separation in Finland between church and state. Annukka alludes to the fact that she is religiously indifferent, but a dour-looking icon of the Virgin still hangs in the school's teachers' lounge.

The fortunes of Tampere were enhanced with the building of the Nokia factory in the twentieth century. Nokia's rise as a tech giant paralleled the first stirrings of reform in the Finnish schools. In the 1990s, when Nokia burst onto the scene with its flip phones, Finland was undergoing its first major education reform program, a series of changes that would take the country out of the nineteenth century and start it on the road toward world-class education.

TEACHING THE WHOLE CHILD: INDIVIDUAL DIFFERENCES

On a typical late-spring day in Tampere Classical High School, the computer room is filled to capacity with big boys surfing the net or playing Tetris and other online games. Students are free to do whatever they want on the computers. There are no filters or blocks. Annukka says that a teacher keeps an informal eye on students in the computer room, but that students – as far as she knows – don't exploit the freedom they have there. Most work on their schoolwork, she says, but when they don't, it's because they need to "blow off steam." It's natural and important, she says.

Concern for the affective health of the students – the keen awareness of a teenager's need to "blow off steam" – seems central to the mission of the school and an integral part of the teaching/learning process. Since the 1990s, all schools in Tampere have had a Committee for Pastoral Care, a group of teachers and other professionals who attend to the emotional health of the students. The committee meets monthly, composed of the school psychologist, the school social worker, the head teacher, the studies counselor, the nurse, and a "teacher member." The teacher member, a rotating position among the teaching faculty, serves as the conduit for communicating to the committee any problems his or her colleagues have encountered with students. Just this fall, the care group has become even more individualized: a new law requires specific case groups to be formed for individual student problems, composed of professionals best suited to student needs.

When I ask Annukka how she deals with serious disciplinary problems, she thinks for a moment and then tells me she's never had any really serious problems. "If a student seems distracted or is talking in class, I usually ask them if they want to take a walk or just leave for a little while. If they have the feeling coming on, they can just get up and take a walk. It comes from them, not me." This confidence in the "self-efficacy" of the student seems part of the core value system of Annukka's school, an explicit learning goal for the teachers with whom I spoke. "Self-discipline comes from within," Annukka says. "We need to teach the students to self-monitor, to understand when they need a break and to not make a big deal about it." A boy who puts his head down on the desk "has ADHD," according to Annukka, and she lets him rest without any admonition. Boys occasionally get up and walk out of the class. Annukka explains that they needed a break or a walk. Again, their behavior is not only tolerated, it is perceived as a normal part of the group activity. There is no scolding, no yelling. The students have a gently sarcastic demeanor, but it is not directed toward adults; rather, it seems like a benign form of self-protection.

According to statistics, almost 35 percent of Finnish students get full- or part-time special education support, and a majority of students will at some point be classified as "special needs," a term that refers to any sort of remediation in core subjects. This astounding number is due to the fact that any weakness is immediately identified and addressed. "Prevention instead of repair," is the coda for the Finnish system.[3] As a result of this doctrine, teachers are required to be keenly sensitive to student intellectual and affective behaviors. And students seem to perceive no stigma in difference.

Juhani, a student with Asberger's syndrome, has volunteered to take me on a tour of the building. With great seriousness, speaking in excellent English, he shows me the various classrooms, each one with its subject name printed on the front: mathematics, chemistry, Finnish, Swedish, and English. We pass a fallout shelter with its familiar and menacing logo. There is also a door with the words "*Opinto-Ohjaaja.*" "That's the teaching coach," Juhani says, "which I think means the room for the psychologist and social worker. I'm there quite a lot." Juhani introduces me to a cluster of friendly girls. Annelia, a tall freshman in a turquoise jacket, greets him warmly, then pumps me with questions. They speak about the good feeling in the school and the "great teachers." Annelia wants to be scientist; she chose Tampere Classical High School, she says, because it has a brand-new science program that is appealing to her. Her friend Maria wants to do theater. "We're all very happy here," she smiles, and pats Juhani on the back as if to say he is partly responsible for this.

It is interesting to see how well tolerated is all idiosyncrasy. Not only in the high school but throughout town, I see old and young dressed in sometimes clownish outfits – men in gaudy hippie attire, with long hair and jewelry, and women with purple or green hair. Annukka says that in a country where there is such genetic physical homogeneity, people look for ways to stand out. Perhaps this explains the high tolerance for individual differences within the school system. People may look odd, but they don't speak out or make a public nuisance of themselves. Instead, these quiet gestures at difference create a general sense of openness and acceptance.

At Annukka's school, the Committee on Pastoral Care is also charged with designing curricular activities that address the emotional needs of the students. Last month, classes were suspended for a "rest period," where mattresses were put down on the floor of the school and students were encouraged to nap and listen to music. This week, "health day" is focused on the "health of the community." The exercise, announced over the PA system, will ask students to consider ways to make the school more responsive to their needs. The school psychologist explains the challenge: imagine the school in 2020; what is the ideal school of the future? What would it look like? How could Tampere Classical High School become that ideal place? Students talk within their desk groups, while Annukka moves around the room. As usual, her manner is both authoritative and playful, unthreatening but clearly in control.

The mental health counselor, a young cheerful woman in tight jeans and a black blazer, comes in during the exercise to ask the group how things are progressing. She is in charge of the day. She stands in the back of the room, listening as each group reads its initial suggestions for improving the school, and as Annukka expands on their comments, asking them to speak in more detail about what they have suggested.

The suggestions are serious and thoughtful. One student, acknowledging the crowding in the common hallways, calls for a student lounge. Another student asks for a bigger library, "more books," she says. "No one goes to the library in the school," a boys calls out. "There are literally no books in it." "We need air conditioning," says one girl. "We need lockers," says another. "These are good suggestions," says Annukka. They will appear the following day, written in a lovely calligraphic hand by a student in the class and hanging on a common wall in the school staircase, along with the suggestions from other classes. To cap off Pastoral Care Day, faculty and students are going to play a soccer match against one another on a field on the other side of the city. Though it is not required, the entire school turns out. After a close game, the faculty wins.

If you ask Annukka what she thinks the school should look like in 2020, she would start her list with a call to eliminate the matriculation exam. These tests, the first "high-stakes" examinations that Finnish students experience, are taken during their final year in school and are used as the basis both for high school graduation and for college admission (although students often have to take another exam for entrance into a specific university). In the course of my stay in Finland, I heard a wide range of opinions on this examination, with faculty and students split about evenly over whether the exams should persist. For Annukka, the formal nature of the matriculation exam and its standardized format inhibit creativity and restrict to some extent the kind of teaching she would ideally like to do with her second- and third-year students. The basis of her complaints largely resides in the arcane nature of the material covered on the examination (its stubborn emphasis on grammar and the "useless" vocabulary it includes) and the multiple-choice format of the test. After years of progressive teaching, an emphasis on choice and individual differences, and a valuing of creativity and collaboration, the exam looms as a rigid testament to the old, traditional system. Annukka describes the arduous and, in her mind, arcane nature of the test: "The questions are really tricky; you hear something only once on tape, spoken really quickly and in an unfamiliar accent, and then it's 'what will the speaker say next: a, b, or c?' To my mind, it's very artificial." The inevitable fact of the exam influences Annukka's teaching in ways that she dislikes. "If there's multiple choice on the matriculation exam, then you have to teach them how to do multiple choice. I mean, does it really test anything? You are guessing.

I would like to have more open-ended questions; I would like to have projects, creative work."

For Annukka and other like-minded teachers, meaningful assessment is self-assessment, public presentations, and interactions with native speakers. "If I can't get a living, breathing native speaker in the classroom, then I use videos. I want to see how well students can interact, reply to questions having to do with real-world skills, something that you would need in real life. Without the exam, I would only teach grammar items that, if you didn't know them, would somehow hinder communication or make you misunderstood. I want more time to teach pronunciation, because you can hear many of the students struggling with basic sounds; we don't really teach (and none of our textbooks have this either) good intonation or just whole sentences or living the text."

There is much talk of imminent reform of the exam system coming down the pike, but no sense of when the promised changes will take place. "I've been waiting for changes for so long," Annukka continues. "Because it's a high-stakes exam, I would be doing my students a disservice if I didn't teach as much grammar as I do, or if I didn't give them these fancy words that they would never need in real life. The matriculation exam controls me. I find that very, very frustrating."

Tuija Laurikka and Kari Talikainen, Annukka's two veteran colleagues, disagree. Both see the test as critical to maintaining standards, which – from their perspective – have already dropped precipitously in the last decade. Kari – a white-haired history teacher with an extraordinary knowledge of English literature – worries that students are arriving at the university with no content and few skills. Indeed, he feels that there should be more examinations throughout the secondary sequence. Tuija is also concerned about the loss of rigor. Students of her generation were required to take three languages, whereas now they must take only two. High-stakes testing is a necessary evil, she says, and the campaign to get rid of it represents another move to dilute standards generally.

Later, in Annukka's afternoon class, there is some discussion about the final exams and about the results of exams that students have already taken in other subjects. The results are due to be posted tomorrow. There is very little secrecy about scores. Annukka checks her laptop to see if any results have come in yet. "Not yet," she reports to the class. The following day, still nothing is posted. As I speak with Annukka in the hall before lunch, a petite girl, with her hair enveloped in a swatch of bright African fabric, stops to speak. "I was hoping to get the results today," she tells Annukka. "I'm kind of excited." "Probably tomorrow," says Annukka, sympathetically. "It's exciting," says the girl again. "Well, you got a nice grade on the oral exam from me, and that's the most important thing," Annukka says. It strikes me that Annukka is more anxious about the scores than is the student. Perhaps, I think, this is because Finnish students are trained in a kind of anticompetitive optimism; for twelve years, they have been told that doing their best is good enough, and there has been for them no evidence to the contrary. In any case, the student who speaks to Annukka seems to perceive the test as merely a formative indication of what she assumes to be her mastery of the subject. For Annukka, it is a reflection on her competency as a teacher and an affront to the integrity of her choices as a professional.

***

Despite the well-earned praise for Finnish school reform that is everywhere expressed, the reality of life in Finnish classrooms is more complex than it seems on the outside. One of the more surprising discoveries for me was the existence of certain familiar (e.g., American) problems in Tampere Classical High School. Budget cuts, both real and threatened, preoccupy teachers and administrators at the school. Contrary to the dazzling images that accompany many articles about education in Finland, Annukka's school was modestly appointed and clearly in need of a facelift. Promised renovations had been stalled because of budget cuts. One large section of the old building was closed down, pending resources for its renovation; the new building (new as of the early 1970s) was a fairly sad-looking cinder-block box. Work on a covered passageway that would link the old building with the new has been suspended. Students must walk, in the bitter Finland winters, across a wide parking lot to pass from one part of the school to another. Cuts have also impacted life in classrooms. In Tampere, three schools were closed down in the last few years, and the remaining high schools have picked up the overflow. Classes are now larger; students are now attending schools they did not choose for themselves, a fact that undermines, according to Annukka's colleagues, the whole point of a choice system, which is intended to promote a sense of empowerment and investment in students attending the school.

Also a source of complaint is the influx of a new school management approach on the national level, one that calls for stricter assessments and more uniformity of instruction. This is fairly alarming to Annukka, and odd to me, when it is clear that such an approach undoes the very strategies that I have traveled to Finland to observe. The new mayor of Tampere, says Annukka, is more enlightened than others and may press back against these new reforms, though Annukka wonders if she has any say in these matters. "The politicians in Helsinki call the shots," she says. These stirrings of retrograde policy seem to be quietly affecting the profession.

Kari, the history teacher, explains that unemployment in general is a major problem for students. College graduates "can't get jobs working at clothing counters," he says, "let alone in more appropriate places." From Kari's perspective, the source of the problem can be traced back to the schools: the policy of providing everyone with the same college-prep education. Since the much-publicized reforms of the 1990s, schools have been restructured to become more egalitarian. After the ninth grade, schooling becomes split into two tracks, the vocational and the academic, or college-bound. According to Kari, too many young people are now going to the academic secondary schools.

Both Tuija and Kari agree that there is little incentive for students to study hard. Both talk of having to lower their standards. Kari holds up a small booklet that was created by his history students as a "project" in lieu of a paper. "They want to use the computers and make this kind of thing," he says. "You do this kind of thing, you get good grades, and then you go to the university and you don't know anything about history! What kinds of students are we producing? Do they have a certain kind of intellectual substance?" Tuija and Kari also question the tremendous focus on technology. "If I would like to buy a book here, then I am in trouble," Kari says. "But if I want to buy a new computer in my class, tomorrow there is a new computer." With students so focused on computer skills and creative projects, they worry, many have forsaken the hard, slow work of textual analysis and the old-fashioned labors of foundational memorization critical to foreign language study or to history. Many students simply do not engage in the higher-level thinking that is necessary for meaningful understanding.

Funding, too, is a major point of contention. As mentioned earlier, funding for building renovations is stalled on the municipal level. But Tuija also complains that funding is misused in the name of "equality," with money being spent on services that have little impact on teaching and learning. One particularly misguided reform, says Tuija, is the movement to consolidate schools. "Small schools are closing down and [being subsumed] into larger schools. We know that students do so much better in smaller schools because everybody knows each other. The teachers can really monitor the students ... if they are facing difficulties or if their behavior is changing suddenly. You can't see this in big schools where [individual] students get lost in the masses."

Kari and Tuija, both highly intelligent and dedicated veteran teachers, perceive their place in the culture quite differently from Annukka. Though both acknowledge that the profession holds more cachet than it does in the United States, they fear that this, too, is changing. "Today in the newspaper," says Tuija, "there was an article about parents and teachers. Teachers find that parents nowadays are contacting them more and more and in a negative way. And now you have the possibility of sending e-mail messages to teachers very quickly, at home and at night if they want to. The majority of them don't, but the minority of parents, who are very often the problem parents, send very nasty messages to teachers, telling the teacher how to teach, as if the teacher didn't know. The parents are becoming experts, saying things like, their child has not been graded properly or has been treated in a bad way for some reason. These contacts are not very productive."

It is hard to assess whether these complaints fall across any predictable lines. Are older teachers more critical of change than younger ones? Are teachers of certain subjects – say, math and foreign languages – more conservative than those who teach literature, given their sense that students need a traditional, factual foundation for any subsequent work? Like all internal politics, it is complicated. But the general sense is that not everyone is happy and that the source of their complaints, as it is in the United States, is related to funding and standards.

On Thursday, Annukka's scores come in, and though we don't discuss it, I can see she is slightly disappointed. Though no one failed, and no one received the lowest score, the percentage of highest-scoring students is a bit lower this year than last. I may be wrong, but I felt it cast a pall on the rest of her day. Periodically, Annukka encounters students who have done very well on the exam, and they exchange hugs. It is sobering to see how much mental and emotional energy is expended on these exams – especially in a country renowned for having freed itself from the chokehold of standardized tests.

CHOICE

Choice is a cornerstone of the Finnish system. In Tampere, there are six academic upper-secondary schools, each with a particular "specialty." Tampere Classical, Annukka's school, is dubbed "classical" because it offers Latin. Other schools specialize in arts or technology or some other subject. Hannu, the math teacher, says that these designations are mostly window dressing, since most schools offer the full range of subjects.

Entrance to any of these schools is through application, and all the schools have minimum GPA requirements, based on a 10-point scale. Tampere Classical's is 7.5. The nearby Theater and Performance School has a 9. The Applied Art School has an 8. These designations are mostly used, according to Annukka, as a way to lower the number of applications to schools that might be most popular to young people. Still, there are rather dramatic physical differences between those schools that have been recently renovated and those, like Tampere Classical, where renovations have not occurred. The Arts High School, where Annukka's close friend Maarit teaches, is a dramatic example of that difference. Renovated two years ago, the school is a model of aesthetic beauty, cleanliness, and high-tech glamour. Maarit's classroom is state of the art, with spotless white desks that slide open to reveal individual computers and headphones for language study. The hallways are decorated with student artwork produced in exquisite painting, print making, photography, wood working, and jewelry making studios, all bright and stocked full with materials. At the arts high school, school and community are literally merged: the first floor library is actually a branch of the city library, and well-dressed older ladies read cooking magazines next to young people listening to music with headphones. The cafeteria is also a public restaurant. Young and old are drinking coffee together there in the well-lit open space on the first floor. Most impressive to me are the teachers' spaces. A large, light, and impeccably clean room functions as the teachers' lounge. It has a cappuccino machine, broad comfortable sofas, clean, bright Marimekko curtains, two bathrooms, and a copy machine. There is a refrigerator and stove, a bank of computers, and a number of telephones. This common space is supplemented by individual workspace within the departments. In the English wing of the building are offices for each teacher. Six faculty share one large space, with dividers separating each of the six areas. Each mini-office has a laptop computer and affords the teacher enough privacy to meet individually with students without disturbing others. All of this renovation is paid for by the municipal government, the same source that has failed to come through with the renovations to Tampere Classical.

ANNUKKA, AT HOME

A constant and sustaining force in Annukka's life is her husband, Jorma Suonio, a tall, soft-spoken man with a kind face and a passion for history. Jorma is currently head of secondary education in the city of Tampere, a position of some authority and one that has taken the former teacher wholly out of the secondary classroom. Annukka met Jorma at Tampere Classical High School when he arrived there as principal in 2000, staying in that position for three years before moving up and out into full-time administrative work. For Annukka, the attraction was immediate, and even though Jorma is eleven years her senior, it is clear that the two are deeply compatible.

Annukka and Jorma live in a lovely blue, wooden house, built in 2000, in a complex of similar homes thirty minutes from downtown Tampere. The house is typically Finnish, with blond wood floors and wood ceilings, with a pitched, ski-lodge ceiling and bright white walls. Jorma is a hunter, and throughout the house, the walls are covered with the skins of his conquests and also their skulls and antlers. Hunting since boyhood, he is adept at cutting up a moose and cooking the meat. Annukka says that before she met Jorma, she rarely ate meat. Since their marriage, she has adapted her palate to his hobby ("Moose is a berry," she jokes, "because it's from the forest!"). Another hobby, this one shared equally by both husband and wife, is art collecting – an activity they have been doing since they met. On the walls, interspersed among Jorma's animal trophies, are dozens of paintings, an impressive and lovely range of works for amateur collectors. There are block prints by Aukusti Tuhka and an etching by Hugo Simberg, one of Finland's most famous nineteenth-century artists. They have collected naïve works by well-known Russian artists and beautiful realist landscapes by members of the nineteenth-century Finnish landscape school. Jorma's sister is a painter, and a large modern canvas of houses has a featured place above the living room couch.

Like many urban-dwelling Finns, Jorma and Annukka also have a cottage in the country – in Sulkava, a village in eastern Finland. They retreat to the cottage frequently, to read and hike and hunt. Annukka and Jorma own a small sailing boat ("really, really small . . . and it leaks"), and they also play tennis together. It is a privilege, Annukka says, to be married to someone in the profession, someone who understands the complexities of the work and who shares a schedule similar to hers. Though Jorma has less time off than she – he has thirty-eight days off per year – it is still considerably longer than it would be if he were employed in other work, and the couple spend a great deal of time together. Over dinner at their home, I was struck by the easy, almost symbiotic way they interact with one another. Like other couples I know who have never had children, they exude a particular kind of intimacy and interconnectedness, reinforced no doubt by their shared professional interests.

In 2012, Annukka was accepted into a summer institute for teachers in the United States, to study American language and culture. The group spent a glorious three weeks visiting Yellowstone National Park; the Mormon Tabernacle; Jackson Hole, Wyoming; Washington, DC; and New York City. For Annukka, the summer proved to be transformative, affording her the opportunity to forge close friendships with many of the participants – friendships that are sustained on Facebook and in visits to France and elsewhere. Annukka wrote about the experience in a national teacher's journal, published for English teachers throughout Finland. "All the friendships," the article concludes, "will live on in my heart. It is truly a privilege to know I gained a worldwide network of friends." Despite the keen pleasures of the trip, Annukka gained a reputation for calling her husband on a daily basis. "Annukka never missed a day on the phone with Jorma," said the program administrator. "We used to joke with her that Jorma was the thirtieth member of the group."

Now, at fifty-five, Jorma is beginning to think about "downshifting," though his plans are still unclear. Finland provides educators with a pension of about 60 percent of their salaries, and medical care, of course, is provided by the state. Both have earned high salaries and are more than comfortable, relative to most Finns. After eighteen years of teaching, Annukka earns about 3000 euros a month after taxes. The textbook writing brings in additional income, as does the grading of final exams, a job for which she volunteers. Teacher pay in Finland is essentially equivalent to other white-collar professions – doctors, architects, lawyers. It is clear that she feels comfortably upper middle class. We talk about shoes and clothes and Marimekko with bourgeois pleasure.

***

It is 10:15 a.m. on a Thursday in early May, several weeks short of the term's end. Before Annukka's first class of the day, she chats with a cluster of students at the front of the room, then shoos them to their seats when she is ready to begin. Annukka is wearing a plaid, knee-length dress with a white sweater and hot pink tights. Her animal print shoes have two little ears on each foot. She wears sparkly brown polish on her nails. Thirty students assemble themselves into their inward-facing desk clusters. Today, the lesson is built around grammar and vocabulary games on the Kahoot program, a form of software that enables teachers to design personalized games and quizzes while integrating music, pictures, video clips, and other materials that appeal to teenagers. Half the class turn on their cell phones; the others work from laptops. Either device can be used to digitally answer the questions that appear on the screen. Annukka begins the program. An image from the film *The Lord of the Rings* appears.

"Is everybody in who wants to be in?" Annukka asks, referring to the digital connection necessary for playing the game. "You're going to see a word in Finnish and then three words in English." The first question comes up on the board, along with a series of pseudonyms (Le Meow, Rooserita, The Donald) that represent either single students or groups of students engaged in playing the game. Dramatic music beats out the passing seconds with game-show drama, and then the scores come up. Sixteen students have answered the question correctly; two have not. The remaining students, it seems, are simply choosing not to play the game or have not logged in their answers quickly enough. In any case, everything is anonymous. "Question two," says Annukka, moving on without comment on the previous outcome. Again, the mysterious music, the projected scores. The game lasts about ten minutes, and then Annukka shifts to a new reading comprehension activity: the screen displays a brief article about a South African editor, persecuted during apartheid. The group is supposed to read the article and then answer questions based on its content. They spend ten minutes on this.

Next, Annukka plays the trailer to *Cry Freedom*, the film about Steven Biko, which stars Denzel Washington. Once again, Annukka offers the class a choice. "You can follow along on the screen," she says, "follow in your books, or just listen to the voice reading." Ten more minutes pass. After completing the comprehension activity, Annukka shifts gears again, moving on to a writing exercise. Despite her ferocious efforts to appeal to her teenage audience, not all students are equally engaged in their work. Some stare listlessly out the window; some do other activities, unrelated to the work at hand. Annukka speaks loudly to a boy who has come up to her with a "problem." "How can you have a book from the wrong class?" she says with mock outrage. "My gray hairs are exploding!" The boy shrugs and smiles, wending his way slowly back to his seat. When students make an effort, they are rewarded with huge enthusiasm. When a struggling student shows Annukka his paper with all the answers correct, she explodes with pleasure: "Feel my hands; they are all sweaty!" she says. "I am so excited! I haven't been so excited in a long time. And I'm very old!"

This is the pace and tone of a typical Annukka Suonio class: one activity following fast on the heels of another, rapid shifts between texts and visual materials, like a well-choreographed dance. Students work in groups or independently, moving at their own pace, candidly acknowledging confusion or difficulty. It is a style of teaching that fits perfectly with Annukka's own personality, her energy and openness. Kari teaches his way. Tuija teaches her way. No one judges which is better or worse, except the students, who make their preferences clear by the electives they choose each term.

***

On the last night of my visit, Jorma and Annukka jointly cook our meal, a delicious dinner of salmon, plain potatoes, and salad (without dressing). Like everything about this country, the dinner is simple, healthy, and unpretentious. We get a bit tipsy on the good wine and laugh about marriage and the differences between our cultures.

Later in the evening, the talk turns back to teaching – its stresses and pleasures, the many differences I saw in the Finland schools compared with those in the United States. Ultimately, Annukka says, people all over the world go into teaching for some of the same reasons: "Teaching works best for people who themselves liked school. Essentially, with teaching, you know what you are getting into. You know what you will be able to provide."

Finally, she concludes by speaking, generally, about all the Finnish teachers she knows, whether in Tampere Classical or through her textbook work or through her personal friendships with those in other schools:

> There are many teachers among us who are single; quite a few who are divorced; many of us have no children; this is their life, these students are their children, this community is their social relationship . . . [The Finnish system] gives you a lot of time to devote to developing your own style . . . Teachers who come here are really keen to be here. I like the fact that in teaching there's no pressure about trying to climb up the career ladder. You start as a teacher, and you end as a teacher. And here in Finland, it's a safe, secure, respected, honorable, well-paid job; a job where you're set for life.

We go on to talk about her students this year, her favorite moments in the classroom. She tells me about a boy who was very bright and bored with the curriculum she designed for the class. She gave him the freedom to do an alternative project, and he created an extraordinary piece of creative work, far beyond anything she had imagined he could do. "That's what you live for," Annukka says. "I wouldn't say that it happens every day; there could be a week where nothing happens, but usually you come home, and you feel like positive feedback has come from a surprising place. If you stay positive, most people surprise you in a positive way. I think what you give is what you get."

2

Taiwan: Tradition and Change

The drive to Huajiang High School in downtown Taipei is an obstacle course of cars and motorcycles, people, pets, and bicycles. The school is located in Wanhua District, known to its residents as Bangka, the oldest district in the city. Amid the shrill noise of the street, one passes the iconic Longsham Temple, crammed with locals leaving offerings to hundreds of separate deities, and the Red House Theater, the first and largest teahouse in Taiwan. One drives through the massive garment district, virtually toppling with decaying signs and storefronts. It is a dizzying, aromatic ride that offers a visitor an intense and immediate sense of the country itself: its energy and ambition, its sometimes-precarious balance between old and new.

Huajiang High School sits in a slightly quieter section of the district, set back from the busy street by a large, gated drive flanked by banyan trees. The school, which has grown to 2300 students in the last decade, has gone through many transformations since its first construction in the pre-war era. The original school was built during the Japanese colonial period and bears the austere look of an aging institutional building: two-story cinder-block, with a stained, gray façade.

Entering Huajiang, however, one is greeted by a square, open courtyard, filled with beautiful mature plantings – pomelo, litchi, orange, and wax apple trees. The schoolrooms are built around this central space, a lush, fragrant garden, cordoned by a chest-level balustrade on which faculty and students have placed small plants. Ten years ago, as Huajiang grew in population, the government added a large, modern extension across the exterior courtyard. The new building, an impressive glass-and-steel structure with an Olympic-sized pool and a giant auditorium and stage, gives the illusion of affluence to an otherwise humble campus. Unfortunately, the extension is mostly unused. When electrical and heating costs proved to be prohibitive, most of the building was sold off to a company that rents out parts of the space for corporate meetings.

Standing on the front steps of the school, Feng-juan Kuo is initially indistinguishable from the mass of students passing around her. She is a tiny woman, barely over five feet tall, with a small, serious face framed by a pixie haircut. At fifty-three, she shows her age only in the fine lines around her eyes and mouth. She is dressed in purple capris with a colorful tunic and platform Mary Janes – a kind of playful attire that she adopts, in one form or another, every time I see her at school.

Feng-juan takes us into the teachers' room of Huajiang High, a large, unadorned space where several teachers sit behind high desks, glimpsing at us as we enter and looking immediately back down at their work. We are introduced to no one, and it is clear that Feng-juan's colleagues try hard to respect each other's privacy, given the open space of the room. Feng-juan ushers us into a tiny anteroom usually reserved for parent–teacher conferences. We sit on a leather couch and talk about life in classrooms, as Feng-juan keeps an eye on a big clock over the door. She has been teaching at Huajiang High for twenty years and has earned her way to seniority and a measure of authority. She is a teacher of Chinese literature but also a class advisor for forty students, a position that exempts her from one teaching class daily. As a result, Feng-juan teaches not three but two fifty-minute classes a day, a genteel schedule that allows her time for curriculum development, grading, and one-on-one work with students.

I am accompanied on this visit to Taiwan by Feng-juan's old school friend Sujane Wu, who is now a colleague of mine in the States and who is here to both interpret and to offer her own retrospective views on how high school has changed since her own time as a student in Yilan, outside Taipei. Having lived in America for almost thirty years, Sujane sees her old stomping grounds through a complicated lens – both nostalgic and anthropological. Sujane and Feng-juan were both Chinese literature majors at Soochow University in Taipei in the early 1980s, bonding over their love of Chinese poetry and their interest in traditional poetry in performance. As members of a poetry club, they sang traditional lyric poems together, poems that dated from 600 BCE and that still form the basis of a Taiwanese literary education. Feng-juan ultimately became a high school teacher, while Sujane took a more circuitous path that led to America and a college position, but both women have much in common, including provincial working-class roots and a deeply intellectual nature that seems to have sprung out of thin air.

The bell rings, and we gather our things and move through the leafy corridor to Feng-juan's classroom for the first of her two literature classes.

More than forty students file slowly into the room, a plain large space with nothing on the walls. Students sit in densely spaced desk groups, five students to four desks. It is late May, and fans mounted on the ceiling blow the hot air back and forth. Within the desk clusters, students seem fitfully engaged, some listening carefully, others talking to their neighbors or checking their cell phones. At the front of the room, Feng-juan presents the lesson of the day, an analysis of a passage in the textbook by a fifteenth-century Chinese philosopher. She calls these kinds of lessons "discussions," though to American eyes, they seem more like lectures, punctuated by structured questioning. Throughout the class, Feng-juan wears a small microphone mounted around her face with an amplifier strapped to her chest. She stands on a raised platform, moving through the lines of the text, explicating their meaning and giving historical context to the material.

Student participation follows an elaborate model of questioning and evaluating, a system of assessment worked out by Feng-juan over several years of experimentation. This assessment system is one of the first things she describes to me when we meet, one that she sees as an example of teamwork and a strategy for boosting student motivation. In advance of each class, Feng-juan sends the students an e-mail enumerating the questions she will be asking, allowing them time to prepare their responses. As class begins, she draws a graph on the board with each desk group represented. Once the preliminary lecture is over, the evaluation system is initiated. First, Feng-juan asks a question about the text. Students raise their hands to respond. If a student volunteers to speak and is called on, the student gets one point for his or her group. If the student answers correctly, he or she gets two points; and if the student speaks correctly and with enthusiasm or particular insight, he or she gets three points. At the end of the period, the group with the most points wins, claiming their material reward. Today's prize is a box of cookies. The group with the lowest score must get a "punishment," which has been worked out in advance by the students themselves. Punishments are usually some form of public humiliation (howling like a wolf, speaking with a mouthful of water, singing an embarrassing song). "Rewards and punishments work best as incentives," says Feng-juan, "as long as they are small and benign."

Feng-juan begins her round of questioning, calling on the first student, a tall girl with a long, thin ponytail down her back. The student stands and answers. "Good," says Feng-juan, "correct answer, good detail." She writes a 3 near the student's name on the blackboard. "Three?!" calls out a boy next to me. "Why three?!" Feng-juan seems unruffled by this interruption and calmly explains to him that his classmate had fulfilled the criteria for the score. The boy puts his head down on the desk in protest. The questioning continues until the passage has been fully parsed.

Feng-juan now moves on to the "group discussion" part of the lesson. "After you read the second essay," she asks, "did you change your views of this author?" She instructs the students to turn to their deskmates and discuss the question. They shift in their chairs compliantly, and Feng-juan stands on her platform observing the animated talk that takes place. After ten minutes, Feng-juan interrupts the hum. "Who would like to share your thoughts?" she asks, and many hands go up, followed by a brief chaos of laughing and talking. Both the group work and the subjective questions have dramatically changed the tone of the class. Feng-juan chooses one boy to speak, and after he rises and offers his assessment of the author, the class applauds. Feng-juan writes a 3 next to his name on the blackboard. A second girl stands up and delivers a longer response; another 3. Three or four more students rise and speak, some receiving 2s and others 3s, always followed by an explanation from Feng-juan. The exercise is punctuated by laughter after class clowns or surly jocks – universal types – give silly or inadequate answers. Students take notes in spiral notebooks, with bright cartoon characters or flowers or pop stars on their covers. No laptops are allowed in Feng-juan's classroom, and no SMART Boards are used to convey material to the class.

As the class period nears its end, attention begins to wane. Students play with their pens, twirling them like batons; they lean across desk groups to flirt or whisper. Feng-juan seems unfazed. She continues to listen intently to each response, furrowing her brow and delivering her summary and assessment of each answer, then noting the scores on the board. Finally, she declares the match over and adds up the points to choose winner and loser. As the winners unwrap their cookies, the losers move to the front of the room to fill their mouths with water while reciting a sentence. Everyone laughs and claps. It is clear that being punished is as good as winning.

TEACHER ARTIST

Teaching two classes a day theoretically leaves Feng-juan time for a life outside her work. But as a single woman, introspective and artistic by nature, her world seems circumscribed. Her greatest passion is poetry, which she reads continuously. In the last decade, Feng-juan has also taken up photography and now keeps a blog that combines her own pictures with poetic descriptions, many of them documenting field trips she has taken with her classes. Feng-juan's photographs are unusually evocative – mostly images of nature at various times of the year and of her students engaged in creative activities she has designed for them. One recent post shows images of flower petals on the spring grass. Beside the images, Feng-juan has written the following poem:

> Before the spring rain washes away the redness of flowers
> We played with the floral puzzle.
> Surviving midterms, anticipating break
> The students are too excited to stay in class.
> We skipped out and went to play with flowers ...

Students have used the petals to form *kanji* on the ground, spelling out images inspired by the flowers. Next to each image is a poetic explanation:

> This group arranged petals into a girl
> With long hair
> This group arranged petals into the word
> "Wedding gift"
> ... the rain comes to wash the West Lake's redness away
> We need to quickly bid farewell
> To the peach blossoms.
> Time does not wait.

The exercise is at once simple and complex, translating nature into word and image (since *kanji* is itself word and image), which is then translated again into photograph and poem. In all, I counted five levels of transposition: nature to *kanji*, *kanji* to image, image to photograph, photograph to poem, paired photograph and poem into blog. This kind of thoughtful, multilayered work seems characteristic of Feng-juan's sensibility, as both an artist and a teacher.

For the most part, though, Feng-juan's photography is not done in the service of teaching. Apart from the blog, which highlights her students' achievements and downplays her own, Feng-juan sees her photography as a private part of herself. Travel is another one, an activity that provides grist for her writing and photography, and one that she says deepens her understanding of human nature and the world around her. During every extended vacation, Feng-juan goes somewhere – most recently to India and Tibet, countries she has visited and photographed in both winter and summer. She has also visited France, Greece, Cambodia, Vietnam, and Japan. These trips are taken with photography clubs, small groups of amateur artists who are strangers to Feng-juan, but whose group status allows for reduced transportation and lodging rates.

In general, there is a kind of self-effacement in Feng-juan that suggests the interiority of a poet. She lives alone; she does not date or engage in an active social life. She is deeply devoted to her students in the way that single teachers can be: remembering small, specific kindnesses directed toward her, quoting correspondence from students who have long since graduated, speaking with deep feeling about the troubles and successes of particular students. She tells a story about a student, a boy in her advisory class who was having difficulty at home and had seemed withdrawn and sad. In his weekly journal entry, he addressed Feng-juan as "Sister Feng-juan," and went on to speak about his life with a candor that was deeply flattering to Feng-juan. To be perceived as an older sister, she says, is the highest compliment she can imagine. When I ask her what she loves most about her work, she says, "Care from the students and trust from the parents." One of Feng-juan's responsibilities as a class advisor is to read the journals of her students, submitted weekly. These private musings are used as a way for teachers to keep track of students' lives and catch problems before they impact academic work. Feng-juan is in charge of forty students, and she spends a good deal of time reading these journals, most of which simply document the surface lives of their authors. Sometimes, though, students choose to reveal more, exposing their fears or the difficulties of their private lives. When this happens, Feng-juan says she sees this as a triumph, a sign that she has achieved her highest goal as a teacher: "to make a real and meaningful connection with another human being."

For Feng-juan, freedom and informality is generally a good thing. She believes that fear-based compliance is antithetical to learning. The least successful teachers in her school, she says, are those who are most strict. "Students want to challenge authority," she says, and if you set yourself up as a strict authority, you invite disrespect and resistance. "I want students to respect me for who I am," she says, "not because I am their teacher."

The notion of teachers involving themselves in the personal lives of students is a relatively new one in Taiwan. Until the late 1980s, the country operated under martial law, and education was rigidly structured and controlled by the government. This was the period now referred to the White Terror, a thirty-eight-year term during which Chiang Kai-shek muzzled free speech and incarcerated thousands of Taiwanese intellectuals. Martial law placed restrictions on the contents of printed material, including textbooks, and on the curricula of Taiwanese schools. But the rigidities of martial law also served to maintain historical norms regarding the role and status of teachers. As the transmitters of cultural values, their role was critical. The inherent conservativism of this anticommunist period, along with the inherited values of Taiwan's early-twentieth-century Japanese colonizers, combined to elevate the teacher into a *sensei* – a person of high moral prestige and social veneration. Sujane says she is shocked by this shift in the teacher's role toward care and confession. In her day, teachers were respected as remote and supreme authorities, unconcerned with student problems. Feng-juan describes high school teachers who were so respected that she couldn't look at them directly. Their dazzle could be taken in only through peripheral sight.

Those days are over in Taiwan, though vestiges of past beliefs and practices still persist. Students still maintain a surface deference toward their teachers. They would never address them by their first names, for example, or direct their misbehavior toward the teachers, expressing their adolescent resistance in quieter forms of distractedness or disengagement. Students still wear uniforms, and in many classes they sit in long rows, listening to lectures. The architecture of the classroom (the raised platform at the front of the class) creates an inevitable and symbolic distance between teacher and students. Other traditional practices seem less institutional and more an expression of Feng-juan's own choice. In some classes, for example, Feng-juan uses a bowl with numbered sticks to call on students. Each student is assigned a number and must respond when his or her stick is pulled from the bowl. Games and other forms of classroom "fun" are strictly separated from the academic work, not organically integrated with it. Feng-juan's system of rewards and punishments creates a festive mood in the classroom but has nothing inherently to do with the material that is being covered. The academic work of the class remains deeply traditional.

For Taiwanese women such as Feng-juan and Sujane, worldly success came through tremendous perseverance and doggedness. Both women are close to their siblings, and neither is married. In both cases, it seems, the effort to extract themselves from the worlds of their childhood and the norms of their culture commanded huge energy and ambition. Sujane tells a story about how she resisted the pressure from her poor parents to attend a vocational high school instead of the academic one, a choice she was required to make at the end of middle school. "What is the point of going to the academic high school if we can't pay for you to go to college?" her mother insisted. "As a woman, you will have no practical skills and be good for nothing." After much conflict, Sujane eventually struck a compromise with her family: if they allowed her to go the academic route, she would spend every waking minute when she was not studying helping her family on their farm. "I would never go to a movie, never see a friend, never leave the house unless it was to help the family." And she kept her promise. That single-minded determination caught the eye of a highly educated and successful cousin, whom Sujane barely knew. The cousin offered her full-time secretarial work in Taipei, a salary and lifestyle that would allow her to attend evening college classes. College itself created new ambitions, and Sujane went off to America, where she gained a teaching assistantship at the University of Wisconsin. From there, the path was cleared for a PhD and a teaching position, first at Swarthmore and then at Smith College.

Feng-juan's story is less dramatic, but it too seems fueled by the same sense of self-preservation, persistence, and self-discipline. She was born in Keelung, a port city in the northeastern region of Taiwan, adjacent to Taipei. Her parents, originally from a rural hamlet and educated only through elementary school, moved to Keelung after their marriage and opened a small grocery store. Throughout her childhood, Feng-juan says, she always felt on the brink of abject poverty. The family store, which had never been particularly successful, struggled increasingly with the rise of convenience stores such as 7-Eleven. When Feng-juan was in sixth grade, her father, facing bankruptcy, joined a ship's crew and left for sea. Feng-juan's mother was left with the store and the children. "I became like a young mother," Feng-juan says, cooking and cleaning, dropping off siblings at school, and then picking them up at the end of the day. The atmosphere in her home, remembers Feng-juan, was "very authoritarian," with almost no time for just "being a kid." Her parents, she says, "cared about their children but rarely expressed love." School, she remembers, was, from the first, a place of escape. In her elementary school in Keelung, teachers were kind and patient, and Feng-juan says she felt a genuine sense of love from several of them. Her first important mentor was a ninth-grade Chinese literature teacher, Shu-yu Liu, who wrote her pupil encouraging letters and even invited Feng-juan to lunch at her own home. Shu-yu lent Feng-juan books by female authors, inspiring in her a sense of possibilities and a love of literature. The next year, another teacher, Daosan Ma, took over the mentorship role. "He was a mainlander," Feng-juan says, "from Jiangsu Province, with a very heavy provincial accent. So, during class time, all the students wouldn't listen to him. I was the only one who struggled to pay attention, to grasp what he was saying. After a while, he only lectured to me. When he made jokes, I was the one laughing." Feng-juan remembers that she was so moved and inspired by this particular literature teacher that she wrote to the head teacher on his behalf. "I said that literature class was the one class where I was reluctant to even blink my eyes for fear of missing one precious moment." Finally, a music teacher, Shengzi Jin, became Feng-juan's first artistic audience. The teacher, a young woman of Korean background, was responsible for reading Feng-juan's weekly journal entries. Jin responded to Feng-juan's writing with such sensitivity and interest that it inspired her to write voluminous entries, filling book after book with her observations about life, family, and school. "She had great respect for her students," Feng-juan says, "so at the time, I really got the feeling that she was like a sister. She cared about me like a sister." That sisterly relationship provided a prototype for the kind of teacher she would eventually become.

Feng-juan's first foray into the world of work was not as a teacher, however. After graduating from college with a literature major, she decided to go into publishing – a position that seemed less stressful and equally prestigious. In the few years that followed, Feng-juan began and quit a succession of publishing positions. "I would work for a year and then get 'occupational burnout.' I would long to travel, but could never get a sufficient vacation to take any kind of interesting trip. So I would quit, travel, and return to look for a new job." After several years of this peripatetic life, Feng-juan ran into a younger female schoolmate who suggested she look into teaching. "Everyone in her family was a teacher, and she knew how to go about applying for private school jobs," Feng-juan says. "She talked me through the process."

In the 1980s, entrance into public school teaching in Taiwan was available only to those who had graduated from normal schools, special institutions for teacher preparation. Those who wished to teach but had attended general universities, such as Feng-juan and Sujane, were required start out in temporary positions in either private or cram schools, and take courses toward obtaining teaching credentials during the evening. Afterward, jobs were assigned based on seniority, often requiring long periods of apprenticeship. Feng-juan waited six years before becoming eligible for her first full-time public school position; many of her colleagues, who had scored lower than she on examinations, never made it into full-time employment, spending their careers as "nomad teachers," moving from one temporary position to another.

Feng-juan began to interview for private school positions. At the first school she approached, she was asked to make a teaching demonstration. "By coincidence, I decided to teach a poem by Du Fu, the famous eighth-century poet, to sing the poem in the way that I had done in college." The main judge, it turns out, was a member of the Ting Yun Poetry Club at Soochow University and was immediately impressed with Feng-juan's performance. "I was hired on the spot, and afterwards, the judge came over and said, 'Actually, I'm from your college and I'm also one of the members of the poetry club.' So it was fate."

Teaching at Tung-hai was challenging. Feng-juan refers to this school as "a gang member's school," a term that refers less to students' behavior than to their general lack of interest in anything studious or intellectual. In Taiwan, as in most of Asia, high school entrance is based on examinations taken at the end of middle school. Students who score well on the exams attend prestigious high schools that serve as conduits to top colleges. Students who score poorly attend either low-prestige public or private schools. Tung-hai was a school for students who had done poorly on the examination. For the intellectual Feng-juan, teaching in the school was frustrating; students were too often unengaged, and the material she was obliged to cover held no inherent interest for her. What's more, the workload for teachers was back breaking. "I taught twenty-seven classes a week," Feng-juan remembers, "five to six classes a day. My microphone was always around my neck; I never took it off."

After three years, she applied for another job, this time in an elite private school, a prestigious institution for the children of government officials. In every way, Guang Ren High School was the opposite of Tung-hai. Students were intensely focused on their academic work, driven by their own ambitions or those of their parents to compete for slots in the best universities. At Guang Ren, the workload was far more genteel, with twelve classes a week, a lovely building that afforded space for private work, and a well-stocked library. But Feng-juan found teaching at Guang Ren even more exhausting than at her previous school. Expectations were unerringly high, students were spoiled and demanding, and Feng-juan's schedule made huge intellectual demands on her. She was assigned four different subjects to teach at both the middle and upper school levels. Feng-juan was expected to design the curriculum for these classes, work she had not done in the first job and for which she had no training. Most stressful of all was the pressure she felt from affluent, well-connected parents. Teachers were expected to maintain continual communication with parents, keeping written transcripts of student contributions to class discussions, and then making them available to parents. "After each term exam, I would receive phone calls," Feng-juan says, "[from] parents demanding meetings and explanations for why their children were performing as they were." Feng-juan tells a story that sums up her experience at Guang Ren. "One day," she says, "I went back to my office and saw a lot of flowers on my desk along with a red envelope. Inside was money – a lot of money." Sujane says that this is not uncommon among elites in Taiwan: "The meaning is clear: 'We hope you give our child special treatment.' Bribery."

Unsurprisingly, then, Feng-juan started to miss the sweet, "kind-hearted" students in her previous school; "gang-members," it seemed, were preferable to the spoiled young people in Guang Ren. After three years, she had had enough. Having taken the requisite courses and gained sufficient seniority to apply for public school positions, Feng-juan applied for and was hired at her present school, a place where she has felt comfortable and appreciated, challenged but not overworked.

Feng-juan remembers her teacher education courses, taken in the evenings at a local normal school, as a combination of dense theory and practical, collaborative work. Since all the students in her classes were practicing teachers (temporary or private school teachers hoping to move full time into the public system), they brought to each course a wealth of daily experiences. Courses were often heavy on reading, with professors assigning as many as thirteen books per term to teachers already burdened by the demands of their daily teaching. Most of the texts that were read were translations of American or British pedagogy texts, painful reading even in their first languages. Feng-juan remembers dividing the reading up between colleagues in the class – say, 250 pages each per week – and then meeting with the group to hear summaries of the material. By far, the most useful part of her teacher training, says Feng-juan, were the demonstration lessons done by her fellow students. Those lessons became grist for conversations about a wide range of issues in the classroom: behavioral problems, special needs, particular approaches to the teaching of a text. Like generations of students in teaching preparation programs, Feng-juan found the practical always trumped the theoretical.

Since the time when Feng-juan was in school, teacher preparation courses in Taiwan have moved out of the normal schools and into the universities, giving access to those courses to a much wider population of aspiring teachers. At the same time, however, teaching positions have become increasingly difficult to land. While larger numbers of undergraduates now get teaching credentials, according to Feng-juan, only a fraction will get a teaching job in the field. This is true, she says, because teaching – as difficult as it is – still holds prestige in the culture, still pays well relative to other white-collar work, and still allows for a degree of autonomy and flexibility that is absent in most professional work in Taiwan. That fact may account for the gender mix I witnessed in Feng-juan's school. Though it is profession that still attracts a majority of women, I was struck by the number of men I saw teaching in Huajiang High, standing on their raised platforms and lecturing.[1]

Teaching for eighteen years, Feng-juan has more than doubled her salary. As a single woman, with health care and pension paid for by the state, she is comfortably middle class. One helpful feature of life in Taiwan is the relatively low cost of living. Taiwan's cost of living index is 40 to 50 percent lower than in the United States. Rents in the city center are quite affordable on a teacher's salary; food is cheap; and even a nice restaurant meal seems inexpensive by American standards. A giant dinner of Taiwanese specialties, abalone and king crab, whole flounder, and stinky tofu, came to less than $20 per person. Clothes are also inexpensive. Shops display racks of shirts on the sidewalk for $1.50 a piece; museums and botanic gardens are either free or inexpensive. A two-hour massage, capped off with a snack of tea and cookies, came to just over $30. Hence, a little salary goes a long way. Ten years ago, Feng-juan bought her present apartment in Taipei, a modern two-bedroom flat that she has converted into a spacious one bedroom. Teachers are encouraged to purchase their own homes through a special teacher loan program set up by the government. The apartment has appreciated over the course of the decade – almost tripling in value. "Pay is excellent; the pension system is excellent." Feng-juan says. When she retires, she will receive 50 percent of her salary, an income she perceives to be quite adequate for buying a house in the country and continuing to travel. For now, though, she is happy where she is. When we visit, she is in the process of painting each room in different shades of mauve and blue. She is doing the work herself, partly because she is thrifty by nature and partly because she enjoys the slow, detail-oriented work of painting.

DAILY SCHEDULE

Feng-juan arrives at school at 7:10 each morning to oversee her advisory students as they clean the outside of the building. All school maintenance is done by teams of students, supervised by their head teachers. This term, Feng-juan's advising group has been assigned to "outdoor cleaning," which entails sweeping around the coconut trees that drop leaves around the interior courtyard and carting away the carpet of other debris caused by frequent downpours. After the morning work, Feng-juan has the first of her two literature classes, an eleventh-grade group of forty-five students. During the free period that follows, she grades papers. At lunchtime, she is again charged with overseeing her advising group as they eat their lunches. The school provides lunches for those who wish to purchase them, and students eat together in the school's unadorned cafeteria. School lunches are delicious, bento boxes with a changing array of dumplings, noodles, pickled vegetables, and sushi. After lunch, Feng-juan meets with individual students, grades students' work, or works on curricula until her second class of the day, in the late afternoon. Then, her final responsibility is to oversee, once again, the students' cleaning of classrooms. At Huajiang High School, virtually all trash gets recycled. Each classroom has six separate bins for different kinds of waste, and students assiduously separate bottles from cans and paper from cardboard, plastic, or wax products.

Feng-juan's second academic class of the day is a literature class for students who are majoring in science. Though literature classes are classified by interest or career orientation, I saw little difference in either content or approach between the morning and afternoon sections, except that this science-oriented group is composed almost entirely of boys. It is dusk – the class runs from 4:20 to 5:10 – and students straggle in with a weary gait. They have come from physical education class, and their exhaustion is palpable. Feng-juan stands, as before, on the raised platform at the front of the room, her microphone anchored to her ear and the amplifier strapped to her chest. "If you need to use the restroom," she says sternly, "do it now." Several students get up and leave the class.

The topic for today is a 200 BC essay about life in the emperor's court, and Feng-juan begins by lecturing. Her presentation consists of a summary of the passages assigned, and then an exegesis of words that are highlighted in the book as difficult, important, or historically resonant. After her opening remarks, Feng-juan distributes a brief critical essay, supplementary material by a contemporary writer, and waits silently as they read it. She begins to lecture again, summarizing the argument in the article and noting key words and phrases. Throughout, the group is serious and mostly quiet, apart from an occasional whisper or the checking of cell phone. There is little personal interaction in the class. Feng-juan never mentions a student by name. When it comes time for questioning, she employs her usual strategy of drawing a numbered stick from the cup on her desk. As the period moves on, behavior begins to slacken. One boy in the back folds and unfolds a tee shirt, another snaps a towel at his deskmate. Feng-juan forges on. Sample test questions have been distributed to the class, and, at Feng-juan's request, students begin reading them aloud in a kind of deadpan chant. The period ends, and the students shuffle out. Their next stop will be home, an after-school job, or cram school.

For Feng-juan, the end of the school day is the end of the workday. She does not bring work home, using the evenings to "clean the house, walk the dog, exercise, read, maintain my blog, and chat with neighbors." Though the day ends late by American standards, usually at around 6 p.m., Feng-juan seems to be able to separate herself completely: "My school life," she says, "does not interfere with my home life. These are two separate realms." In order to maintain that separation, Feng-juan needs to use her school time efficiently. At work, she is constantly reading and grading. Her eighty-five literature students write three long essays per term, each of which receives detailed written feedback as well as individual conferences. As a head teacher, she is also responsible for reading the weekly journals. With forty students in her advising group, it is a constant weekly chore.

Five times per semester, Feng-juan meets with all the other subject teachers to discuss their classes and the curriculum and to share best practices. In these sessions, one teacher at a time takes the lead, presenting to the group what the teacher learned in a conference or in his or her teaching of a particular portion of the text. Teachers decide together what texts to use. Since text choice can change every three years, there is much talk of the text's efficacy and how their individual classes responded to the material. The text they currently use includes excerpts of great Chinese poetry, essays, and history, with substantial footnotes and annotations at the bottom of each page. To an outsider, it seems like a very slim text to cover over the entire year, but Sujane explains that each of these brief sections represents complex and difficult material, in terms of both content and form.

Weekly department meetings are spent parsing out the lessons in the book over the course of two semesters, thirty classical readings that form the cornerstone of the literature curriculum, nationally. Fifteen lessons are covered each semester, broken up into three groups of five. School-wide exams are given in each department after each five-week period. Feng-juan and her colleagues have worked out a clear, systematic approach to each set of the five lessons. In the first, she introduces the author and key characters in the text, usually using supplementary media – a film clip or a news commentary program. In the second, third, and fourth lessons, she moves in great detail through the content of the chapter, writing brief summaries of each paragraph on the board. Students need to retain the names of all characters in these dense, historical primary texts, and Feng-juan says she gives them tricks and mnemonic devices to remember, punning the ancient names with terms like Starbucks or McDonald's. Students copy her work from the board or use their smartphones to capture the material. The final class within the series of five is for more open-ended discussion. During this class, students are asked subjective questions about the text

("How did this passage change your view of the author? Why do you think Li Si is such a great writer?"), and a range of right answers is possible. Exams, given after this sequence of five lessons, are multiple choice.

Though Taiwan ranks consistently high on PISA and other international measures in 2012 (fourth in math and seventh in reading out of sixty-five countries),[2] criticism has been leveled at the education system for its rigidity and the lack of an affective and creative focus. The government responded to this criticism with a lengthy White Paper, issued in 2014, that sought to humanize the system.[3] The report touches on almost every aspect of the education system, from the creation of new counseling systems for students and programs for fostering "social responsibility" to an increase in sports, arts, and "health literacy" programs. Indeed, the policy mandate went so far as to call for the experimental withdrawal of entrance exams between middle school and high school. Under the proposed new system, students would be judged on school-based examinations like the kinds Feng-juan gives at the end of each five-week term. The government has instituted the change in only a small number of schools, and there is surprising resistance to it. Critics claim that the shift will put even more pressure on students and teachers – on students, who will come to perceive all their tests as summative and not formative measures of their growth, and on teachers, to inflate grades so that students will not miss out on entrance to preferred high schools.

The White Paper also addresses the "employment crisis" within the field of teaching, the fact that so many college graduates are vying for so few positions. Most Taiwanese teachers hold on to their jobs for life. The retention rate within the profession averages over 80 percent.[4] The new government report seeks to exploit the glut of talent on the market by increasing standards and assessment for practicing teachers – establishing "teacher professional standards" and "teacher performance indicators." The report calls for local governments to "establish initiatives to re-assess incompetent teachers" and "reward and recognize outstanding teachers."[5]

Feng-juan says she knows nothing about the White Paper recommendations. Clearly, policy initiatives and the politics of reform are beyond her concerns. Like every teacher I have ever interviewed or worked with, Feng-juan's focus is on the daily – the literary passage she is teaching, the particular needs of a sullen student, the burned-out light bulb in the overhead projector. Feng-juan already integrates the arts into her classes through student blogging; she already maintains communication with parents by giving them access to those blogs; she "breaks down walls between school and community" by taking students on field trips to beautiful parks and historic districts in the city. These recommendations don't concern her. The changes that Feng-juan herself would like to see are much simpler: "There are too many people in each class," she says. "I think classes should have no more than thirty students. First-years and sophomores should take only six classes a day, leaving the seventh and eighth for elective choice – for clubs or exercise or special interest classes."

On my last day in the school, I observe the once-a-week class meeting that Feng-juan oversees in her role as a class advisor. Like other kinds of reform that have been instituted to humanize the schools, this "social gathering" is intended to build school spirit and rapport among the students. From the start, the class is wholly student run. Two boys enter the classroom singing; one girl puts her sneakers up on ledge of the blackboard. Feng-juan stands and watches as students trickle into the room, then make announcements about yearbooks, school trips, and cleaning assignments for the week. "We need five people," calls out a pony-tailed boy over the din of chattering students. Still quietly tucked into her place at the side of the room, Feng-juan watches as a class leader gets up and starts a Simon Says–like game where students must form rapid groups of two or three, clinging to one another before sprawling onto the floor. Anyone who is left over once the groups are formed gets "punished." Bodies rocket around the classroom, as each new grouping is called: "Two girls and one boy!" "One boy, one girl!" "Two girls, three boys!" At the end of the period, the losing students have to eat sour lemons in front of the class, grimacing and laughing. Feng-juan continues her silent watch, smiling when students take their rewards and punishments. "In my day," Sujane says, "when the teacher entered the classroom, the students fell silent."

In conversations, Feng-juan admits that her own attitudes about teaching, about the new freedoms of students, are different from those of her peers. Most teachers, she says, miss the old authoritarian ways, the blind respect for the teacher. Throughout our time at Huajiang High School, I have been introduced to no one – not one fellow teacher, not one administrator. Autonomy, in Huajiang, is coupled with a sense of discretion, a sense of everyone going about his or her own business. This may be true, to some extent, because of the large size of the school and the sheer numbers of bodies that must be moved and managed over the course of a day. But the anonymity seems connected, too, to a deep, traditional sense of privacy, one that speaks to the essentially conservative values that still pervade the school. The solitary atmosphere at Huajiang High School reinforces the essential purpose of the high school: to help students pass their exams. Even the reading of student journals seems intended less as a way to break down personal walls than as a vehicle for early intervention, a proactive strategy for addressing problems that might scuttle academic success. Despite talk of reform, that goal still seemed central. Whatever fun and merriment I observed during game day was done in service of that aim – because hard work requires the occasional reward of play. The most frequent explanation I heard for the hour of games is that "students do better on their exams when they can blow off steam."

Since she is a solitary person by nature, teaching is a perfect profession for Feng-juan. She is never forced to compromise her essential nature in the classroom. She knows precisely the parameters of her role, and they include all the things she most likes to do. "I like helping students, one on one," she says. "I like correcting compositions, because I get to understand their ideas. I like introducing my favorite writers to my classes. These are the pleasures of teaching." Low pay, low status, poor resources, misbehavior: when I ask Feng-juan her thoughts on these endemic problems that teachers encounter throughout the world, she waves her hand at me. "These problems don't exist for me," she says. "I'm very pleased with the way I am treated. I am very happy to be a teacher. I am very, very lucky."

3

Greece: A Week of Austerity

From my hotel window near Athens' central Plaka, the view is staggering. The creamy Parthenon rises on its great hill, lit on four sides and wrapped in lacy scaffolding. Even after two and a half millennia, the Acropolis radiates an unparalleled sense of harmony, beauty, and balance. Everywhere beneath it, however, the city rumbles and grouses, horns honking, homeless people wrapped in their blankets, panhandling cripples and burn victims blocking the small, trash-congested roads. In the open squares that punctuate this ancient city, tourists buy evil-eye key chains, wooden bottle openers in the shape of phalluses, and endless reproductions of the beautiful friezes and busts that line the walls of the new Acropolis Museum. The city's crises – its financial miseries, its strikes and protests, its pervasive graffiti – stand in ironic counterpoint to the ruins of Athens' glorious past, the still-gorgeous temples that overlook the complexities of modern life in Athens. Day and night, cranes work to restore the marble façades of the Parthenon, the temple of Athena Nike, and the Erechtheum, while the city suffers from the draconian cuts of Greece's austerity measures.

International press has documented the extraordinary price paid by Greek citizens to stay in the European Union – the slashing of salaries and services, the humiliating restructuring of businesses. Spending time with ordinary Athenians drives home just how painful those cuts have been. Austerity measures have closed down schools, public offices, and private shops; millions of seniors have been stripped of their pensions. Greece's public hospital budget was cut by 25 percent between 2009 and 2011, and recent statistics report that nearly a million people in Greece are now without access to health care. Infant mortality rates are rising, as are levels of HIV infection among drug users; malaria has returned to Greece; and (perhaps unsurprisingly) there has been a spike in the suicide count.

Greece is suffering, and the light at the end of tunnel – for those who choose to believe it exists – seems very far away indeed.[1]

Vasiliki Michailidou, a thirty-four-year-old, thirteen-year veteran English teacher, considers herself one of the lucky ones. She is employed in what she considers to be a good and fairly secure position. She has her own apartment, at a rent she can afford, and her life is still rich with friendships and hobbies. When we meet on the first morning of my visit, at the Panormou bus stop down the hill from her school, she exudes a kind of young-teacher vitality. It is 7:40 on a Monday morning, the start of what will be, from my perspective, a bruising week of teaching and duty responsibilities at the Athens Varvakeion Model Experimental School.

Vasso, as she is called by friends and colleagues, is a tall, slim woman with waist-length hair, a long nose, and broad smile. Her youth stands out among her colleagues, all of whom are older and more conservative in their attire. On this first day, Vasso wears a long gray sweater and baggy black pants, the same outfit she will wear tomorrow. There is a slightly bohemian quality about her – the attractive scruffiness of an artist.

Typically, Vasso's first period is reserved for parent conferences; today, however, no one has contacted her, and she is free to review the lessons of the day and grade papers in the small teachers' lounge on the first floor. The lounge is filled with perhaps seven or eight faculty, several of whom sit down at the table with us. There is no coffee pot or refrigerator in the room, or any of the other ubiquitous objects found in teachers' rooms around the world. One teacher has brought in a bag of pastries and hands the bag around to some colleagues. Outside on the macadam driveway, I can hear students kicking a soccer ball; then, from the outside courtyard, comes the sound of the daily opening prayer, each day led by a student. Perhaps two dozen students have joined in, gathering near the front door of the school. When the prayer ends, the soccer game resumes until the passing bell.

Vasso gathers her materials and goes upstairs to unlock a classroom door. The hallways are painted a deep salmon color and punctuated periodically by bits of adolescent graffiti. Each of Vasso's classes is assigned to a different classroom, and each classroom must be locked and unlocked between the ten-minute passing periods. Inside, the second-floor room is devoid of decoration, filled to capacity with old double-desks, many covered, again, with graffiti. A gray Formica floor carries sound jarringly in the chill air, projecting every movement of the metal chairs. There is an old-fashioned television and a whiteboard covered with writing from a previous teacher's class. Above the board, a small, painted icon looks down with a tight smile.

Students enter slowly, dumping their backpacks on the desks and depositing themselves noisily into their seats. Most wear sweatshirts, sweatpants, low-hung jeans, and Ugg boots. Settled into their places, they are loose limbed, sleepy, and barely attentive. Ten minutes into the period, twenty-seven students have arrived, and Vasso begins to speak, explaining the nature of the day's lesson. "We are going to start with the second song on your sheets," she says, passing out a Xeroxed page. At the top, the title explains the point of the exercise: "Review of the Indicative Present, Future, and Imperative Tenses." She turns on the audio system, and a rock beat blasts into the room. The song, entitled "Crawling Back to You," by the Arctic Monkeys, describes an obsessive infatuation, a surreal hymn to adolescent love. The handout shows the lyrics of the song with key words omitted. Students are to listen carefully and then fill in the empty spaces.

Because of the idiosyncratic nature of the secondary system in Greece, many subject-area public school teachers find themselves in a peculiar situation: Vasso's ostensible job is to prepare her students to pass their grammar proficiency exams for college entrance. But because the curriculum designates only two forty-minute periods of English per week, almost all college-bound students know they must attend private cram schools in order to learn sufficient English to pass the test. Students then take their proficiency tests at the soonest possible moment, often during the second or third year of high school. As a result, close to three-quarters of Vasso's fourth-year students have already passed these Basic English exams, and enter her classes with no incentive to learn more grammar. At the same time, however, all students are required to enroll in English through their last year of high school, creating an essentially captive audience for teachers of examination-required subjects. To make matters worse, the grades that students receive in their public school classes are not factored in to college admission. In other words, Vasso and her colleagues hold no leverage over their pupils, their assessment means nothing, and their only instrument of motivation is the teacher's own capacity to entertain and engage. It is hard work, even for a young, gifted teacher like Vasso.

To motivate her students, Vasso uses music, games, open-ended writing assignments – anything that can pull teenagers into the subject. Each class I observe is pitched to adolescent interests and popular culture, as Vasso's endless patience nudges students into participation. "What is this song about?" Vasso asks the class. A cluster of girls in the front rows watch her carefully as she stands, arms folded in front of her, near the computer. "A guy is in love with a girl," says a girl seated by Vasso's hip. "Does he love her? If he is 'crawling back to her,' does she have the same feelings? It says, 'we could be together if you wanted to.'" The same small group of doting girls continues to answer Vasso's questions, while the hum of distracted conversation drifts from the back of the room.

"Are you familiar with the video?" Vasso asks a cluster of boys studying their cell phones near the window. "Yes? If someone read the lyrics without the video clip," she coaxes, "would they understand? Yes? No?" The period moves on, with students in the back tuning in and out of the lesson. Vasso plays the song again, then distributes another worksheet, then speaks to the group about an upcoming essay assignment. It is cold in the room, and most students wear their coats. Later, Vasso explains that a recent scandal involving the theft of funds for heating the building has meant the furnace will not be turned on in the foreseeable future. In the face of everything her colleagues have already withstood, this latest indignity seems almost comic.

CUTS, CUTS, AND MORE CUTS

Every teacher with whom I spoke at the Athens Experimental School made reference to the draconian austerity measures enacted since 2012. Those measures have had a particularly devastating impact on Greek schools. Within minutes of my first meeting her, Vasso described the chaos that has accompanied the budget cuts. The greatest blow by far was the wholesale shutdown of dozens of programs and subject departments in the public schools. Many of those eliminated subjects were vocational in nature, with working-class families suffering worst of all, since it was their sons and daughters who utilized those programs the most. Vasso's mother was one of the first casualties of the cuts. A veteran health teacher, she left the field two years earlier when the government simply deleted all health-related fields, including programs for nurses' aides, hospital orderlies, and other vital, but low-status jobs. Like others in her situation, Mrs. Michailidou was told she could either leave with 50 percent of her promised pension or accept a part-time position far away from her home. She chose the former; relocating for part-time work seemed untenable for a woman in her sixties.

Teachers' salaries have also suffered dramatic cuts. In the last two years, Vasso's pay was halved, from approximately $24,000 to $12,000 a year. Still, she has a job. "Even friends with PhDs in chemistry and computers are out of work," she says, "even engineers and doctors." Vasso's brother, a telecommunications expert, took a job in Sweden at the height of the cuts and has now decided to stay. Vasso says his choice to abandon the country is commonplace among college graduates in

Greece. "This is becoming a country of old people," Vasso says about the exodus of young professionals. Saddest of all, says Vasso, is that people have given up. "There are solutions to these problems, but politicians don't want to apply them to education and to programs that would help the underclass. Money is thrown away. There are so many abandoned buildings," Vasso says, yet "so many homeless."

Presently, Greece has an unemployment rate of approximately 20 percent, but conversations with working friends of Vasso's suggest that the employment situation is even worse than those numbers would suggest. As part of the stimulus, the government has paired with corporations to hire new employees, splitting salaries as an incentive for hiring. The share program was intended as a way for companies to hire and promote workers into full-time company jobs. Instead, Vasso and her friends say, corporations are simply firing these government-sponsored employees after a year and hiring a crop of new ones.

School cuts have been accompanied by all kinds of large and small indignities. Vasso tells me that when austerity measures were first implemented, government officials wielding measuring tapes would come into the classrooms as she taught, and start measuring the dimensions of the room. They had been sent to see how many students could be fit into one classroom, to work out the numbers "scientifically," and to report back to the government with their recommendations. It was concluded that forty students could fit into an average classroom space, a finding that meant the teacher–student ratio should be set at 40:1. Part-time positions were cut by 50 percent, and permanent teachers were required to teach two additional hours a day, without compensation. Austerity measures also meant the firing of all secretarial staff. Teachers now take on the secretarial duties themselves. Vasso and other teachers rotated the job of the janitor as well, cleaning toilets during their free periods. Several mornings a week, Vasso spends 8:00 to 10:40 on secretarial work, providing paperwork for students transferring out of the school, overseeing students who come into the office to collect class rosters for homeroom teachers, and monitoring the surveillance camera outside the school. At one point in the morning, she moves into the principal's office to cover for her as the principal conducts her morning review of the building. The principal, a middle-aged woman who was, until this year, a Greek literature and language teacher, is herself a temporary fill-in, since the previous principal moved to another school. She, like most principals in Greece, continues to teach six hours a week; the assistant principal teaches twelve hours.

Vasso and her colleagues say that protests against the cuts have been futile. Last year, teachers went on a one-week strike but ultimately went back to work, having negotiated no concessions. "Some teachers in our school were threatened by administrators," one teacher says of the strike. In a fragile economy such as Greece's, fear of layoffs gives teachers little leverage in negotiating salary or work hours. Indeed, there is little leverage for teachers in designing or reforming the curriculum as well: as teachers struggle with scant resources, mandated reforms are constantly being imposed from above. According to Vasso, many of these reforms are very minor, but all are inconvenient and meaningless. More annoying is the fact that the reforms cost money, money that is not being spent on salaries, facility maintenance, and other achingly necessary changes.

***

During Vasso's second-period class on Tuesday, she takes time from the lesson to introduce her American visitor and invite questions from the students about life in America. Several boys in the back, chronically distracted earlier in the week, immediately raise their hands. "Why does America love war?" asks a boy in a gray T-shirt, with a pencil behind his ear. His expression and tone is both curious and provoking. The class laughs uneasily. "What do you think about all the racism in America?" asks another boy. "Why is there so much bullying in your country?" says a third. Their candor, and Vasso's response to it, offer a window into the power dynamics in her classroom and her philosophy of education. Freedom of speech and behavior is at the foundation of Vasso's style of teaching. If she cannot offer much in the way of content knowledge – given the vicissitudes of the public-private system – she can still teach her own private principles and values. Those principles are nurtured by deeply progressive beliefs and a sympathy for socialist ideals, ideals of classlessness and egalitarianism. The informality of the teacher–student relationship (and indeed, the adult–child relationship) in Vasso's classes emerges, to an outside visitor, as a kind of political act: a way to nurture activism and, in the process, fight back against a system that oppresses her on a daily basis. Vasso, however, is not an ideologue. After I speak to the class about America's crippling fears after 9/11, Vasso reminds the boys in the back that in their own country, a significant percentage of voters had supported an infamously racist candidate in the last election, many out of fear of immigration and a changing population. Another boy counters this by saying that "immigrant kids beat up native-born kids, so it's natural that the native born would grow up racist and anti-immigrant." "You see?" Vasso says. "It's always more complicated than it seems on the outside." That remark incites more animated discussion, and the debate continues for the rest of the period.

Not all Vasso's colleagues see their work as teachers in the same way. A male teacher, Dimitris, represents an ideological counterpoint to Vasso, and his attitudes offer insight into how more veteran teachers see the transformation of the profession. Dimitris is a religion teacher who has been teaching for more than twenty years. "Nobody understands how hard the work is," Dimitris says. "'Oh, you get out so early every day; you have summer vacations,'" he mimics his nonteaching friends. "The prestige of the profession," Dimitris says, "has drastically diminished since I was a boy. Because the values of the society have changed." As Dimitris sees it, as the culture became less conservative and more open politically, education went too far to the left. "Students must feel free; they must feel good about themselves at all cost," he says, sarcastically. (At one point, when speaking about another issue, I ask teachers if they can touch or embrace a student; Dimitris responds, "Can you embrace a student in Greece? Yes, but you must embrace all the students! Otherwise, it is inequality!") As for this new equality, he says, "The teachers bought into it. They lost control." Dimitris traces the laxity to the early 1980s, when the Panhellenic Socialist Movement (PASOK), led by Andreas Papandreou, won a majority of seats in Parliament. Social and cultural changes happened very rapidly, as progressive reforms brought a sense of economic stability among the middle class. As Dimitris perceives it, that sense of plenty led to the breakdown in values. As a child, when he would imagine a prestigious occupation, he would envision a doctor, a lawyer, or a teacher. Teaching, at that time, he says, was perceived as a "sacred occupation." "My parents revered my teachers, and that certainly also influenced my decision to teach." Dimitris has two children. "At this point, I would be fine having my children become teachers," he says, "but they won't even think about it. Most students now wouldn't think about it. They want to be engineers, polytechnical workers; no one wants to work this hard."

Though Vasso is far less concerned with prestige in general, she is not unaware of the change in the profession. She shows me a cartoon in which a parent is holding a student paper with a bad grade on it. In one block, labeled "1970s," the parent is yelling at the student. In the next block, labeled "2012," the parent is yelling at the teacher.

HIRING AND FIRING

In Greece, newly graduated aspiring teachers almost always begin their careers in private cram schools, the controversial schools that exist to supplement public education and prepare students for their all-important exams. To move from the private to the public sector, teachers take a national examination, then hope to be transferred to public school, usually, to start, in an undesirable location. As they continue to work, teachers accumulate "points," gradually earning their way into better schools in more coveted parts of the country. All hiring happens on the national level, with points accrued only through years of service. Before there were licensure exams, created in the 1980s, Vasso says, aspiring teachers could wait for years to be appointed to openings around the country. "We had people fifty years old waiting to get a job in the public sector," Vasso says. "Growing up, my teachers were very old. I never had a young teacher." Now, with an examination to screen candidates, the system is more transparent.

Experimental schools like Vasso's differ in their hiring policies. Teachers in these schools can also earn points through formal qualifications such as advanced degrees or through ancillary work with students, in-service training, and seminars. Teachers create "portfolios" that are used to transfer from one special school to another. These portfolios offer a broader picture of the candidate, Vasso says, and make securing positions in the experimental schools more competitive and less arbitrary. Experimental schools are also allowed to call on faculty from the University of Athens to offer input into the hiring process since student teachers tend to be placed in experimental schools and because, theoretically at least, they are intended to serve as crucibles for new strategies and techniques. Vasso attributes the fact that she won the position in the experimental school to her having completed her master's degree in both theoretical and applied linguistics, a degree she attained gradually while working in the private sector.

Tenure in public schools in Greece is still fairly automatic, granted after two years of full-time teaching, not necessarily in the same school. After this granting of permanent status, only the most egregious behavior is grounds for termination. Vasso is herself ambivalent about the way the tenure system works in Greece. On one hand, she feels impatient with the disengagement and ineffectiveness of some of her colleagues. "Some of the people you met at my school are not right – even not appropriate, I would say – for working in a classroom with students. It's not about being physically inappropriate, but [being] psychologically inappropriate. With personal problems that don't allow them to perform well." The system, she says, ultimately undermines the overall educational experience for students: "Schools just keep [incompetent teachers] in their positions, paying them, and just try to avoid bad things happening." Teachers who complain about lazy or ineffective colleagues are stigmatized and shunned, she says. There is also, according to Vasso, a good deal of nepotism in the system. She describes a teacher she encountered in one of her earlier schools who was wholly incompetent: "His brother was one of the union's top leaders. This teacher stayed at school, but he never entered the classroom, because we, as fellow teachers, could not trust him with children. But he was still paid . . . At the end of the year when the austerity measures forced them to cut teachers, he would get to stay there. The other teachers who actually performed his duties [were] asked to go to another school far away." Even as she relates these stories, however, Vasso says she and others will resist the new forms of teacher assessment that have been proposed by the Ministry of Education, including peer assessment and self-assessment. "We're not sure whether this is going to be applied in the proper way, so we're fighting against it," she says. Then, seeing the contradiction in what she has said, she adds: "Our fault as teachers, I suppose, is that we do not have anything to offer as a counter to their proposals."

***

On Wednesday, Vasso's third-year class writes compositions on an open topic, using the title from one of their favorite songs. She is asking for 150 words, not an extraordinary challenge for second-year students, especially those who have received private lessons outside school. Initially, there is the usual commotion. Students are chatting and singing, digging into their backpacks. "Miss!" calls a boy in the back, "Miss! Miss!" Vasso cannot hear him, and he settles down after a moment, turning instead toward his partner, who is assiduously writing on the desk with a fine-tip marker. Vasso has given the class a choice to work alone or in pairs, and most choose to work in pairs. She walks around the room, smiling at her charges, answering questions, and making kind comments. As they finish, students pull out cell phones. The boy who had called out to Vasso at the start of the period has produced a full page of writing; he is now engaged in a slapping match with his partner. The compositions themselves, inspected after the students file noisily from the room, represent a range of adolescent preoccupations: crack cocaine sales that end in violent death, fights with parents, letters to boyfriends or girlfriends who have betrayed them. The English, in all of them, is surprisingly good.

In addition to her regular English classes, Vasso teaches a "project class," a curricular reform intended to enliven the conventional offerings of the public high school. In project classes, the teacher is allowed to propose a topic based on his or her interests or hobbies. In Vasso's school alone, the topics have ranged widely, from entrepreneurship to ancient art to women in religion. Vasso chose to lead a project class in contemporary music, and it is a part of her week she particularly enjoys. In project classes, faculty help students in untraditional ways. There is no formal instruction. Instead, students define the contours of an independent project, work in teams, and conduct research. At the end of the term, each team writes a paper and gives a public presentation. It is a kind of teaching that resonates well with Vasso's own style, structured as it is around open-endedness and creativity.

Back in a regular third-year class, Vasso puts on another rock song and begins the process of reviewing the lyrics. She had hoped to use the laptop computer for this class, to project an Internet word game onto the wall, but another colleague was already using it and refused to share. In a place of scant resources, it seems, it is hard to be generous. Vasso recites to me a few examples of bad behavior by fellow teachers, behavior that seems to derive from a culture of cuts and a lack of adequate support. "Sometimes," she says, "cooperation is difficult. For example, today: I was like, 'Could we share?' She was like, 'No. I want to finish showing this movie today.' End of discussion."

The class finishes the review of the lyrics and pulls out their vocabulary workbooks. Vasso is using a new edition of the book this year, after assessing and rejecting the one she inherited from her predecessor. Most of the book is composed of fill-in-the-blank exercises, many of which would stump an average American teenager or, for that matter, an American English teacher: "Language _____ along side technology, and certain works take on new meaning. A. advances B. progresses C. grows D. evolves."

One of the few advantages of the separate tutoring system is that it allows her a level of freedom in designing her own lessons. Together with her colleague, Vasso chooses a book from among a range approved by the Ministry of Education. She tries, she says, to choose the cheapest she can find, since students must purchase the books on their own. In making the selection, she always involves her students, asking them to assess what they liked and didn't like about previous books and what their interests are. "I would do much more with media, with technology," she says, "but we are ultimately so limited by what the school owns. Which is not much. And we are one of the most well-equipped schools in the city."

After the class, we return to the hall outside the teachers' room. The principal asks Vasso to get her something to eat because her "blood sugar is dropping," and Vasso runs off to the commissary, arriving back just in time to begin her next class. Here again, thirty-five students crowd the room, waiting for her. As Vasso fishes through her bag for their essays, some draw on the desks, some listen intently to their iPhones. The class begins a vocabulary exercise, and Vasso moves energetically through a list of difficult words: nonchalantly, disclaimer, nascent, pluck. Again, a cluster of girls in the front rows listens intently and responds to Vasso's prompts. Those in the back are periodically engaged, moving back and forth between attention and distraction. Vasso speaks to whoever is willing to listen.

At 4:00, Vasso goes home to get some lunch. She's eaten nothing all day.

PROTEST

One afternoon, Vasso and I attend a "Pan-Hellenic, Pan-Education" rally in front of the Parliament House in Athens, a broad-based protest of education policy in Greece. Vasso tells me that these protests take place regularly, but that the police and the government have done everything they can to put a stop to them. Today, police have closed down most of the subway entrances and exits en route to the Parliament, so Vasso and I walk some distance to get to the gathering spot for the protest. When we arrive, there are 2,000 to 3,000 people in the street, grouped by constituencies representing all factions of education: college students, high school students, professors, teachers, teacher unions, "suspended" teachers, and so on. Each group has its own banners and placards, and all are chanting slogans and singing protest songs. One group of high school students chants about a teacher who was killed during an earlier protest. Solidarity among the disaffected, however, is hard to achieve: Vasso says that the Communists refuse to participate in these protests, choosing instead to launch their own protest marches at the same exact time in a slightly different part of the city. They feel that the mainstream protest is too accommodating of government mandates, and as a result, the Communists will not lend their voices to the rally. Vasso is sympathetic to their stance; she claims that the Communist agenda is really more correct and that the regular protesters are already mostly resigned to the inevitable defeat of their cause – as evidenced by the relatively small numbers at the gathering.

Last year, she says, there were tens of thousands in the streets. Protesters threw rocks and were tear gassed. Now, what's left of the activists are torn between many different agendas, between different and sometimes competing goals for education reform. The right has the advantage of unity, she says. They are not split into interest groups in the way the left is.

At the rally, we run into a friend of Vasso's, a man named Alexis with whom she taught in Naxos eight years earlier. He is attending the protest with a fellow teacher named Hercules. Alexis is a technology teacher, and Hercules teaches economics. They talk about their careers and their sense of dismay in the recent reforms. Hercules lays out what he sees as a strategy by the government to commit a kind of class warfare through the education system. The most recent reforms, he says, have made graduation exams much more difficult for ordinary, working-class students. Two years ago, 6 percent of the student population failed the graduation tests; last June, 25 percent failed. Students who could once get a diploma are now leaving school with nothing or dropping out before the third year because they are so demoralized. Programs that target working-class students – particularly those in the vocational and health fields – have been most drastically cut. As the school population shrinks, the government can lay off more and more teachers, and it cuts off basic facilities, making teaching more difficult. Alexis says that the conditions of his employment influence every aspect of his life. Last week, he says, he was buying a winter jacket and based his choice on whether he could lift his arms easily in the coat, knowing he'd be wearing it to write on the blackboard, indoors. At the same time as these cuts are being made, he complains, the Ministry of Education is continuing to create experimental schools that draw the best students out of the regular public schools – a strategy very similar to the charter school phenomenon in the United States. "Like *Waiting for Superman*," Hercules says, referring to the American documentary that excoriated the public school system.

Vasso and her colleagues tell me that the shrinking turnout at these protests is partly because of the sense of demoralization and impotence, but also because of fears of government reprisal. Teachers have been beaten in their own schools, and police routinely use tear gas to dispel the crowds. Media, they claim, has been bought off by the government, showing a very one-sided view of the protests: news coverage plays down the numbers of protesters and focuses on the violence of the crowd and the "thugs" who invariably show up at the protests. Vasso thinks these hoodlums are brought in by the government to besmirch the validity of the teachers' cause. Even amid the peaceful assembly I observed, riot police stood guard, flaunting guns and plastic shields.

On the metro back to my hotel, a middle-aged man talks loudly into his cell phone: "I'm going to be late because of the bullshit student demonstration," he says. Vasso says, "This is what we are dealing with."

THE TEACHER, IN PRIVATE

Vasso's home is a clean, simply furnished, ground-floor apartment in a lively, largely immigrant section of town, a short bus ride to her school. This is a new apartment for Vasso, who spent the last three years living with a boyfriend, John, in another part of the city. John was a technology teacher in a primary school; he is still clearly a painful topic for her. Though his failure to commit and his basic immaturity made it clear that the relationship should end, the wound still persists. On her modest salary, Vasso is able to afford a one-bedroom flat, with a small, eat-in kitchen, an airy bedroom, and a living room that serves as her office space. Her rent is about $350 a month; with electricity and utilities added, she spends approximately $500, leaving little for other living expenses and virtually nothing for indulgences. Luckily, Vasso says, she is not a "clothes" person and certainly not the type to covet expensive handbags or pricey restaurant meals. The apartment came furnished, and the few bits of decoration – a colorful throw on the couch, artwork by friends – speak to her travels and her personal relationships. Drawings by Vasso's godson are taped to the wall beside the couch. The child's mother is a close childhood friend of Vasso's, who will be moving soon to Germany to find work. Vasso's bulky and beloved accordion sits on the floor beside her desk. She has been playing for many years and considers herself as much a musician as a teacher.

Vasso grew up in Thessaloniki, the daughter of two teachers. She attended local public schools and then, from the age of seven, after-school music classes. Both her parents encouraged her musical abilities. "My father really liked playing the guitar," she remembers. "He had a band when he was a teenager, and he sang." Vasso selected the accordion as her instrument of choice when she was eight years old. She has been playing ever since, moving from one band to another and performing in public whenever she can get a gig. Vasso's best teacher in high school was a man named Papaphilippou, a Greek language teacher who set high standards and whose instruction surpassed anything she received in the private cram school she attended in the evenings. "He was the person responsible for getting me to pass the exams for university entrance," she says. Papaphilippou taught ancient Greek, and the examination was notoriously difficult, including the requirement of translating an unfamiliar passage from an ancient text. "He did his job at school with great competence and without hubris."

Once Vasso got to college, teaching seemed like a natural choice, a logical way to support an interest in music and a viable career option for someone interested in languages. At the University of Thessaloniki, Vasso studied English language and literature. Knowing she would emerge from school as a teacher, she enrolled in the three required courses for teacher preparation. In Greece, Vasso says, teacher education – at least as she experienced it – is minimal, and what is offered is virtually all theory-based. I had been surprised earlier in the week when Vasso's colleague told me that her own student teaching experience had lasted all of five days. Vasso tells me that she never spent a single day in a real classroom. "This may be changing," Vasso says, "since last year, for the first time, we had some student teachers visiting us. They stayed three weeks, and one of them taught [altogether] for like three or four hours in my classroom."

Vasso spends her free time playing music. She has been in two bands and plays her accordion periodically for gigs around Athens. On so small a salary, she never eats out in high-end restaurants, but she shows me some small coffeehouses that offer sandwiches and drinks at very modest prices. When we meet at one of them, a women's collective slightly outside central Athens, the sandwich and wine are delicious and cheap, the walls covered with local artists' work and flyers advertising intimate concerts and recitals. Vasso is a friend of one of the owners, a tiny lesbian in a boy's shirt, who greets her warmly when she enters. The café seems a world away from the school.

Vasso does not regularly socialize with her colleagues. The one other English teacher in her department, Clara, is someone with whom she has little in common. Clara is married to an engineer and has two young children. Though Vasso likes her and acknowledges that they share a love of subject, their worlds seem light years apart. Another colleague in the school, a single technology teacher and fellow musician, sometimes does karaoke with Vasso on the weekends. Otherwise, all of her close friends are people she has known since childhood. Many of them still live in Thessaloniki or are now scattered around the world, exiles who have gone to find work in other places.

A PERIPATETIC CAREER

Like most teachers in Greece, Vasso has spent the thirteen years of her career moving from one school to another, trying to earn enough points in the advancement system to end up in Athens. At thirty-four, she has worked in two private language schools and eleven public schools. Virtually every teacher with whom I spoke in Athens had followed a similar path to his or her present position, gaining points to move to better locations. Vasso's first position, at twenty-one, was in a school situated about half an hour outside her home in Thessaloniki. There, Vasso worked afternoons for twenty-one hours a week, moving on, at the end of that year, to a second private language school in the same region. Again, she taught students in afternoon supplemental classes, this time learning to use a range of new technologies (video cameras, SMART Boards, etc.) and, liking this new challenge, stayed on for three years. Next, Vasso passed her licensure examination and applied for full-time public school positions where her salary would be higher and she would receive benefits. Her first public school job was in Naxos, one of the Aegean Cyclades, where she taught six hours per week in two primary schools, and twelve hours per week in a high school located forty-five minutes away. The Naxos jobs lasted one year. Vasso then moved to what is called an "intercultural school" in Thrace. Intercultural schools educate large numbers of nonnative Greeks or native-born Greeks whose minority status creates language and culture challenges in the regular public schools. At the school in Thrace, Vasso explains, "70 percent of my students were Muslims whose first language was Turkish. There were also Greek immigrants repatriated from Russia, and Pomaks, immigrants from southern Bulgaria for whom Greek was not their second language but their fourth – after Pomacian, Turkish, and Arabic." The experience was challenging, especially in the first of her four years at the school when she was teaching middle school–aged children. During her third year in Thrace, she moved to yet another school, this one for regular Greek children. The first year in Thrace was the hardest of all. Vasso could hardly control her class of twenty-three boys. "There was only one Muslim in the class," she says, "which was also illegal. You are required to have at least 10 percent of any minority in class together." Halfway through the class, Vasso found out the entire group of students hoped to enter the military or go into police work. "If I'd known that from the start, I'd have taught differently," she says. "Less literature; less creative work."

In her last two years in Thrace, Vasso moved into the adult education program within the school, working mostly with Muslim women who had not completed their basic education. Working with this population was again challenging, but also satisfying. "There were so many different restrictions imposed on them due to language problems, to social

problems, family problems, whatever, so they were really motivated ...
Some of them needed evidence [of school graduation] in order to work, so
they attended classes. They worked in the morning, and then they had to
come to school and stay there until 8:00 at night, even though they had
their own families." Vasso remembers these adult students as being especially grateful for their time in the classroom. "They really respected us
teaching them. We had a very close relationship. I still receive e-mails from
some of my students. We shared personal problems, and we shared
advice."

Finally, after five different teaching experiences, Vasso applied for and
won a position in the school of her dreams: an arts-focused high school in
Athens. "It was one of the best years ever," Vasso remembers. "Athens was
new to me. The children were really inventive; full of ideas." But Vasso's
move coincided with the start of the financial crisis in Athens. "These
schools – art schools and music schools here in Greece – are supposed to
have buses ... that bring students from different places to the few schools
that offer these arts programs. But these buses do not exist anymore [after
the austerity cuts]. It was the last year we had the buses." Vasso's position
was soon cut. One more primary school position followed, until Vasso
finally secured her present job at the experimental school.

Another teacher in Vasso's school told me he has had seventeen jobs in
seventeen years. "How do you grow as a professional when you are
constantly relocating?" I ask him. "Exactly," he says. "You don't grow.
You shrink."

THE NEW DARK AGES

On the last day of my visit, Vasso, now sniffing back a cold, has another
very full day ahead of her. She starts with an hour-long jam session. The
school is preparing for one of its three all-school celebrations, each com-
memorating a critical moment in Greek history: October 28, marking
Greece's renunciation of the Nazis; November 17, marking the end of
Greece's 1974 junta; and March 25, the all-important date of liberation
from the Turks in 1821. Earlier in the year, short of key ancillary staff,
teachers divvied up responsibility for planning the programs. Two language teachers, Vasso and a tech teacher, have volunteered to run this
particular event, a day of singing and theatrical performances.

The choir rehearsal takes place in a small, second-floor classroom where
forty students press together, sitting on window ledges and on the floor.
Two boys come in with an electronic piano and set it up, serious and

focused, while the rest of the group, mostly girls, waits respectfully for them to finish. Then two more boys enter with acoustic guitars. Vasso has brought her accordion. She begins by leading the group through a series of vocal exercises, and for the first time, I hear her clear, inflected, and lovely voice, demonstrating each note while waving an expressive hand. The students are silent as she speaks, smiling and engaged. When they start to sing, they seem like different children from the ones I watched in English classes the day before: now focused, compliant, cheerful, and respectful. The scene is a powerful testament to me of the power of arts education.

Too soon the period ends, and Vasso rushes off to her next class, locking and unlocking doors along the way. Here again is another group of twenty-seven students, restless as ever. Vasso begins by distributing another Xeroxed sheet of lyrics, similar to the one she had used in her previous class. Before the formal lesson begins, a tall boy in a conservative sweater and slacks stands to make an announcement; the student government, he says, has decided to change the mode of transportation for an upcoming school trip to the interior of Greece. To rein in costs, they will be taking buses instead of trains. A girl in the first row calls out angrily, claiming the buses are dangerous on the high, winding roads they will travel. The debate escalates into angry argument as Vasso listens from the sidelines. Half a dozen girls join in to defend the first girl's concerns. More animated debate ensues, even after the young man yells back that the nonrefundable tickets have already been purchased. The debate lasts most of the period. Later, Vasso tells me that she allowed the discussion to continue all period because it was clearly important to the students, giving them an opportunity to express their frustrations. The impotence of the resisting students in the face of the inevitable (the fact that the tickets were already purchased) reminds me of the teachers' protests – protests that can yield no change but allow them to "express their frustrations."

As the students file out of class, Vasso prepares for the next one, fiddling with an amplifier she has brought from home and with the old computer provided by the school. Without a proper screen, she will project a music video on the stained wall of the classroom, asking students to interpret the images. This period's song is by the group Bad Religion. A ballad throbs through the speakers: "These are the new dark ages ... " "Why does he describe the present as 'the new dark ages'?" Vasso asks. The hubbub in the back of the room continues; a boy throws his pencil kit across the room. A girl in the front of the room answers the question, but I cannot hear her. "Is that a gerund or an infinitive?" Vasso asks her.

Despite everything – the inadequate salary, the extra duties, the bureaucratic mandates, and oppressive cuts – Vasso loves to teach. It is clear in every interaction she has with her students. Her endless patience, her calm and unflappable demeanor, her willingness to volunteer for more than is required of her are all testament to a deep and abiding connection to her students and her work:

> I think that even the worst day you may have [as a teacher], the most tiring day, the most stressful day, is diminished to nothing [when set against] a very medium normal day. I mean, even a day when nothing special has happened is a really very, very, very nice day for me ... It's the communication, the sharing. I think I've found [in teaching] a way to stay alive and young. It's my subject that allows me to have this philosophy, because I have no specific syllabus from the ministry and I can be creative and do things I find interesting, and focus on other things besides English grammar. Because, really, you can learn English [anywhere]. You can go to private school and learn English at any point in your life when you really want to. I say that to my students. It's okay you may not want to learn English now, because you're a teenager. You have other stuff [on your mind]. I see education as something holistic. Even though they may not learn the grammar rule today, I may teach them something about life, nice behavior, politeness, fairness, equality. I think we should be equal in class. I mean, I don't like to be the authority.

"This is my philosophy," Vasso concludes. "Other people see it other ways. I would never judge them."

4

Azerbaijan: Teaching in the Shadow of War

Driving from the Baku airport into the city center, half-completed construction projects glitter on the horizon, eerily lit from within, like elegant ghosts. Flame-like buildings shoot up into the sky. Massive rococo fountains stand empty of water. Oil has brought great wealth to Azerbaijan, which proudly compares itself to Dubai in its rapid modernization and architectural bravura. Unlike Dubai, however, Azerbaijan is – at least officially – an adamantly secular country. Women are mostly unveiled, they drive and drink; and youth in the streets and cafés have a distinctly Western manner and slouch. A statue in the center of Baku depicts a young Azerbaijani woman lifting off her veil, a powerful symbol of secularism and modernity.

In the midst of this modernization, however, Azerbaijan's painful history still lingers just below the surface of daily life. Starved and culturally strangled by the Soviets, the country broke free from its oppressors in 1990, only to be battered again in the terrible war that ensued. January 20, 1990, the date of the brutal Soviet occupation, is now commemorated as "Martyr's Day," a national day of mourning. Those who witnessed the invasion in Baku describe tanks rolling down the broad boulevards of the city, shooting women and children in an indiscriminate slaughter. "Tanks ran over ambulances," a local tells me. "Grandmas were shot through their apartment windows while preparing dinner; schools and television stations were shut down." Today, there is equal or greater animus in Azerbaijan for the Armenians, who are presently engaged in Russian-backed and bloody conflict with their neighbors over disputed territories. "Do not mention the word Armenian," says my guidebook. "You will upset and offend your hosts." Armenia has seemingly taken over the Russian fight to reannex Azerbaijan, appropriating border territories and banishing longtime residents. In the last twenty years, more than a million people have been relocated into school buildings and other temporary shelters throughout the country, waiting for disputed towns and cities to be returned to Azerbaijan – something that is not likely to happen soon.

In terms of Azerbaijan's education system, the shift from Soviet rule to independence created complex and seemingly intractable problems. As scholars of Central Asia have described, the decline of Soviet power opened the way for competing philosophies, including liberal secularism, reformist religious movements, and varieties of fundamentalism. In schools, goals that were once sharply defined by Soviet policies – equality, achievement, and sacrifice for the nation – grew less clear. Schools in Azerbaijan still seem to be looking for an alternative sense of mission, one that can accommodate the freedoms of capitalism and the cosmopolitanism that comes with Internet access, while struggling with scant resources and old-style bureaucracy.[1]

***

Four hours from the capital of Baku, in the riverfront city of Mingachevir, Gulnaz Haciyeva teaches English language and literature to students between the ages of ten and seventeen. She is in her forties, with center-parted, chin-length hair and fashionable glasses. On the day we first meet, Gulnaz is wearing a camel pencil skirt, black hose, and high black platform boots that seem not to restrict her movement as she runs from home to school to town and back again throughout the day. Indeed, the most immediately striking characteristic of Gulnaz is her energy, a kind of compacted dynamism that allows her to follow a grueling daily schedule of teaching and tutoring, traveling, mothering, cooking, and volunteering.

Gulnaz's school, like all schools in the country, is designated simply with the number. A glum-looking building, with a faded, 1940s exterior, School No. 13 is shaped like a large T, with two floors of classrooms to the left and right of the main entrance. On a broad wall across from the front door of the school hang the images of Mingachevir war heroes, those struck down in the war with Armenia. On either side of this memorial are the names and photographs of students who have achieved high scores on the national graduation exam, the test that serves as the focus for all Azerbaijani education.

The school is unheated in mid-January, and mold rises up the walls like dark stalagmites. Ceilings are peeling. The rooms have not been painted in decades. The teacher's lounge, serving sixty teachers, is a small, spare room, without so much as a mini refrigerator or coffee pot. There is no

Xerox machine, no ornamentation, no sofas or comfortable chairs, the usual accoutrements of faculty lounges worldwide. Gulnaz tells me that until this year, the second floor of the school (which now houses the high school classes; lower level classes are on the first floor) was used as a warehousing site for war refugees. For twenty years, "displaced persons" from Garaba, a disputed region now under Armenian control, lived in the dank cement classrooms. "We could constantly smell their cooking," Gulnaz says, as hundreds of people tried to live their lives in these temporary quarters, sleeping on mattresses laid out on the floors. Gulnaz says she was the only teacher who ever came upstairs, ever spoke to the second floor tenants and offered empathy; but still, she says, "One hand can't do anything." Besides, she says, other refugees in the country were living in worse conditions – in open-air camps or tents in the desert. The recent relocation of the school's tenants to the outskirts of town may have been prompted by the coming European Games, beginning the following summer. Like so much of what is new in this city, outside show seems to be the motivation for rehabilitation.

Though inching toward reform, education in Azerbaijan still seems mired in a system inherited from the Soviets. In most classrooms, students sit in formal rows and recite their responses in unison. Instruction is built around periodic tests that themselves serve as dry runs for the major test at the end of the high school sequence. Teachers in Azerbaijan, as in most countries in the world, focus their instruction necessarily toward this single examination. The test itself is shrouded in mystery. Gulnaz says that questions arrive by helicopter on the morning of the exam, sent directly from the office of the Minister of Education in Baku. During the test, teacher-monitors are chosen who do not know the subject, to ensure that no cheating takes place. The secrecy and fastidious rules associated with these tests represent a relatively new strategy in Azerbaijani schools. During the Soviet era, each department within each secondary school administered its own examinations orally. After independence, the method was deemed unfair and inefficient. Most areas in Azerbaijan have now moved to computer-scored exams, which has cut down on bribery and other scurrilous activities that were once rampant in secondary schools. Recent studies have shown, however, that the problem of corruption has simply moved from one arena to another, from cheating on tests to bribery for access to particular university scholarships.[2]

When I ask Gulnaz how many of her students fail the test, she tells me that no one fails it. She is constantly monitoring their progress, she says, by giving them versions of the test throughout the year. This way, she can tell who needs extra help and in what areas. Various schools prepare practice tests, then sell tickets to students to take them. Between the in-school practice and the tutoring, all students who are willing to persist will pass. Those who wish to continue their studies into post-secondary education take a second exam in July and August that ranks them for university entrance. Students' scores are evaluated on a mean, with passing scores shifting from year to year, depending on overall student performance. Students with scores above a certain number are eligible for a free university education. Below that score, they must pay. Students scoring above 500 have access to the most coveted majors. Those scoring above 600 are celebrities in their towns and cities. In numerous towns I visited, posters bearing the names and faces of these high scorers graced giant billboards. When students do well, their success reflects back on their teacher. "It is a small city," Gulnaz says of her own relationship to the test. "All the teachers around this city know each other. If your student doesn't pass the exam, there is shame."

In Azerbaijan, school teaching alone cannot provide a living wage. School runs until 1 p.m. each day, and Gulnaz, like most of her colleagues, teaches only two or three classes, for a total of twelve classroom hours a week. For this, she is paid 150 manats a month, or about $150. The system, as it is presently structured, is difficult for both students and teachers. Students who hope to further their education by attending college enroll in afternoon tutoring in individual subjects, paying out of pocket for these private lessons. According to a recent survey on private tutoring in Azerbaijan, more than 90 percent of students take private lessons or attend preparatory courses for entering higher education. Indeed, private tutoring, according to the study, is becoming increasingly like school itself and often becomes a substitute for mainstream education.[3] In Mingachevir, as in most communities, afternoon lessons are held not in the school building but in the homes of each tutor. Gulnaz's three children, for example, walk from one tutoring site to another after each formal school day, arriving home between 8 and 10 each evening. Tutoring takes up a large part of Gulnaz's own day, as she meets with individual students throughout the afternoon and evening. This work supplements her income and is critically important to the family. She charges thirty to forty manat a month to each private English student, depending on the student's age and level, the equivalent of about thirty to forty dollars.

A typical day for Gulnaz is very long and very complicated. It begins at 7 a.m., when she makes tea and breakfast for her three children and her husband, Vivadi, and oversees their daily preparations for school and work. From 9:00 to 10:20, Gulnaz prepares the lessons for the day, then walks to school to teach her first class. Some days she teaches two classes, some days three. At 1 p.m., she returns home, lays out the midday meal, and calls her husband to let him know that lunch is ready. This is the one meal that the family eats together, before both children and Gulnaz begin their afternoon marathon of work and study. In the afternoons, she tutors individual students, and on Mondays and Wednesdays she goes back to school again at 4 p.m. to teach a special supplemental class for students from neighboring communities. Gulnaz returns home by 7:00 for a light dinner with any family members who can attend – usually her husband and mother-in-law. At 8 p.m., more private tutoring students arrive, and she teaches until 10:00. At that point, Gulnaz begins cooking for the following day. On the weekends, she frequently travels to Baku for various school and leadership related programs.

Gulnaz is an astute "networker," using her keen intelligence and boundless energy to forge connections with anyone who can help her teach better. She attends every in-service or professional development program offered for teachers; she applies for every grant and travel opportunity. She has won fellowships to study in Poland and in the United States and has made useful connections with aid organizations such as the Peace Corps – all of which have helped her improve the conditions in her own classroom. She persuaded the American Center in Baku to give her three computers for her classroom, though connection to the Internet is often a problem. The English Teachers Association (of which she is branch manager) raised money for the set of cabinets that sits in the back of her room. Peace Corps volunteers helped her write a grant for some curricular support. Soon after this occurred, however, Azerbaijan outlawed Peace Corps volunteers from the country as a gesture of appeasement toward the Russians who have pressured the government to remove Western aid workers. Every improvement seems to come with great effort, persistent agitating, and, ultimately, a political agenda.

***

Gulnaz's first class of the day is a fifth-grade group of twenty-three eager, energetic ten-year-olds. They are dressed in sweatshirts and jackets with Western logos, sneakers, and jeans. Gulnaz has explained that this is the weakest of the three groups of fifth graders in the school, and it is hoped that her teaching skill can bring them up to par with the other groups. To me, they seem uniformly engaged and good-natured, trying hard to please their teacher and wholly on-task throughout the class.

Gulnaz's classroom is a colorful retreat in an otherwise bleak building. The walls of the classroom are filled with hand-drawn vocabulary posters, enumerating colors, shapes, and parts of the body. "Question words," one reads. "Who? What? Where? When?" There are maps of America, maps of the world, maps of Azerbaijan. Having created or acquired these bits of ornamentation, Gulnaz sees the classroom as her space, not to be shared with other teachers. She locks the door each time she enters or exits, even for a few minutes.

"Who is present? Who is absent? What is the date today?" Gulnaz shoots her questions at the class in the rapid clip of a game-show host. Students strain forward and wave their raised hands, begging to be called on; then jump from their seats to answer the questions. Rising to respond seems ingrained in Azerbaijani children from early elementary school.

After this opening exercise, Gulnaz begins the day's English lesson using vocabulary describing the geography and cultural attractions of Mingachevir. She draws a large circle on the board, writing the city name in the center. "This is Mingachevir," she says in a slow, lilting voice. "What are some of the nice places you visit in this city?" Again, students' hands shoot into the air, and Gulnaz calls on one after another: "The history museum!" "The art museum!" "The Kur river!" "The beach!"

"In what season do you go to the beach?" she asks the girl with a long braid who just volunteered that answer. She hesitates briefly, and a boy sitting next to her jumps up and answers, "Winter!"

"Do we go to the beach in winter?" Gulnaz asks with a mock scowl. "Noooooo!" says the class. "No," says Gulnaz. "We go to the beach in the summer." "In the summer!" the class echoes back.

This vocabulary drill goes on for ten minutes, and then Gulnaz changes focus. "Now, I will divide you into three groups," she says slowly, enunciating each English word. "Group one will choose a place in our city and will write about this place. Group two will choose a place and will draw a map, showing how to get there. Group three will choose a place and write a 'short information' brochure about it." She looks at her watch. "You have eight minutes to complete this. One, two, three: start!"

The students move quickly into their places and lean into their groups, straining to see the paper that is being collaboratively composed. Not a single child is off-task. Gulnaz moves from group to group, gently looking down on each tight cluster of bent, whispering heads.

"Don't be afraid to make a mistake!" Gulnaz says, and then, "You have three minutes." The whispering continues more loudly. "Chop, chop!" says Gulnaz. "Two minutes!"

When the minute mark comes, she claps her hands. "Put your pens on the desk," she says, and pens clatter onto the tables. One by one, she invites each group leader to come up and present what he or she has written. A round-faced girl in a jean vest comes up to the front of the room. "The beach is small. Beach people play games." "Just two sentences?" says Gulnaz, motioning her back to her seat with a wave of her hand.

Group two is represented by a small-boned boy whose group has chosen the topic of "School No. 13." They have drawn a map that identifies the park, the shoe store, the line of apartments across the street. "Good," says Gulnaz, and the group leader punches the air in delight.

The third group has chosen to present information on Mingopark, the large park in the center of the city. A tall girl with hair ribbons on two braids reads out two sentences, which both mention grass and trees. Gulnaz fake-pouts in disappointment.

"I now want to evaluate you," she says. "Group two was the best."

The remainder of the period is spent identifying cities in Azerbaijan on a large map of the country at the front of the classroom. Again, students practically fall from their seats, straining to be chosen, then run to the front of the room to point out their answers. They have opened their primers to a page that lists English vocabulary for geographic directions. "North!" says Gulnaz, and they recite back to her: "North!" "South!" "South!" The catechism continues until all the vocabulary words are recited. Then the class is over.

"Goodbye, students!" Gulnaz sings. "Goodbye, teacher," the students respond, gathering their books and running out into the dreary hallway.

***

Gulnaz Haciyeva was born in Balaken, a town on the border of Georgia in northwest Azerbaijan. The youngest of four children, Gulnaz remembers her childhood as a very happy one – a rural childhood where money was scarce and much was left to a child's imagination. Neither of Gulnaz's parents were educated. Both worked at manual jobs in town, just making ends meet. Then, when Gulnaz was in the tenth grade, her father died, a catastrophe for the family, and briefly, a moment when Gulnaz's future was in profound question.

Some people are born to teach, Gulnaz says, and she is one of them. From the time she was very young, she loved to play "teacher." One of her early memories is of being inside her brother's new home, a house built for him by her father. She is holding a branch and moving through the rooms, tapping the chairs and asking them questions. She remembers her father's delight in watching this and his prescient observation that she would someday be a teacher. Seven years later, when he became gravely ill, Gulnaz's father made her brother promise to see that Gulnaz fulfilled her destiny. "Please, help Gulnaz to be a teacher," she quotes her father as saying on his deathbed. "I know that she wants to be a teacher. You should help her to study." Gulnaz was in tenth grade; her brother solemnly promised to see her through to her goal.

During that penultimate year of high school, Gulnaz had a teacher, she says, who solidified her ambition to teach. "He was very young and handsome and single," she says, "and he was a great teacher. I was amazed at how a teacher could be so motivated, so encouraging of the students. I had him for English and German, and he encouraged us to love these languages." At that time, Gulnaz says, she was so sheltered and naïve that the notion of speaking a second language seemed extraordinary. She had been brought up speaking Avar, a dialect of Azerbaijani. Learning the primary language of her own country seemed in itself an achievement. "I was shocked," she says, "how a person could speak in the language of a whole other country." The influence of the handsome young teacher solidified her ambitions. "I am going to study foreign languages in Baku," she concluded, and turned her energies to that goal.

A year later, Gulnaz took the examination for the University of Baku and scored so high she earned a full scholarship to the school. With her brother supporting her living expenses and the government covering her tuition, Gulnaz spent five years learning German and English, moving directly from her bachelor's degree into a one-year master's program. In the first two years of her bachelor's work, she focused on refining her language skills and fluency. In the third year, she began to work exclusively on teacher preparation. This began with a kind of intensive pre-practicum experience, she says. "We would sit and observe the teachers' classes to learn how they are teaching. This was called a 'passive practicum.'" By her fourth and fifth years, she was required to take over classes and to move students through the prescribed curriculum. These teaching stints lasted between one and three months, each time in a different school, teaching a different level. In addition to the work she did in classrooms, Gulnaz took courses on pedagogy and psychology. At the end of this program of classes and internships, Gulnaz took the state teachers' examination, notoriously difficult, and failed it. Undaunted, she took it again. Gulnaz says that her mother was deeply proud of her decision to become a teacher and pressed her to persist, even when things got tough. After the second try, she remembers, her mother stood at the door of the house, waiting to hear the results. Gulnaz's mother, the source of her toughness and ambition, had warned her in advance: "'You mustn't cry [if the outcome is not what you hope for]. You must simply try yet again.'"

After graduating from Baku University, Gulnaz was delighted to receive a job offer from her old high school. Without her knowledge, the principal of that school had been following Gulnaz's achievements at the university and had contacted the rector at the time of her graduation, telling him that the principal was keen to recruit Gulnaz for a job. At his urging, the Ministry of Education, which oversees placements of new teachers, sent her back to Balaken. "It was a secret," Gulnaz explains. "He [the principal] had been following my progress all along."

Gulnaz remained in Balaken for only a year, teaching English in the local high school. In 1996, she married Vivadi, a man she had known since childhood, who now lived in Mingachevir. The marriage happened at a moment when her career was just taking off. She had been offered a position in Baku, to serve as a German secretary and to work at the university. Instead of accepting these positions, she chose marriage and motherhood, giving birth to three children over the course of four years. Though the loss of income was not a problem for Gulnaz (in Azerbaijan, new mothers receive three years of subsidized income for every child they have), she missed her work and her independence. As it is for many mothers, finding a job after the hiatus was not easy. Then, in 2000, she received a call about an opening in School No. 19, teaching ten hours a week. Soon after, another position opened at her present school, No. 13. For a while, Gulnaz spent some time teaching in both schools – mornings on one side of town, afternoons on another. After a year, she quit the first job, and took on more hours at the second. The change has made her commute much easier: School No. 13 is literally across the street from Gulnaz's apartment and around the corner from the shoe store in which Vivadi works.

TWO PERSPECTIVES ON AZERBAIJAN

Much of my research around Azerbaijan was made possible by attaching myself to a group of American sports disability experts whose State Department–sponsored trip around the country, to cities, small towns, and rural areas, gave me access to schools and other sites no tourist would ever see. With our own van and fluent translator, we spoke to and saw a great range of people, schools, and community programs in places far off the beaten track, in Sheki, Ganja, Sumqayit, and other smaller towns. Disabilities education is new to Azerbaijan. During the Soviet era, children with disabilities were hidden away in their homes, their very existence shameful. Though traditional schools themselves still do not accommodate either the intellectually or emotionally disabled, some communities have moved forward in developing special programs for them, and there is small but keen interest in inclusion as a model for further integration of these children. Part of the work of the group with whom I traveled was to figure out ways to persuade parents to utilize these new resources. Even with the expressed change in attitude toward "difference," however, most of the sites we visited were drastically underresourced. The American disability experts were constantly frustrated by what they saw: programs that served hundreds of children from surrounding towns by offering a mere one hour of rehabilitation services a week, throwing a bocce ball in a small gymnasium.

Two native Azeris accompanied us on our trip around the country, offering interesting and often counterperspectives on what we were seeing. The first was a twenty-year-old college student named Anna who was assigned by our sponsoring organization as an informal translator and hostess. On holiday from her university classes, Anna came along with us everywhere, offering the youthful take on everything and often sparring with the older "official" translator, to whom she was theoretically subordinate. With Buddy Holly glasses and a short, asymmetrical, two-tone haircut, Anna seemed to emerge over the course of the weeks as the best possible symbol of Azerbaijan's future. Born in a post-Soviet world of relative openness and Internet access, she had been educated through the public school system and was now receiving a free college education, thanks to her strong performance on the university entrance exams. She liked Green Day and American television; she wore miniskirts and Doc Martens. She was tech savvy and compulsively checked her accounts on Facebook and LinkedIn. Though her interests were varied, Anna was studying economics and planned to move directly into graduate work in that subject. Like other young people with whom I spoke (first, a friend of Anna's, and then a hotel clerk who worked assiduously – and unsuccessfully – to fix my television set), Anna hoped to go abroad, building her "real life" in the United States or Britain, while simultaneously voicing her ambivalence about this. Change is in the wind, she acknowledged, and if she stayed in her country, she might be part of that transition, one of the architects of the new Azerbaijan. Still, she told me, life at home was predictable and provincial, and the lure of a larger world would probably prevail.

Our second translator, Asaf, represented another perspective on Azerbaijan – less cheerful and more sobering. Born into wealth, a child of Soviet privilege, he had grown up in the most beautiful and affluent section of Baku, attended the very best state school, and experienced the kind of elite upbringing that was available to only a handful of families. Asaf described a childhood of lavish formal dinners, nannies, and rides on the carrousel in the manicured park across from his home in the same beautiful Beaux-Arts building where the Communist leader Bulgarov hosted lavish parties that spilled out onto balconies above the boulevard. In those days, he said, Baku was a truly international city – French, Russian, Egyptian, Greek, and Turkish could be heard in the streets. Rather than becoming an apologist for the old system, however, Asaf had a positive loathing for it. His commentary on the past painted a picture of mass suffering and repression, of starving people collapsing in the streets.

Despite his fierce criticism of the past, however, Asaf was no optimist when it came to present-day Azerbaijan, which he constantly reminded us was problematic in other ways. Corruption and graft were rampant, he said. The dazzling architecture of the capital city represents a shallow surface that hides deep and enduring poverty. Historic buildings are torn down to make room for luxury hotels; beautiful old houses and synagogues are deemed "damaged" as an excuse to level them. Asaf showed us a place where the wall of the old, historic city had been torn up to make way for a Four Seasons Hotel. Indeed, the old city itself has recently lost – after three warnings – its World Heritage Site designation, as renovations have sanitized and stripped bare the crumbling beauty of the area's medieval past. Asaf pointed to one renovation project after another. No sooner is a road rebuilt, he said, than it is torn apart and built again – all in the service of laundering money. Asaf had himself moved to Malta, a place that he claimed to be, in comparison, a paradise on earth. His skills as a translator brought him back to Azerbaijan again and again, and each time his contempt, he said, was renewed.

As a gay man in a homophobic culture, Asaf's reactions were necessarily those of an outsider, the victim of untold indignities both small and large. Still, studies of Azerbaijan and other central Asian countries tend to reinforce his perspective. A 2005 Freedom House study ranked the central Asian countries, including Azerbaijan, as among the least democratic in the former Socialist Bloc. On a scale of 1 to 7 (with 1 representing the highest and 7 the lowest level of democratic development), Azerbaijan scored a 5.86.[4]

Anna and Asaf continually argued about the future of Azerbaijan. Like many young people, Anna was an optimist who saw the intolerance and poverty as a temporary step toward a better, freer, and more affluent country. Even the fundamentalist impulse that is attracting some of her generation, she assured us, is temporary – a fad that will dissipate as the wealth is spread more widely. Indeed, she likened that process to the way that her "hippie friends" ultimately gave up their "lifestyle" to become economics graduate students and small business owners. Ultimately, Anna saw the future in terms of her own personal ambitions, and the relative privilege of her place as a university student with educated parents.

Asaf saw the rise in fundamentalism as a more serious threat to the country's future. As a boy, he said, Baku was the number-one place for Jews to emigrate in the Russian republic. There were Yiddish schools and a thriving cultural community. Now, it is all gone. When he meets up with expatiate Jewish Azerbaijanis in New York or California, he tells them it is inconceivable that they could ever live in Baku now. "The anger is everywhere beneath the surface," he said, "and we are millennia ahead of Chechnya and the Caucasus. They just want to kill." Persistent poverty combined with the glamour of jihad has moved poor neighborhoods toward a rising conservatism. Asaf laid out his views on the present and the future:

> Women are covering themselves more. Men are wearing short pants and long beards. This has been going on for a while. As anyone with an education and the economic wherewithal leaves the country, rural people move into the city, bringing their poverty with them, their superstitions, their prejudices. What people don't see in the West is that huge numbers of former Soviet Muslims are offered money to fight. They're mercenaries, but also highly ideological. Muslims are building mosques in all the former Soviet republics. It's a powder keg waiting to explode. If you love your family and you have nothing to eat, and someone offers you bread if you will pray in the mosque, you do it.

This is what is happening everywhere, according to Asaf. When he heard Anna's assessment of the situation, he rolled his eyes. "Baby-talk," he said.

Despite the fact that Azerbaijan calls itself a democracy, there are still cloudy overtones of bureaucratic control that harken back to earlier times. A visit to a rehabilitation center for the disabled was canceled because the mayor was not included in the original correspondence about the visit. Another visit to a program in the city of Ganja was interrupted by a coifed, Russian-style bureaucrat who insisted the group visit the local history museum. The Azerbaijani airline lost my luggage because the airline tag had been ripped off. Once they found the bag, new problems arose; after many conversations in which all the contents of the bag were enumerated, the bag could still not be returned because "the tag was missing" – a Kafka-like scenario that one senses is commonplace here. Anna told us not to write any e-mails that were critical of the government because "they could read it and we could get in trouble." Whether she was exaggerating or not, it is a sobering thought.

***

During my stay, I witness paroxysms of high-end building and renovation in those sites fortunate enough to host sections of the 2015 European Games. Mingachevir, with its wide Kur River, would serve as the location for many of the water sports. Here, the boulevards seem newly paved, wide and clean, with fir trees lining the main roads, and behind them, open storefronts flanking both sides of the street. A giant white statue of two hands holding a dove greets a visitor entering the city. There is an expansive, curiously unpopulated feel to this modern city; few people walk in the streets, and the hotel I stayed in, Western to the hilt, seems as vacant as an unused movie set.

Gulnaz's home stands in a residential part of the city, a neighborhood of small apartment houses and shops. There is a friendly, village-like sense of familiarity in the streets. Everyone knows everyone, especially Gulnaz. She a friend of the bus driver who will take me from Baku to Mingachevir; she knows the cab driver who will stand ready to transport us each day; she is on first-name terms with the hotel staff and the people who work in the restaurant. She navigates the city like one who sees her neighbors as extended family – having taught or tutored many of their children and having worked in so many different kinds of support positions in the city.

Gulnaz lives in a five-room apartment filled with memorabilia and books, stuffed toys, and small, decorative objects. It is a warm, colorful home with three bedrooms, a small kitchen, and a living room that doubles as a dining room. Gulnaz and Vivadi have two sons, Nemat, seventeen, and Kamil, sixteen, and a thirteen-year-old daughter, Ulkar. Gulnaz's mother-in-law lives in the apartment next door, a stooped woman in a headscarf who clearly represents an earlier generation of Azeris. She received no education and rarely speaks, presiding over the hubbub of family life like a silent admonition against modernity: the children who come and go, the vodka and homemade wine that is consumed with guests, and the television that chatters in the background. Nemat, Kamil, and Ulkar seem to Western eyes as lovely, compliant, and family-oriented young people, clearly devoted to their parents. Nemat, the most fluent in English and the most academic of the three, has set his sights on a future in finance. He is compulsively studious; his small room is piled with books and study guides; he neither drinks nor smokes, is largely vegetarian, and has no interest in partying or in any other activity that young people engage in to relieve the pressures of adolescence. He is also deeply conservative in his view of culture, descanting on one occasion on the differences between the sexes and the appropriate roles of each. When challenged by an American visitor, he retreats from the discussion: "I prefer the Azerbaijani way," he says, with a small smile.

Despite her busy schedule, Gulnaz provides lavish lunches and dinners for us, laying them out on a long table that takes up the entire living room of the house. One platter after another is brought in: beet salads with nuts, eggs, and pomegranates; marinated chicken; *plov,* a rice dish served with chestnuts and meat; stewed beef with potatoes. Vodka flows from start to finish, lubricating the conversation, especially among the men. The devotion among family members is striking. At one point during the meal, Vivadi moves to share a seat with his son, and they wrap their arms around one another with perfect joy. "I love my father," Nemat says, and they hug again. Gulnaz seems to be the dominant force in the family. Her values – of education, family loyalty, and hard work – undergird all their behaviors and interactions. Following his mother, Nemat works with a group he founded with his friends called "Charitable Juniors," thirty high school students who volunteer together on civic projects. His most recent success was in collecting 300 signatures to agitate for more trash bins in the community. The group was successful; Mingachevir was recently named the cleanest city in Azerbaijan.

Gulnaz herself is extraordinarily civic minded. In the last few years, she has volunteered in an orphanage, teaches teachers in Genja through the British Consul, is head of the Azerbaijani Teachers Association, has developed a community theater, and, until recently, has taught classes at the local pedagogical university. When we first met, she had applied to the European Olympic community for one of two slots as an English-speaking representative to the games. She is waiting nervously to hear if she will be chosen, explaining that the position would mean taking a leave of absence from her job. In December 2014, she was named Teacher of the Year in Azerbaijan. According to Gulnaz, the award has special meaning because it was achieved without paying a bribe to move one's application from the local to the national level. Gulnaz says she is the first person to win the honor without the benefit of money exchanging hands.

For her distinction as teacher of the year, Gulnaz is interviewed by the Mingachevir newspaper, the one paper in the city. We walk together to the office to meet the reporter who will be conducting the interview, a well-known poet named Ismayil Imanzada. Gulnaz tells me that Imanzada has written twenty-five books and that his work is taught in the schools, but that he also works to support himself as a stringer for the newspaper. At the newspaper office, he greets us at his desk, a sweet-faced man in his mid-seventies, wearing a tweed cap, a sweater vest, and a tie under a sports jacket. Six people sit in the open area of the office, with only one computer between them. Imanzada writes his notes by hand in a small notebook. He has nothing on his desk but the pad and a glass bowl of candy. Gulnaz is asked about her career; her many roles as teacher, tutor, and teacher-trainer; her views about school reform; and her hopes for the future. Once the interview is over, the three of us discuss Imanzada's favorite author, Theodore Dreiser. "We are both newspaper men," he says, referring to Dreiser's career as a reporter for the *Chicago Herald*. "We both believe in writing about real life."

***

Gulnaz's second class of the day is an eleventh-grade group that is focusing on grammar in preparation for the final exam. She has warned me that there would be few students in the room because most feel it is no longer necessary to attend English class. At this point in the year, the tutors are taking care of test preparation. Six students, led by Gulnaz's son Nemat, take their places in the front row of desks. Here, because the group is the most advanced in the school, Gulnaz speaks only English and peppers the students with questions.

"I want to speak today about study habits," she begins. "Are you a good reader? What kind of books do you like to read? Fiction books, nonfiction books? Who will start the conversation?"

Gulnaz's son Nemat begins: "I like science books," he says, "and I like *Sister Carrie*."

"You like Dreiser," Gulnaz says. "Does anyone else like Dreiser?"

"I like fairytales," a girl offers. "Cinderella. Also Jane Austen. Also Mark Twain."

"Good," says Gulnaz. "Do other people like fairytales?"

The class is sluggish to respond, and Gulnaz chastises them: "Are you sleepy this morning? You are eleventh grade. You should know how to speak."

The drilling continues for several more minutes as Gulnaz pulls bits of information from each student. Some like William Shakespeare. Some like John Steinbeck. A boy with a grunge hairstyle says he doesn't like to read at all. He likes football. This draws a laugh from the class.

"Today, we will go back to our text by Mark Twain. I wanted to show you a video today about the life of Mark Twain," says Gulnaz, "but the Internet isn't working. So I will give you some information to write down in your notebooks." The group dutifully opens their notebooks, and Gulnaz delivers a brief historical lecture on Mark Twain. Then the class begins to read aloud an excerpt in the book from Twain's memoir, *Life on the Mississippi*. Each student in turn reads a sentence aloud and then translates it into Azeri. Though Mark Twain was the first American writer translated into Azeri, he seems a difficult choice for a class first learning formal English, since the idioms and navigational terms in the story render it particularly challenging. Still, the class plugs along, moving from line to line in their charming, Azeri-inflected English.

With the passage completed, Gulnaz goes on to review vocabulary. "What is scald? What is lean? What are cowboys? What is gratify? Ghost? Wrath?" The students respond, and Gulnaz adds an observation or comment after each answer, sometimes praising and sometimes correcting pronunciation.

Next, Gulnaz's questions change, becoming more affective and friendly in tone: "Did you like the story? Why? What did you like about it? Did you identify with the story? When did something like this happen to you? What would you do if you were Mr. Bixby?" she asks, referring to the character of the steamboat pilot who is training the fledgling Twain. Though the students are slow to answer her questions, Gulnaz ultimately draws out some extended responses. One boy tells a story about something that happened to him in sixth grade, an interaction with a teacher that was humiliating to him. Gulnaz congratulates him on his courage. "He was so brave to say, 'I don't know,'" she says to the class. "It is good to say, 'I don't know.'"

On more than one occasion, Gulnaz has praised her students for admitting their uncertainty, for taking risks, for speaking up even when they are not sure they are right. This clearly sets her apart from the other teachers I observed in her school. Gulnaz says that she is explicitly striving to develop critical thinking in her students, a concept largely absent from educational goals in Azerbaijan.

"I want you to write your opinion about this story," Gulnaz says, passing out paper to the group. "Work in pairs; talk first about similar situations you have experienced in your own lives. Then, compose a reaction paper together." The students sit silently for several minutes; no one has picked up a pen.

"Use your imagination!" Gulnaz cajoles, and gradually students begin to speak, then write. At the end of the period, she collects the work. "Tomorrow," she says, "I will read these out loud."

Between classes at School No. 13, younger students run through the halls in a chaotic, unsupervised rampage – a powerful contrast to the decorum and tractable focus of the classes themselves. Gulnaz and the other teachers make their way through the ricocheting bodies, seemingly oblivious to the noise and commotion. Without a gym or a cafeteria, the bottled energy of these preteens and adolescents is palpable. And the unrelenting cold of the unheated building, too, would seem to encourage running. I am tempted to join the disorder, if only to warm up a bit.

The director of Gulnaz's school is a biology teacher who has been in her position since 2006. A smartly dressed blonde woman, she sits in a well-furnished office decorated with photographs of her family and with plaques and citations won by students in the school. Her office is the one heated refuge in the damp, cold building. Before being placed in School No. 13, she worked at a wealthier school, and her success there made the President (who makes all appointments in the country) reassign her to No. 13. The director continues to teach two biology classes a day, and her salary for those classes is the same as any other teacher's salary. She takes me on a tour of the building to show the awards that the students have achieved in the area of "ecological solutions to civic problems": a gold medal, and several silver and bronze medals. The director's daughters are themselves highly accomplished: one is a philosophy teacher in the school; the other is a "well known" doctor in Baku. Her questions to me offer insight into the way news of America is communicated in Azerbaijan. "Why is there terrorism in American schools?" she asks. And "Why don't black and white students attend the same schools?"

***

At 4:00 on a Wednesday afternoon, Gulnaz goes back to school to teach in the English Access Microscholarship Program, a program established by the American Consulate to improve English-speaking skills for students from other communities planning to attend university. Ten students are waiting for her when she comes into the room at 4:30 sharp, a combination of boys and girls, with open notebooks on their desks. Access students have traveled a distance to get to the school, and their motivation is apparent from the first minutes of the session.

On this day, Gulnaz takes them through an extended list of facts about the United States. "What is the national bird?" she asks. "The eagle," they recite in unison. "Who was the first president?" "George Washington," they call back.

Next, they turn to their workbooks. The topic of the day is "Special Occasions." The class moves through another set of vocabulary words: Flag Day, Halloween. "What are some special occasions?" Gulnaz asks. Students respond informally, enumerating the characteristics of each holiday, including many facts that no American would know ("There are eleven state holidays and three non-state holidays." "Four holidays call for a flag at half-mast").

"What is the difference between a vampire, a zombie, and a witch?" asks Gulnaz, when the class is speaking about Halloween. Everyone seems to know the answer.

Gulnaz asks the group to talk about their own favorite "special" days. One girl responds that her favorite day is her mother's birthday, and describes what she does for her on that occasion: cooking, cleaning, and organizing a party. Another girl says her favorite day is Women's Day, an Azerbaijani holiday in which women exchange presents with one another.

"Do you prefer to give or receive a present?" asks Gulnaz.

"Receive!" the class says in unison.

***

Several years ago, the Ministry of Education developed a comprehensive reform agenda that was supposed to change the nature of teaching in Azerbaijani schools. The thrust of the reforms was progressive: teachers were supposed to move away from Soviet-style drill and move to what was dubbed "interactive teaching." Select teachers were trained in the new method and were charged with passing those techniques on to other teachers. According to Azerbaijani law, teachers must engage in professional development courses every five years to maintain their positions in the school. These classes take place at the Mingachevir Teachers Institute and also in Baku, at the university. In the case of the new interactive method, however, Gulnaz seems to take the lessons to the teachers themselves, traveling to other cities to demonstrate the techniques. She has recently been assigned to go to Ganja to observe twelve teachers, staying two nights at the expense of the Ministry of Education. She has also attended at least ten conferences, sponsored by the Azerbaijani Teachers Association, in which guest speakers from America and England presented materials, templates, and theory to explain the student-centered strategies. When we speak about the content of these sessions, Gulnaz lists the "stages" of a good, interactive class: warm-up, motivation, presentation, practice, production, and review. Strategies for questioning and follow-up are built into the training. "I have been taught not to [spoon-feed] information to the students; to ask close or related questions, and draw the answers out." It is clear that Gulnaz has mastered this technique. Her classes are full of talk, and one activity leads into another with an almost dizzying rapidity. Observing other classrooms, however, I see none of this, just solemn recitation. And with the exam system unchanged, no teacher evaluation system, and few opportunities for teacher exchange, it is not clear how the old system will change.

Gulnaz sees her work as a teacher extending far beyond the boundaries of simple test preparation. If she is to work as a teacher, she says, she must teach more than English grammar. "I want to teach them life," she says, "how they can be a good citizen." Now that she has visited other countries, it's clear, she says, that there is a difference between Azerbaijani children and Western children: "In other countries I saw that children, even very young, can stand on their feet. They can do everything. They can speak freely in front of even a television camera. In America, parents and teachers develop self-confidence. Here, I would like to open students' eyes, to help them to do volunteer work. They should know that everything isn't so good around them. They should see everything." Spurred on by an international group with which she became affiliated, Gulnaz attended a conference in Poland focused on how to inspire volunteer work in one's community. She came back fired up. "I mentored thirty-six people. We searched for problems in the community. We made action plans." One project was designed to promote more reading among young people in the city. Volunteers went into schools and read dramatic excerpts from library books, stopping short of the dramatic conclusions so as to encourage students to visit the libraries and read the books on their own. Another group decided to have students make commemorative books for the veterans of Victory Day, the annual celebration of the Nazi defeat, and invited the survivors to the school to talk with students, who recorded the presentations and then anthologized them. All of these activities are part of what it means to be a teacher, Gulnaz says. It's not just about teaching to the test; it is about improving the community.

***

Everywhere we go, the ongoing conflict with Armenia saturates consciousness. In the Creativity Center at Bazar, outside Mingachevir, ceramics classes make small figurines of dead mothers and children. One display features a doll, dressed in traditional costume, with her apron covered with blood; a book on display lists the names of the 300 locals who died in the war: "This depicts our fate," it says, "But we are a proud nation." A mural display in another youth center includes a collage by a child that consists of tanks, bombs, rocket grenades, and other weapons. One particularly memorable presentation occurs during a student talent show in which children demonstrate their puppeteering skills, dance traditional dances, and perform a dramatic presentation about the 1991 Khojaly massacre, reading from handwritten scripts in the most agonized and plaintive voices. During the presentation, Asaf leans in toward me to explain: "They're saying how horrible the Armenians are."

One afternoon, Gulnaz accompanies our group to the Pedagogical University in Mingachevir. We are greeted in typical Soviet style, by a battery of solemn, formally dressed men and women who usher us around a large oblong table, bearing bowls of sweets. The director begins with a formal statement extolling the benefits of exchange and enumerating the hard work of their staff. Since most of our contingent are specialists in disabilities, the conversation turns to that subject very quickly: "Work with the disabled is the priority for our government," the director says.

The hour proceeds with frustrating double-talk. Deans from each wing of the university deliver elusive answers to the group's questions. "Do teachers receive any training in how to work with students with disabilities?" I ask. One teacher responds, "I went to a December conference where one of the suggestions was to introduce this preparation into primary school teacher preparation. Now, the suggestion is to expand upwards; all teachers would have to receive this training." "Does this mean there is or is not training for teachers at the present time?" our translator presses. "This is an issue that is awaiting resolution," says the director. "During Soviet times," another dean adds, "the disabled were isolated. Presently, the issue is gaining traction." Again, it is unclear what this means. An officious, barrel-chested woman explains that once a child is assessed with special needs, the teacher and parent decide together on the best strategy for placement, including the developing of an Individualized Education Plan (IEP). Later, one of our Azerbaijani hosts, himself from the Ministry of Education, says that this kind of talk has been going on for years and that it bears no relationship to what is actually happening.

***

On our last day together, Gulnaz and I sit in her living room nursing a glass of tea. We have spoken about the day's classes, Nemat's dream to study abroad, and her own next steps in life. She has two announcements, she says. First, she has landed the job with the summer European Games as a hostess and translator. This is a delightful turn of events in that it will pay a good wage and give her a chance to meet people who might possibly help her carve out a better future. Second, she confesses, she is thinking of leaving for Baku to accept a job at the university. Her plan is not completely clear, but since Nemat will be graduating, it seems like a time to consider shifting gears. Given what I have seen of her lifestyle and schedule – the low pay, the pieced-together hours, the conditions of the school – I can understand her readiness to move on. As if reading my thoughts, Gulnaz defends her decision: "Nowadays," she says, "very few young people in Azerbaijan aspire to become teachers. It's mostly the salary. But also they see how hard the teachers are working, how difficult the job is, how much responsibility teachers have, and how hard it is to care for family while doing it. Most young people want to learn English and then work for companies." The profession of teaching has changed drastically, she says, since she was a child when, under the Soviet system, teachers were venerated. "When I was young," Gulnaz says, "we looked at teachers like they were angels. We couldn't eat in front of them, run in front of them, touch them. Not just me, all people in Azerbaijan; we thought that teachers never ate." She goes on to tell me a story that illustrates, she says, her childhood sense of the teacher-as-goddess: "When I was in the eighth grade, I never went to the cafeteria. I was very shy. Once, my classmates made me go with them, forced me to go with them, and I bought some cookies and soda. When I wanted to bite my cookie, I saw my teacher and couldn't swallow it. First, I bit it and I wanted to drink the water. My mouth was full, and I couldn't swallow. From that time till graduation, I didn't go to the cafeteria again. That's how much I respected the teachers!"

According to Gulnaz, the change in attitude happened gradually. "At that time, we hadn't any computers, any telephones, any information or Internet." People didn't have perspective on their lives the way they do now. "Now, for the people, everything is easy. They see everything. They know everything. Maybe the teachers also, they don't expect to be [venerated]. Not only in Mingachevir, in Azerbaijan – it all changed. Now, teachers are not so important. In Azerbaijan, it is a tradition that when you see old people, you stand up. You should give them a way. Now it's changed. If we take something from abroad, from other places, it should be good things, not the bad things, not this new disrespect."

"You should know," she concludes, "I am very happy being a teacher. If I had a chance to be born a second time, I would choose the profession again. But that attitude is not common among the younger generation, and sometimes I think, what will happen to my children's children if nobody bright and capable wants to be a teacher anymore?"

5

France: Defending Rigor

Lycée Jean Jaurès is a sprawling, three-story building, located a short, uphill walk from the metro Mairie de Montreuil, the last stop on the green line of the Paris subway. Set within a large gated complex and housing 2,000 students between the ages of eleven and twenty-one, Jean Jaurès is a culturally and racially mixed school in Paris. Rich and poor, African, Arab, and native-born French, Jewish, Catholic, Protestant, and Muslim students are enrolled in both traditional and accelerated programs that cater to the wide-ranging population. Entering the school's main gate, signs point to separate buildings housing the administration and the classrooms, linked by scruffy walkways. The school was built at the end of the 1950s under the leadership of a Communist mayor, and an aerial view of the campus would show that it is shaped like a hammer and sickle. Cement-colored and unadorned, the building reflects the aesthetic ideology of its Marxist designers. There are few plantings, bare hallways, and a simple open courtyard where, whenever I visit, the same two boys are throwing a basketball.

Laurence Manfrini, forty-one, has been teaching English at Lycée Jean Jaurès since 2001. On a spring morning, when we arrive together at 8:30, Laurence meets with a group of five students, four girls and a boy, who are part of her second-year *classe préparatoire*, the university-level program that prepares students for examinations to enter the top post-secondary schools in France. Because it is the end of the year, the class has been entirely focused on the subject of one of their imminent final exams, flawless translation of a literary text from French into English. As we enter, twelve students look up, nod, and resume what they are doing: Several are reading the newspaper. Others look together at a problematic note in the text. A boy and girl discuss the recent election and the frightening rise of extremist candidates. While this talk continues, Laurence takes roll.

There is a quiet tension in the room, and Laurence, respectful of their stress, asks the group how they would best like to use the time. The consensus is to continue with a discussion of the text they have been orally translating, *Les Enchanteurs*, by the French writer Romain Gary. Without prompting, the students begin to take turns reading a Xeroxed passage aloud, translating into English as they move through the paragraphs. The goal, Laurence tells me later, is to help the group sharpen their "translation reflexes," reflexes that make most translation almost second nature. To do that, they must internalize idioms and syntax; they must be capable of making instantaneous decisions about word choice. As the students read, Laurence follows along, occasionally correcting pronunciation or making a comment about tone or other stylistic details. Once they have finished the Gary passage, they move on to the next assigned translation, a work by the contemporary French author Alice Ferney, *La Conversation Amoureuse*, which deals with a love affair between a thirty-six-year-old woman and a seventy-two-year-old man. The class again begins to translate, then turns to a detailed parsing of the text, addressing voice, point of view, style, word choice, grammar, rhythm, tone, and finally content.

"Note the change in vocalization," Laurence says, pointing to a sentence in which the female protagonist, Penelope, suddenly realizes that her lover is getting older.

"What do you notice in terms of point of view?" A serious-looking boy in a sweater vest responds, noting how the lover, Paul, briefly becomes the central consciousness, before the text shifts back to an omniscient narrator.

"Why the shift?" asks Laurence. "Why here?"

Two students speculate on the meaning of the change, speaking directly to one another in a tone of friendly argumentation.

"Look carefully at the first sentence of the next paragraph," Laurence presses. "Look how Ferney creates a foreshadowing of what will happen next." The class bends to the passage, writing notes to themselves in the margins. "Then look, it's a flashback – an analepsis," she says. "Starting in line 2 and running to where?"

The class continues poring over the text, noting changes in tenses, shifts in attitude, ruptures in the rhythm of the sentence. The hour moves like a well-choreographed dance. Students resume their oral translation without prompting. Laurence interrupts with an observation; others extend her point or argue it, directing their comments to one another as well as to their teacher. Slowly, the text unfolds.

When the period ends, the students stay in their seats, stretching like runners after a marathon.

"Before beginning to translate any passage on the test," Laurence says, "you need to focus on the text with this kind of close attentiveness."

Everyone nods. Still, they remain seated. Laurence packs up her bag, and we go off for coffee.

***

Lycée Jean Jaurès, like most French high schools, offers a three-year program capped by the baccalaureate exam, the national test for graduation. In France, college-preparatory secondary education is available through two different types of high schools. First, there is the *lycée général*, which offers the standard range of subjects. Within these general schools, students can choose particular topics of interest, such as literature, science, or social science. Second, there are technical high schools that specialize in subjects such as engineering or horticulture, where students prepare for particular technical careers.

At Jean Jaurès, Laurence teaches in a special program within a *lycée générale* called *classes préparatoires*, a two-year, university-level enrichment sequence available in some high schools in France. These enrichment classes themselves can be focused on literature, social science, or science. Laurence teaches in the literary *classes préparatoires*, also called *hypokhâgne* (for the first year) and *khâgne* (for the second). All *classes préparatoires* serve as a national winnowing process for those who wish to compete for places in the Grandes Écoles, the most elite postsecondary institutions in France, existing outside the main framework of the French university system. Only France's very best teachers are allowed to teach the *classes préparatoires*, and only the best students are allowed to enroll. Indeed, the statistics on enrollment illustrate how extraordinarily competitive these programs are for French students. Only a small fraction of those who enroll in the sequence eventually pass the examination for entrance into the Grandes Écoles. Still, it is a great privilege to have even gained entry into the *classes préparatoires* program, and students who are not admitted to the Grandes Écoles will still receive two years of university credit in any other higher education institution in France.[1]

In recent decades, the equity of the *classes préparatoires* system (or *classes prépas*, for short) has been called into question. Historically, the *classes préparatoires* programs have existed only in affluent high schools around the country, accessible mainly to privileged students with long-established "French roots." In an effort to encourage diversity in the top schools, these elite programs have been expanded to the less privileged areas of the city. The first *classes préparatoires* in Montreuil were created in 2001. "The idea was to create a center of excellence in a part of the city that had not been the focus for elite education, to attract students from different social, cultural, and ethnic backgrounds," Laurence explains. Laurence herself feels strongly that social and ethnic diversity adds to the quality of the program. At Jeanne Jaurès, a quarter of the *classes prépas* students have North African, African, West Indian, Asian, or other European origins, or else are Muslim or Jewish. Still, it is not easy to attract qualified immigrants or disadvantaged students to the program, let alone the literary program in which she teaches. Given the opportunity, most high-scoring North African immigrants, for example, tend to go to scientific *classes préparatoires* rather than literary ones. Several years ago, as part of a national effort to recruit, Laurence went to Morocco to help promote literary studies. "People there told me that the humanities there were not as highly regarded as the sciences," she sighs.

***

Laurence lives on the Boulevard Voltaire, in the 11th arrondissement. The area is a lovely, gracious neighborhood, outside the glitzier inner spiral of lower-numbered arrondissements, but still close enough to the center city to retain the historic architecture and the aesthetic charm of those areas. The broad street, flanked by creamy Haussmann apartment houses with grill balconies and mansard roofs, is a ten-minute walk from the Place de la République, the hub for the massive Charlie Hebdo demonstrations in December 2014 and the terror attacks the following year at the Bataclan Theater. The restaurant, La Belle Equippe, at which so many were killed, is literally five minutes from Laurence's front door. The neighborhood still retains a large Jewish population, with kosher restaurants and small boutiques selling menorahs and ornate mezuzahs. A Jewish school is guarded night and day by machine gun–wielding soldiers. Laurence tells us that her neighborhood is changing both ethnically and economically: in the last decade, the trend toward gentrification has accelerated in the 11th arrondissement, making home ownership harder and harder for young professionals like herself – and even more so for the working-class families that once dominated the district. This change in demographic is happening all over Paris, Laurence says, even in areas on the outskirts of the city like Montreuil, where she teaches.

Neither Laurence nor her partner, Nicolas Tondre, are native Parisians. Nicolas, a tech designer for a start-up software company, was born in Montreal to a Canadian Jewish mother and a French journalist father who moved the family first to Poland, then to Thailand, and eventually to France. Laurence was born to a blonde, French mother and a Nigerian father, an Oxford-educated judge whom her mother divorced when Laurence and her sister were very young. Laurence's mother had moved the family from Nigeria to Marseilles, where Laurence herself was born, and Laurence never saw her father again throughout her childhood. After settling in Marseilles after the divorce, Laurence's mother became a civil servant for the Ministry of Economic Affairs and Finance, a position that forced her to relocate to Paris, 480 miles away from her children. "It was a big dilemma for her, because she had two young kids, and being a single mother with two little girls in Paris, and no relatives around to help her out would have meant a hard life ahead." It was a difficult decision to leave Laurence and her sister, Stephanie, with their grandparents in Marseilles, but it ultimately worked out for everyone involved. "Each weekend, my mother came back to see us. It was an eight-hour trip . . . Then, during the holidays, we would all go to see her in Paris." After five years, Laurence's mother finally got a transfer to Marseilles, but the prioritizing of the mother's career set a strong example for the daughters, modeling independence and the importance of meaningful work. "In the meantime," Laurence says, "I developed a special link with my grandparents and with my sister." Laurence's sister continues to play an important role in her life. Stephanie, she says, was hugely supportive of her decision to become an English teacher, though she herself was focused on a career in science and technology. Stephanie went on to help found the software development company that eventually hired Nicolas, and Laurence was first introduced to Nicolas at her sister's company party. Today, both sisters live in Paris, both juggling young children and busy work schedules, much as their mother once did.

The combination of her parents' genes produced in Laurence a physically striking woman. She has thick, wild, gold-flecked hair and honey-colored skin, and her features bear something of the look of those beautiful, computer-generated faces that combine all the races of the world. Her easy smile and her curves make her seem more Mediterranean than Parisian. Laurence dresses simply, in black pants and boots, tight dark sweaters, and, outside, a jaunty knit cap with a soft brim that manages to look chic even in the sodden cold of midwinter. In 2014, Laurence and Nicolas had a baby, Victoria. The baby soldered the link between the two.

Mothering, combined with the intense demands of the *classes préparatoires,* have taken a toll on Laurence. On the first morning we meet, she tells me she has slept three hours the night before, and made it only halfway through the fifty essays she had promised to return the following day. Despite the hectic nature of her life, Laurence knows she is lucky. Nicolas is a hands-on father, and his parents, now retired, live locally, taking Victoria for a full day every Sunday. "I think it was and is not always very fun for Nicolas," Laurence smiles. "In general, being with somebody teaching in *classes prépas* means having to deal with a lot of work brought home, invading the private sphere. Many teachers in *classes prépas* are childless, or divorced!" she says.

Nicolas himself comes across as calm and affable, a handsome man of forty, with red cheeks and high, arched brows. Though in conversation he refers to Laurence as his "wife," the two are not legally married – a not uncommon condition of couples in France where the marriage rate (and birth rate) have fallen dramatically in the last two decades. In the case of Laurence and Nicolas, it is she who is the hold-out, seeing little reason to engage in the formality of a wedding when the pair are clearly bound to one another ("If it turns out that it's better for Victoria's sake for her parents to get married, I will accept," says Laurence, "but it won't be because I fancy wearing a long white dress"). When I ask Laurence to speak more about her feelings about marriage, she is the model of Pascalian rationality:

> It's just a contract. It does not tell anything about the nature, the solidity of the relationship. If you want to cheat on someone, whether you're married or not, this is not going to change anything. For me, it has to do with the ... quality of this commitment, but also honesty, trust ... a relation does not depend on any social, public contract. The couple must work on the problems they face, whether they are married or not. I better understand the idea of getting married after being with somebody for a long time than getting married after being together just for a couple of years. It makes more sense to me to marry late.

Nicolas and Laurence's two-bedroom apartment is a beautiful oasis of calm and culture. Long windows open out onto the boulevard, and the white walls are punctuated by floor-to-ceiling bookcases filled with novels and CDs – including a good deal of jazz by Miles Davis and Thelonious Monk. Nicolas and Laurence visited Ghana several years ago and came back with artwork: masks and paintings, small wood statuary and textiles, and these have been placed throughout the rooms in a pleasing and sometimes striking way. A giant circular mask sits above the mantel in the dining room; a beautiful cubist-looking tempera piece hangs beside the bookcase.

The living room is cluttered with baby toys and blankets, but it still retains a cool, urban feel, filled with light and a cheerful sense of French chic. It is the home of well-educated and highly cultured people.

The much-vaunted childcare system in France seems to have little impact on Laurence's life. She received one week of home nursing after Victoria was born, but shortly thereafter, she was wholly on her own. Because Victoria was born in May, Laurence had no child care leave, either. She simply took the summer vacation months to adjust to mother-hood, and then returned to school at the start of the new school year. But having no help in the summer meant she was not able to prepare her classes for the fall. This is particularly problematic for a *classes prépara-toires* teacher since, each year, the syllabus of the exams changes, and summer months are necessarily used to develop new curricula around those texts. Other factors have complicated Laurence's transition into motherhood. Though the state runs excellent early childhood services (charging on a sliding scale, depending on family finances), low-income families are prioritized. She and Nicolas did not get Victoria into their first-choice childcare center because their income was too high. Nicolas says that though their present, private arrangement seems to be working fine, the public daycare would have offered more socializing for the baby. Though the state affords parents some tax cuts, paying for their own childcare means finances are tight. Rent is 2,000 euros per month, and Nicolas and Laurence rarely eat out.

Unlike some of her colleagues who consider themselves "born teachers," Laurence assumed teaching was the last thing in the world that would interest her as a career. Though she is not sure precisely where that resistance came from, Laurence does remember feeling, as teenager, that teaching was neither sufficiently prestigious nor a good fit, given her sensibility. "What I wanted to do was to be a museum curator," she says, "until I entered the *classes préparatoires* in my own high school. That was the beginning of change in attitude. I remember thinking that if I had to become a teacher, that would be the kind of teaching I would like to do." Then, once she entered university and became immersed in literary studies, "I realized that it was not easy to find a job that would give me the freedom to continue learning every day. I slowly realized that maybe becoming a teacher would give me this opportunity to read, analyze, and exchange ideas, and would be something that I would love to do as a profession."

Her experience as a student in the *classes préparatoires* also introduced Laurence to a new kind of teaching style, one where students were allowed to pore over texts, to discuss and speculate. One particular *lycée* teacher, a

Latin teacher named Monsieur Adam, emerged as a role model for this kind of approach:

> He was cultivated, and his lessons were very well structured and organized. He was very kind, and he was also fair: you always had the grade that you deserved. I don't know, there was something of equality in the way he taught that I really appreciated. He tried to raise every one of us from one level to a higher one, and he gave us the way, the method to follow to improve ourselves. He was very much concerned with our evolution. This is something that I liked, the sort of teaching that I was attracted to. *Classes préparatoires* changed my perception, and then when I went to university, the love of literature closed the deal.

Laurence began her university work at Aix-en-Provence, where she studied both English and Spanish. Her two years in the *classes préparatoires* meant she needed only two more years at the formal university. From there, Laurence moved to Paris to prepare for her teaching career at the Sorbonne. In France, teacher preparation is a challenging and extended program of study. Teachers have the option of taking one or two exams, the CAPES (*certificat d'aptitude au professorat de l'enseignement du second degré*) and the *agrégation*. Coursework required for passing even the first is highly rigorous, especially compared with American standards. All aspiring teachers are required to pass the CAPES exam; those who wish to teach in the *classes préparatoires* are required to hold a master's degree and to have passed the *agrégation*.

For Laurence, preparation for teaching English meant taking courses in literature, civilization, and translation. These three areas of study corresponded to sections on the two examinations, and each had a written and an oral component. "The main difference between CAPES and *agrégation*," Laurence explains, "has to do with the number of books (for the literary section) and subjects (for the civilization section) on the syllabus. The list of requirements for the *agrégation* is much longer. In both exams, you are asked to comment on texts, discuss subjects, and translate passages from novels." After the year studying for the formal written part of the teacher tests, aspiring teachers spend a second, government-funded year as an intern in a real classroom. For Laurence, that meant a year teaching in a high school in Marseilles, taking over two classes and continuing to study pedagogy. Under the Sarkozy regime, efforts were made to cut costs by folding the internship year into the content coursework year. "In one year, the students had to prepare the exam and do internships in schools," Laurence explains. The new, abbreviated system proved to be too challenging for aspiring teachers; under the presidency of Hollande, the policy was ditched. "The government realized that shortening the time to become a teacher was a disaster for everyone. A whole year of professional training in the classroom is vital," says Laurence.

After the rigorous literary training she received for the *agrégation*, Laurence found her first year of intern teaching to be challenging in a different way: "Because the *agrégation* meant studying at a very high level, I had no clue as to what I could expect from a fifteen-year-old kid," she explains. "There was such a gap between what I had been taught and what I was about to teach, that at the very beginning I found it very hard just to understand the students' obstacles. Just to put myself in their shoes was something that was very difficult for me. I wasn't used to it." Luckily, the pedagogy courses provided a forum for talking about the gap between theory and practice. A sympathetic professor helped to make the connections and ease the transition into the classroom. Without that help, Laurence says, the first year of teaching would have "been a complete catastrophe."

A MODEL CLASS

Laurence's *khâgne* (advanced, second-year) class meets on Tuesday morning in a large, bright, slightly shabby-looking room on the first floor of the building. There is a giant map of France near the door; a painting of a bird and a winter landscape hang over the whiteboard. In the back of this room there is a table with a microwave, coffee cups, and a half a bag of chips. No one gets up to eat or drink, however, or to use the bathroom throughout the course of the class.

The twenty-five students are discussing a passage from *Jane Eyre*, and the class begins with each student reading a few sentences aloud. They read with feeling and fluency. Once the passage, a single-spaced, single page, is completed, Laurence thanks the group and then begins soliciting a narrative context for the excerpt. "Who can tell us what happened right before this passage?" she begins.

Students respond without being called upon. "She was dining with Mr. Rochester and she thought he might have some interest in her. But then she finds out that he is with Miss Ingram."

"There was a fire, and it was a romantic scene," volunteers another student.

"There is something between the two of them that is hinted at," Laurence summarizes. "So when the scene starts, she is in what kind of mood?"

"She swims in happiness."

"Swims in happiness. Good," Laurence smiles. "So what happens here; what is the new understanding?" The class responds by teasing out the changes in Jane's state of mind as she realizes Mr. Rochester is engaged to another woman, Blanche Ingram, who is more wealthy and beautiful than she. At this point, the discussion takes an analytical turn. A girl with a short haircut and high boots lays out the basis for comparing the two characters, Blanche and Jane, noting that Jane's view of her rival is based on "an exaggerated idealization."

"Let us try to develop this theme," Laurence says, "the difference between these two characters." On the board, she writes: "Blanche is the reverse image of Jane."

"Blanche is dressed in white; the image of purity; angelic. She's 'graceful' and 'beautiful.' What kinds of words are these?" she asks.

"They are subjective," responds a student. "It is from Mrs. Fairfax's point of view."

"Very good. This will become important. There's a list of physical features. Different parts of the body described in a poetic way. So Blanche's description is laudatory. And how is Jane described?"

"She's almost beast-like. She is described in pejorative terms."

"Can you give us examples?"

"Full of defects, harsh, irregularity, poor and plain, disagreeable, displeasing," says a student.

"She is disconnected from the group that represents beauty," says another.

"Notice," Laurence points out, "the prevalence of the prefixes dis- and irr-. I'd like us to focus on the word 'disconnected,'" she says. She reads aloud from the text: "' . . . portrait of a governance: disconnected, poor and plain.' What is the comparison here with Blanche?"

"She's a poor dreamer, and that is why she is disconnected from the world," suggests a girl in the back. The discussion continues for several minutes, and then Laurence shifts the focus.

"I'm interested in the phrase 'portrait of a governess.' It's as if she is fictionalizing her life. She has created a fictional Blanche who is perfect, and she has created a fictional self, who is the opposite," Laurence states, and several hands go up.

"She is socially marginal, as she points out earlier," someone says. "She is neither servant nor guest. So she is disconnected." Another student notes that in the passage, each member of the group takes up a different and distinct space in the room.

"Good," says Laurence. "And what are the characteristics of the social group to which Blanche belongs?"

A student reads aloud, "They 'sing,' they 'wear jewels.' It's a 'spectacle.'"

"So there is this notion of theatricality," Laurence says. "These social classes go to the balls to be seen."

Another student extends this idea: "It's more than opposition of two social worlds; they are associated with gods, dressed in white, singing, the crown, the jewels, the queen."

"Yes," says Laurence, "there is a deification of the upper classes. And there is the lexical field of light. Can you pick up some words to show that?"

The close analysis of language continues, as words are chosen and parsed.

"So we have two characters, physically opposed, socially opposed; what conclusions should we draw from this?"

"Jane Eyre has no chance."

Laurence speaks about "the tragic irony of the dialogue between two selves," in which Jane Eyre talks herself into "coming back to reality."

"It's like a trial," a student interjects. "She weighs the pros and cons. Her reason stifles her imagination."

"Yes," says Laurence, "she pronounces a very hard sentence on herself. Can you find words that bear on this vocabulary of trial?"

Again, the students are fast to respond: " . . . my own bar," "the use of the 'second person.'"

"She becomes a kind of split personality. The judge and the judged one. The one who has self-esteem and one who seeks to destroy it. Reason and feeling."

Again, Laurence makes the class look to the text: "What are the stylistic devices that reason uses to win the case?"

"The imperative mood." "Rhetorical questions." "Repetition of address: 'You! You!'"

"What is this called?" Laurence interrupts.

"Anaphora," says the class, in unison.

"Who is behind that voice? Is it only Jane?"

"The society. The moralizing society. The collective voice of Victorian society," various students respond.

"And what does this society believe?"

"Separation of the classes." "Respect for decorum." "Respect for social conventions."

"So when Jane says 'you,' it is the collective voice of Victorian society," Laurence concludes. "And who is the other Jane?" Laurence continues.

"The books she reads. The human self; the hopeful part of her as a human. Or Jane the rebel, trying to overcome these differences. Almost an instinctive voice that cannot be repressed."

Next the discussion turns to the question of whether Blanche and Mr. Rochester would be happy together in marriage. A boy notes that they are described as having the same eyes, the same musical talent, and that there is a "metaphorical harmony" in these similarities. When the two sing a duet together, it is "excluding," like a marriage bond. Another girl questions whether this kind of social and physical harmony necessarily translates into a happy marriage. Laurence points to hints of ill-suitedness, again within the passage itself. "Prolepsis," she says. The laws of entail will restrict Blanche from inheritance. "Hyperbole," she says, her beauty is exaggerated; the character has been elevated and mythologized. "Conversely, Jane's description of herself is based on meiosis," Laurence concludes, "exaggeration in order to debase the self."

"If one is a myth and the other is a nobody," Laurence concludes about Jane and Blanche, "what is the place of women in Victorian society? Women were either angels in the house or nonentities. So, on the one hand, we have mythification; on the other, vilification. In both cases, the portraits are distorted. Let's try to understand the reasons for this creation and deconstruction of two feminine portraits." After some discussion about the difficulty of self-representation, Laurence concludes, "Maybe the message is that if it is difficult to see others as they really are, it is just as difficult to see oneself clearly. The author is playing with the notion of realism here – a genre that was in fashion at the time the novel was written. Brontë may be challenging Stendhal's assertion that 'the novel is a mirror walking down the road.'

"But we can go one step further. What Jane decides to do at the end of the extract is literally to paint two contrasting portraits, of herself and of Blanche. This is a *mise en abyme* of the art of self-portrayal: Jane the character literally makes a portrait of herself through painting, just as Jane the narrator draws a portrait of herself through words by writing her (fictional) autobiography, an autobiography entitled *Jane Eyre*. This extract can be construed as the whole novel in miniature."

The class ends, and the students stay on, talking between themselves about the passage, about Laurence's interpretation, and about the difficulties of self-representation.

***

More than anywhere else, France emerged for me as a place where debate, argument, analysis, and disagreement were a kind of pleasurable exercise. It was apparent in informal interactions in the faculty room, in after-school discussions in cafés, in one-on-one joisting with Laurence's colleagues. Verbal provocation is a kind of flirtation in France, one of many differences between the United States and this language-loving country.

Laurence and I have lunch with two of her colleagues, Claude and Pierre, in the airy teacher's cafeteria. We move down the cafeteria line with our trays, taking two kinds of salad (bean or hearts of palm) and then a hot course ("No choice," says Laurence). Today's lunch is an omelet with squash; then apple tart or yogurt and fruit (today's fruit is stewed apples). We sit together in a quiet open space and talk about teaching and prestige. Pierre, a philosophy teacher, is highly opinionated, a trait that comes, he says, with being a philosopher.

"Arrogance is a nice way to be frank," he says to me, "though in the Anglo-Saxon tradition, there is a strong prejudice against arrogance."

"Pierre loves stichomythia," Laurence says. "The verbal duel."

When I ask him how he thinks his students perceive him, Pierre says, "To students, teachers are eunuchs. And their parents see us as losers. Lazy people. To the upper classes, teachers are the types who eat in the street," he says. Pierre himself has a PhD; he worked in the television industry, was a speechwriter for the mayor of Paris, and then decided he didn't want to be around people who constantly told him what to do. Teaching gave him autonomy and a stage of his own, and he's been teaching for twenty years. Perhaps because of his own illustrious pedigree (he is a graduate of the prestigious École Normale Supérieure), Pierre seems particularly prickled by issues of status. He has contempt for the teachers at the so-called high-class schools, the ones that "produce the politicians," he says; places such as Henri IV, the most prestigious public school in France, situated right next to the Sorbonne and to the École Normale Supérieure. "It's is filled with snobs," he says.

Claude comes across as a very different personality. While Pierre is dressed in jeans and a worn wool sweater, Claude wears a pinstriped suit, and speaks slowly and seriously. For him, Claude says, teaching was something he wanted to do since he was a little boy. There was never any question about what he would become.

"My parents were teachers," he says. "As a kid, I loved books, I loved studying and talking about ideas."

He is now a history teacher with a particular interest in the history of the discovery of evolution. He has written a book on the subject. He is not interested in issues of status or prestige. We spend the rest of the lunch hour talking about the American controversy over the teaching of evolution and his own research on the subject. Pierre listens distractedly, as if waiting for an opportunity to contradict or disagree.

"I love teaching," Claude says.

"I'm glad for you," says Pierre.

LAÏCITÉ AND THE PROBLEM OF DIVERSITY

Even given the ethnic mix of Jean Jaurès, I saw no tension among students, nor did any of the teachers speak about challenges in working with students from such diverse backgrounds. This was a happy surprise and contrary to what I suspected I would find at the school. Shortly after the Charlie Hebdo massacre, colleagues in the United States had circulated an article, written by a *lycée* teacher in a predominately Muslim school in France who had been effectively driven from his job after publishing a piece calling for a return to "the true values of Islam," and criticizing the extremist response to injustice. Students and colleagues had called the teacher a traitor to the religion for expressing these moderate views and had made vicious threats against him. When I showed the article to Laurence, she reminded me that the school in question was a *lycée privé sous contrat* (a private high school under contract with the state), exempt from some of the mandates common in public high schools. "I'm not really surprised to read this," Laurence says. "The Ministry of Education should inspect these kinds of places, and dismiss their fishy supervisors. But they don't do that as often as they should. The ministry just operates under the assumption that this kind of thing does not happen."

The failure of the government to intercede in such cases raises questions about how effectively the core mission of French schooling is being regulated. Public education in France is framed by the principle of *laïcité*, the French term for secularity, and by the 1989 Law on Orientation in Education, which affirms the individual right to freedom of conscience. In practice, these two principles have come into conflict, particularly with regard to students belonging to religious minorities such as Islam: even as they endorse freedom of belief, French schools are bound by the fundamental mission of teaching "Frenchness" and of separating church and state. The controversial episode a decade ago, when French schools banned the *kippa* and hijab, illustrates the complexity of the issue. After the banning of the hijab, French Muslims created their own Islamic schools throughout the country. Critics of *laïcité* argue that it is a disguised form of and an infringement on the individual right to religious expression; that, instead of promoting freedom of thought and freedom of religion, it prevents the believer from observing his or her religion. This is a problem – both practical and philosophical – that the country has yet to resolve. There is clearly a tension between core values and political realities, a tension that is worsening as the population of the country becomes more diverse. While Jean Jaurès has so far managed to remain unscathed by protest or ethnic tension, the shadow of what is happening elsewhere hangs overhead.

On Tuesday morning, Laurence meets with her section of the *hypo-khâgne*, the first-year class of the *classes préparatoires* program. This is a small group, composed of students who are taking English as a second foreign language (German or Arabic being their first) and so are less intensely focused on literary study. Laurence is working with them on nonfiction essays, focusing on grammar, content, and interpretation. At the start of class, we talk informally about schools, teachers, and the teaching profession. Thillali, an Algerian student who has just recently come to France, is first to say she is not interested in becoming a teacher; then she backtracks and states that she would consider the work as a fallback if nothing else comes through. Her lack of interest in the field is partly explained, she says, by the indifferent education she received growing up. Education in Algeria, she says, was a mixed bag, at best. There was little interest in investing in the schools.

"When the education is bad, it is good for the government," she says, an interesting idea that opens the way to a lively discussion in English about the relationship of free thought to democracy. Once you educate the poor, someone says, they start to question the system; they start to agitate for change.

Martin, a young man in a T-shirt emblazoned with the English words "Give a Shit," turns the discussion to social class. "The best teachers want to teach in schools where the students are smartest; it creates inequalities in the system," he says.

We talk about Montreuil and the fact that Fox News classified the neighborhood as a "No-Go Zone" for American tourists, claiming that the district is controlled by Arabs. The mayor of Paris sued Fox for libel and won.

"Language influences the way people think," another student, Alban, says. "You make a statement like that – that Montreuil is a dangerous or unsavory place – and then it is impossible to change people's minds."

Laurence joins the discussion, saying that one fundamental difference between France and America is embedded in the language: "French is a language of nouns, of concepts. English is a language of verbs, of action and doing." American history is about cowboys; French history is about philosophers.

The class turns to the text they have been assigned for the day, an article describing an exhibition dealing with the history of human liberties that is currently at a city museum. Laurence begins, as I have watched her do before, anchoring the discussion in facts: "Who is the author? How might her status influence her perspective? Who are the various people highlighted in the exhibition and what did they do?"

With these points established, Laurence moves to analysis and critique. "This is an exhibition dealing with the past, the present and future. What is the author suggesting to us about the present and the future?"

Thillali speaks first: "She is trying to give a sense of guilt."

"Guilt? Interesting. How do you see that she creates that feeling?" Laurence presses.

"She talks about rights and says our time is dangerous for rights, because many governments in the Western countries want to cut liberties because of terrorism and we do not react."

"Okay," says Laurence, "One rhetorical strategy is to compare the way people behave now with how they behaved in the past. What other rhetorical devices does she use to make her point?"

"She refers to the various historical documents like the Magna Carta, using hyperbolic language," says Alban.

"Good. So you're saying that the importance of the Magna Carta is illustrated in the laudatory phrases the journalist uses to refer to it?" They look together at various nouns and adjectives in the text.

"'Treasure trove,'" reads a student. "It's a word that connotes material value; but here, the wealth it brings is not material."

Thillali points to the admonishing tone of the language: "'this exhibition should serve . . . ' When we say 'should,' we want to warn, to alert; so if she is teaching us a lesson, then her aim is didactic. The tone is didactic. 'Should' is a 'moralizing' word."

"So understanding this strategy leads us to focus on the main question this text raises," says Laurence. "Are these rights threatened because of terrorism or because of indifference?"

Thillali brings up the example of the assassination of Archduke Ferdinand before World War I and the way Europe responded by demonizing innocent civilians. The conversation turns to 9/11 and the Patriot Act, and the similarities and differences in national response.

The class goes on to discuss the role of government in the lives of individuals, drawing on another assigned article the group has read the night before that deals with habeas corpus, the 2005 London terrorist attack, and the fact that terror suspects in England can now be detained for twenty-eight days without evidence. This then leads to a discussion of security cameras and the pros and cons of urban surveillance.

"Would more cameras have helped catch the Charlie Hebdo attackers more quickly?" Laurence asks.

Thillali says the problem is not yet big enough to justify the loss of civil liberties.

Alban disagrees: "Cameras influence the way people act," he says, "so they also serve as a kind of prevention for crime."

Two hours pass easily in serious debate. Throughout the discussion, everyone speaks, pushing through their grammatical limitations. The ideas are sophisticated, and each listens to the others with interest and sympathy. It is another impressive class.

"Next time," Laurence says, "we'll try to articulate the middle ground between pros and cons." The period ends with her distributing a mock exam in preparation for the real one the following week. The students have brought their lunches to class, and they will work through lunch to answer the sample essay prompt. An hour later, Laurence will return, collect the exams, and then review them with the students.

***

On Wednesday, I accompany Laurence to a different school, the Lycée Horticole de Montreuil, where she teaches an extra section of the *classe prépa*. The Lycée Horticole is about a fifteen-minute walk from Jean Jaurès, up a long hill lined with small shops and a giant cemetery. Laurence has elected to teach here – as a paid overload – in part because it represents such a contrast to the world of Jean Jaurès; this school is focused specifically on students who are interested in going into landscape design and architecture, and the building and its occupants reflect those interests and concerns. Unlike the massive institutional buildings of traditional suburban high schools, the Lycée Horticole is a pleasing series of wood, slatted structures, sauna-like, flanked by attractive plantings already in bloom in March: cherry blossoms, gladiola, forsythia. Each classroom is entered from the outside with its own door, and desks are arranged in a large, inward-facing rectangle. Because these are art and architecture students, Laurence says, their English is, for the most part, not as strong as the students' English in Jean Jaurès, and the test she is preparing them to take puts less emphasis on literature. "Their passions lie elsewhere." Students at Lycée Horticole are hoping for entrance into particular Grands Écoles that specialize in their areas of interest, such as the National School of Landscape Architecture of Versailles and the National School of Landscape Architecture of Blois. Like the *classe prépa* students in Jean Jaurès, these students can still enter the regular university with two years' worth of post-secondary credit, if they fail to pass the qualifying exam.

Physically, I can see immediately that this is a different kind of youth: artsy, dressed in black Converse sneakers, vintage dresses, and black-framed glasses. The desks are covered with drawings, pencil cases, and large sketch pads; the walls, with students' completed art assignments, some quite accomplished. It is the day before the final exam, and again, Laurence has warned me that very few students might actually show up, since they have the option to work on their assignment – corrections to an essay – at home. Still, twelve students out of twenty-four are present when we arrive.

As Laurence sorts through her papers at the start of class, the previous hour's teacher comes in to wish the group good luck on their exams. "*Bonne chance*," she says. "Stay calm and focused, and you will do well." The students laugh ruefully at this. "No chance of that!" a boy says to his friend beside him.

Because of the close proximity of the exam, the class will spend the day reviewing grammar. Generally, grammar is studied in context, not through worksheets or discrete lessons. But the students are worried about the coming test and have asked for a review session. They take out a worksheet they have completed for homework, covering the subtle distinctions between the "simple" and "habitual" present tense, and move through the exercises, taking turns responding to each prompt, correcting the mistakes of their peers, and listening to Laurence's explanations when those corrections fall short. The complexity of the grammar rules, the investment of the students in understanding them, and the general good-will with which all this activity is taking place underscore the special nature of the *classes préparatoires*. These students know why they are there, how high the stakes are, and how valuable their teacher's input will be in helping them achieve their ambitions.

At the end of the class, the students stay seated, turning to converse quietly with one another or pulling out a newspaper to read privately. A student opens the classroom door to let in the cool, spring-scented air.

UNIONS, STANDARDS, AND A CHANGING SYSTEM

One afternoon, I sit in the faculty room with Alain, the head of the teacher's union, talking about the different role of unions in France and the United States. I begin by speaking about the growing insecurity of American teachers with regard to the solvency of their pensions. Alain explains that French teachers have the same concerns: "In France, we have a deferred system, which means each generation pays for the people who are retired. The government says the system is not sustainable because the population is getting older and older." Alain explains that the government's pension reform proposal is a choice among three unappealing options: first, to raise the age of retirement; second, to reduce pensions; or third, to change the system at the margins so that everyone is saving up and contributing to their own retirements. French unions, he explains, have lost a good deal of their power in the past thirty years, as conservative politics and recessions have eroded teacher support and confidence in the union. Alain is a member of one of the more militant education unions, the Force Ouvrière, and his perspective reminds me of the views of older lefties I know in the United States. He is articulate and full of integrity, but his manner is resigned and a bit tired. "When I defend the interests of education workers," he says, "I'm fighting for the population as a whole – and families especially. But my union is not the majority union." Indeed, only 12 percent of teachers vote in professional elections for candidates in the Force Ouvrière; most teachers now belong to a secondary school association called the Syndicat National des Enseignements de Second Degré (SNES), the equivalent to the state associations that drew American teachers away from the American Federation of Teachers in the 1960s and 1970s. Division within the Force Ouvrière (also known as the Confédération Générale du Travail) is partly to blame for the dissipation of interest in the union. Ideological conflicts within the union undercut its potency. In 1948, Force Ouvrière split into two parts, one linked with the Communist party and one linked with the AFL-CIO (amid rumors that the CIA was funding the split). The mess turned many teachers to seek a new independent forum, one they found in the SNES. Union membership among teachers is now down below 50 percent.[2]

"Many people mistrust the union," Alain says. "This is because, for many years, trade union power was associated with political power. So you don't defend the teachers, you defend the political party. But it is also because of fatalism. The idea that we can't do anything to change things. It's all about politics."

Even changes that work to his benefit as a union leader also send a bad message: "Now, when you make a voluntary contribution to the union," he explains, "60 percent of that is tax deductible. I don't think that is healthy."

One of the current battles being fought by the union reflects directly on the status of teachers in France. Since the early 1950s, teachers had been hired to teach courses only in the subjects in which they were educated. "Now," Alain explains, "the government is asking teachers to teach students outside their area of expertise." I suggest that the shift toward multidisciplinary teaching might be seen as a positive, albeit challenging new way of thinking about subject matter and curriculum. "Among people of good faith," says Alain, "that may well be true." But this is not about inventive curriculum and interdisciplinary instruction, he says. The motivation is simply about saving money, "with getting the most out of a 'multi-functionary' teacher. So the qualification is devalued and we're not doing the students any favors." Many French families, however, see this cross-disciplinary teaching as money-saving and harmless, and this complicates the moral imperative for the unions that, theoretically at least, are championing the needs of working people: "What's very difficult at the moment for the trade unions is that the wishes of the families are different from the wishes of the unions." The government, according to Alain, plays on this divide; French teachers have prided themselves, for example, on maintaining clear standards for passing a class. The government contends that repeating a year in school is a waste of time, and parents tend to side with the government.

Evidence of the falling prestige of teaching can be found in the shrinking numbers of students taking the CAPES exam, the exams leading to teacher licensure, especially in the sciences. "Now," Alain says, "some schools must go outside the system to find teachers." In general, teaching is losing ground for three reasons. The first is pay and working conditions; these are deteriorating as funding is rerouted elsewhere. Second is the fact that values have changed among ordinary French people; they are less cultured than in the past, and they see education – especially rigorous education– as a lower priority. Finally, he says, French people see their society in crisis, and education and culture are not perceived as a defense. This attitude, he says, is class based – a fact that is particularly insidious. "Bourgeois *lycées* still seek out high quality teachers, while the poor and working-class are less and less interested. In Montreuil and in rural areas, they say: 'Oh, Greek and Latin aren't necessary for the poor; the caviar isn't necessary for the poor.' And the people say, 'No Greek? Okay, no Greek.' The essential skills set is only important." Even the trade unions have sided with this "practical" perspective, a decision that Alain himself opposes: "Ultimately," he says, "this will simply reinforce class division."

At lunch, Laurence has arranged for all the English teachers in the *lycée* to meet in the faculty room for a discussion about the differences between teaching in America and in France. Antoine, Sandrine, Maryse, Isabelle, Jean-Marc, and Pauline are all veteran teachers, ranging in age from their mid-thirties to their late fifties. Isabelle has brought a large plastic container of rice with vegetables and ham, and we serve ourselves on paper plates and sit down around a large wooden table.

What, I ask, are the key issues and concerns you have as teachers in the French system? Several teachers respond at once, citing the workload, the burgeoning class sizes, the gradual whittling away of teacher discretion and authority. Maryse addresses the first of the complaints. "Class size," she explains in perfect English, "is something that inhibits our ability to teach well. The law states that we should have no more than twenty-four in a class, but most of us usually have more."

"The workload is truly difficult," Sandrine adds. "We have six or seven classes a week, each of which meets 2½, 3, or 4 hours a week. Some days are lighter than others in terms of actual teaching, but when we are not in front of the classroom, we are meeting with students, grading papers, developing lessons. Even on lighter teaching days, it's a long, hard day."

Most of the teachers I speak to work from 8:30 to 6:00 p.m. in the school itself; then go home to work well into the night. A regular, full-time load is fifteen to eighteen hours of instruction time per week, Laurence reminds me, but most teachers take on more classes as an overload, for which they are paid additional salary. Under the Sarkozy administration, these extra courses were tax exempt. Now, however, they are taxed, making the additional work less lucrative. The group begins to calculate together the sweet spot where extra work is actually a winning proposition, salary-wise.

For teachers, the tax exemption for extra work was, evidently, the only good thing about the Sarkozy administration. In general, the teachers said, the period under Sarkozy was devastating for the schools. Budgets were dramatically cut. Student assistants, previously hired to help students with after-school work, were terminated. In the old days, teachers taught fewer students and fewer classes. Now, everyone is stretched thin and exhausted. At the same time, the expectations only increase: expectations about pass rates for the exams, expectations about technology and accountability. The upshot of all this austerity, say the teachers, is that no one wants to go into teaching anymore. In the past, the profession was highly competitive and prestigious. In a country that valued ideas, culture, and debate, the work of teaching was the highest art. In the past twenty years, things have changed dramatically. Now, notes one of the teachers, you have to put ads in the paper to recruit teachers.

"My granddad was a teacher," says one of the group. "The priest, the mayor, the teacher – these were the most important people in the village."

Standards have also fallen. In recent years, the success rate at the baccalaureate has been about 80 percent (with top *lycées* achieving 100 percent). The test, which was once a measure of real knowledge, has been dumbed down. Poor performing students are passing the "bac" and then failing in university. Maryse, a woman in her mid-forties, described how, in high school, she went to Marin County, California, for an exchange year. An indifferent student in her own country, she found that she was the best student in that California school. The experience showed her how much more rigorous and demanding the French schools were, and how intellectually sophisticated the teachers were in comparison to those in the United States. That was in the old days. "Now, the profession is simply not glamorous enough," someone says, "to attract the kinds of teachers it once did. Money has become the criterion for choosing a career. Parental complaints and demands for grade equity have made teachers lose discretion over their classes. For so many reasons, teachers have to compromise their standards."

"The focus has moved from teaching to social work," someone else volunteers.

Changes in benefits have also begun to erode the appeal of the profession. The requirements for receiving full pension benefits keep inching up. One veteran described how she had signed on decades ago with the promise of full benefits after 37½ years of service. Then it was changed to 41, then 42, then 44. The unions have not succeeded in stopping the momentum.

All of this started under the Sarkozy administration, and the outcome has been "catastrophic" for the schools, they say. "No one is going to want to do this work of teaching over the course of career. If you create a profession where it takes forty-four years to get a pension, you are essentially asking for a temporary work force."

***

Laurence has nothing but goodwill for her colleagues and feels especially close to those who are teaching in the *classes préparatoires*. "The way we work is very interesting, because we are all very much connected," she tells me. "Each time there is a student who is not doing well, we work together to find ways to help him. Each time one of the colleagues does not feel well, then there is always someone trying to help, to fill in. It's quite precious to me that the group is so supportive." Laurence says that in other schools, especially the elite schools in central Paris, this kind of camaraderie does not exist. "In Paris, the most prestigious *classes pré-paratoires* are generally known for having a rather difficult atmosphere, because there is competition between teachers and between students. Who is the smartest, the cleverest, the most intellectually impressive; it is from these traits that prestige is derived. That mindset is not something that exists here," says Laurence, "maybe because we're not in central Paris, but also, I don't know, because Montreuil is a bit special, a bit independent. There is this relationship to authority which is looser." The newness of the program itself, the community's communist history, and the diversity of the student body all contribute to a more affable environment. "In the center of Paris, if you're close to the Sorbonne, they compete for the best students and the best teachers, and it affects the feeling of the school."

The irony of this snobbery is that the French system is consciously built on egalitarianism. The university is free or very inexpensive, and the system of "school mapping" for elementary schools, middle schools, and high schools is designed to promote social diversity by obliging pupils living in one district to attend their neighborhood schools. Yet in practice, Laurence says, school mapping is not adhered to by those with cultural capital: in problem areas, people who want to avoid the nearby school either change their home addresses or send their children to private schools.

In the context of the larger culture, Laurence feels that, as a teacher, she is often on the defensive. Even though she is teaching university-level classes in the *classes préparatoires*, the assumption is that she is not working hard and that the work requires little intellectual effort. "Whatever you teach, people think the same thing: teachers have too many holidays, they strike too often, they do little work or preparation, they do the same thing every year. When I ask them, 'Would you like to become a teacher? Would you like to come and take my place?' they say, 'No,' because they don't want to do that disciplining, they don't want to face disrespect, low salary. People assume the job is more about disciplin[ary problems] than knowledge. This is why it is difficult, both for the teachers, I think, and for the students."

This kind of attitude did not always exist in France. Indeed, the country was long held as a model for championing the intellectual and cultural values that eluded the United States. Alan Bloom, the scholar and cultural critic, noted in his widely discussed book, *The Closing of the American Mind* (1982), that French culture has long been a culture of the book. Certain literary and philosophical texts – Voltaire, Montaigne–were so profoundly embedded in French consciousness, Bloom wrote in celebratory terms, that they formed a kind of shared second language or a second religion of cultural literacy.[3] Teachers, as the purveyors of that culture, carried special clout in the society. Laurence dates the beginnings of cultural change in attitude toward education to the revolution of 1968, and the reforms that were implemented in middle and high schools in the decade that followed. Starting in the late 1970s, under the administration of Giscard d'Estaing, the French government moved to transform the traditional system with the establishment of a single middle school education for all pupils ages eleven to fifteen, and a new goal of having 80 percent of all students pass the baccalaureate exam, a goal that necessarily changed the rigor of the exam itself. The mission was to encourage more students to remain in school for the full range of free public education. Laurence calls this "the massification of education," and though the new policy did encourage more participation, it also "dumbed down" a system long known for high standards and intellectual rigor. "I would say that, from that moment on, and later under François Mitterrand, the level of education became lower, the prestige attached to teachers also became lower, because people considered that it was less demanding, less intellectually challenging to be a teacher if the level was then lower."

These changes that began decades ago have also impacted the material rewards associated with the profession. In France, high school teachers still earn more than elementary school teachers. Though all salaries have been falling off against inflation, salaries in the lowest grades are especially meager: Laurence says her cousin is a primary school teacher in Paris earning approximately 1,800 euros a month, or $2,000. She is looking for an apartment, and, given the law that renters must earn three times their monthly rent, she is hard pressed to find decent housing. "The best you can get for 600 euros," Laurence says, "is a ten-square-meter flat. In other words, you get nothing for this amount of money." To make matters worse, French teachers have not received a raise in six years. Under the Eurozone austerity measures, government salaries have been frozen. "This is why there are so many strikes," Laurence says. "Salaries have not gone up, but the cost of living keeps rising."

As a *classes prépas* teacher, Laurence earns the same as her colleagues teaching in the regular high school, approximately 3,000 euros a month. Laurence is lucky in that her base income can be supplemented by additional funds available only to *classes prépas* teachers: "For example," Laurence explains, "the *khôlles* [the mock oral examinations that Laurence administers to her students] are paid separately, and this adds to my salary. If I was doing only the ordinary job, without the *khôlles*, my salary would be exactly the same as regular high school teachers in the school, around 2,500 to 3,000 euros a month." With the *khôlles*, which are paid by the session, she earns what is essentially a bonus.

***

On the last day we are together, I ask Laurence to speak generally about the things she loves and doesn't love about being a teacher in France. She answers the second part of my question first, because it is the easier one to articulate. The downside, she says, is in the demanding nature of the work: "The amount of time I spend grading and preparing. I think it has an impact on my social life and on my emotional life. [The challenge of] trying to find a better balance between the public sphere and the private sphere is difficult for me."

As for the pleasures of teaching, Laurence summarizes her work in what seems to me to be a tribute to the special nature of teaching in France's *classes préparatoires*:

> I would say working with people who are stimulating, really. The fact that they are young, discovering the world . . . it's a fuel for me. Their appetite, their curiosity is so challenging. It pushes me to know more, to find more information, to seek precision in what I teach, to question more. This is something that is never-ending . . . You cannot really rest on your laurels . . . you learn all the time. They ask you questions, and they are thirsty to learn. They like to confront points of view. I like this stimulation. I also like watching them evolve. This is another very satisfying thing. At the very beginning and at the end, the way they mature, the way they change, the process of transformation. I like this moment when, reading a student's paper, I come upon a brilliant idea. Helping them to think, helping them to challenge, question, have a critical attitude, this is something that I really love. Giving them the tools to become free thinkers, to have critical independence. The power of the mind; this is something that fascinates me.

6

Chile: Revolution and Resignation

Downtown Santiago is pulsing with life. Wide boulevards at the intersection of Teatino and Huerfanos are cordoned off for pedestrians, and the streets are packed with people – working people, tourists, bearded men with long, sad El Greco faces, beautiful young couples kissing passionately on benches. The avenue is lined with clothing stores and bodegas, makeshift kiosks selling pantyhose and bracelets, serious-looking bookstores. Open coffee bars with elevated tables for standing and leaning punctuate the business district. It is also a city of protests, where demonstrations seems like a way of life. On Moneda, a traffic-clogged avenue leading to the elegant Presidential Palace, one cannot walk for long without passing protesters chanting in front of the businesses that exploit them and groups of students marching through the middle of the street, calling for reforms. Protest seems deeply engrained in the DNA of the Chileans, whose long history of internal conflict and revolution still lingers just below the surface of everyday life.

Many of Chile's institutions also seem to straddle old and new; Pinochet-era restrictions and the progressive, aspirational policies of the current, liberal regime. Augusto Pinochet's rise to power in 1973, following a U.S.-backed coup-d'état, struck a massive blow to Chile's poor, many of whom had relied on subsidies and services offered under the regime of his predecessor, Salvador Allende. Pinochet withdrew federal support from schools, hospitals, and other public institutions, and engaged in a well-documented series of human rights violations, the full extent of which will probably never be known. According to the Latin American Institute on Mental Health and Human Rights (ILAS), at least 200,000 Chileans were exposed to "situations of extreme trauma."[1] Among the primary targets were intellectuals and students, many of whom were secretly abducted and murdered. In his campaign to transform the leftist policies of Allende,

Pinochet abolished civil liberties, dissolved the national congress, banned union activities, prohibited strikes and collective bargaining, and erased the Allende administration's agrarian and economic reforms. All this happened in the lifetime of Mauricio Ramirez, veteran English teacher at Liceo 1 Javiera Carrera in downtown Santiago. The recent history of his country, its struggles and its deprivations inform every aspect of his sensibility and his views of teaching. As a child of his time, he is acutely aware of the distinctions between what he calls the "left hand" and "right hand," the one that gives and the one that takes. In all our conversations throughout the course of my stay, politics and the injustices wrought by power are never far from the center of discussion.

Mauricio is forty-two, with a round, unlined face and the high coloring of his countrymen. Born in Valdivia, in the south of Chile, Mauricio describes his childhood as "traditional," typical of Chile's rural working class during the early 1970s. When Mauricio was seven, his father abandoned the family and his mother moved her children into their grandparents' home. This proved to be fortunate, he says, because it allowed Mauricio to thrive under the influence of his grandfather. "He was a very responsible man, very clean," Mauricio remembers of the surrogate father. A railway worker with a high school education, the grandfather was also concerned with the education of his grandchildren. "I remember that he bought me magazines from Walt Disney every month, and because of that, I learned to read and write very early." In his way, Mauricio says, his grandfather always tried to engage with the larger world. "He read the newspaper every day"; and there was always talk in the family about politics and the changing conditions for the poor.

When Mauricio was a teenager, his grandfather had a stroke, and money became a more acute concern. Mauricio was now nearing high school age and, resigned to the family's economic situation, he chose to go to a vocational high school, assuming he would be consigned to manual work. But in high school, things changed. After almost twenty years of autocratic rule, Pinochet was voted out and the Christian Democrat candidate Patricio Aylwin came into power. Among the rapid reforms that followed was the sudden availability of funding for education. In 1991, when Mauricio was a sophomore in high school, a school counselor noticed his good grades and encouraged him to think about higher education. When Mauricio explained the family's economic situation, the counselor applied on his behalf for a newly available government scholarship. "You have good grades so there are now lots of possibilities for you," he remembers the counselor saying. Mauricio's scholarship application was successful, and from then on, he received monthly stipends for living expenses, money that not only helped the family but also allowed him to begin thinking in new ways about his future. From that point on, he says, opportunities continued to open. He took the university exams and received a good score. More scholarship money materialized. Now under the Aylwin administration, university fees were largely covered for top students, and post-secondary education became possible. He applied and was accepted into the southern Austral University, where he received a 95 percent tuition scholarship. It was an extraordinary turn of events for a young man who had five years before imagined a very different future for himself.

Teachers were always spoken about with admiration in Mauricio's family, and several of his own teachers made a powerful impression on him. But the profession itself had seemed out of reach for Mauricio. After all, it required a college education and a level of sophistication he could hardly imagine. Now, as a college student, he could consider entering the field. "I was enamored with the idea of helping others," he says, "of changing society. When you are at the university, you're very idealistic. You know, in a vague way, that you're going to have problems with salary [if you choose to teach], but I think you only really understand what that means when you are part of the system." Mauricio chose to major in English with a focus on earning a teaching license. He loved languages, history, and literature and English seemed to comprise all three. "With English," he says, "I figured I could do any number of things – work in a high school but also do translation, tutoring ... all kinds of things to make money."

In those days, progress toward licensure meant following a strict course of study. Having chosen to study English, he spent the first four years taking classes in a range of English-related subjects: literature, including prose, poetry, and drama; then grammar and linguistics. The final fifth year of study was devoted to pedagogy, including one class of student teaching. For this internship, Mauricio was placed in his own former high school, taking over two classes. Though Mauricio loved the students and they loved him, his mentor teacher was less than ideal. "He was nice but fairly remote," he says, "not really helpful in showing me new techniques or explaining things." Mauricio says he wondered if the teacher felt intimidated by Mauricio's rapport with his students. Looking back, Mauricio sees his teacher preparation as a mixed bag: most of the pedagogy courses were less useful than time spent in the classroom. "Professors at the university have read a lot," he says, "but they had a disconnection between theory and the reality. Though my mentor teacher did little for me, time spent in the classroom was still the most useful. It's there that I learned to teach."

In the last decade, the road to licensure in Chile has been shortened from five years to four. Reformers have reduced the number of required literature courses for aspiring English teachers, removing content requirements such as separate courses on drama or poetry. Internships are also shorter. One of the consequences of the change, according to Mauricio, is that more students are pursuing teaching degrees, and the field is glutted with aspiring teachers, especially in the humanities. What's more, he says, with the rise of private universities in Chile, more and more poorly qualified candidates are being accepted into teaching programs. "Where once it was special," Mauricio says, "now everyone gets in."

THE POLITICS OF SCHOOLING

Mauricio's school, Liceo 1 Javiera Carrera, is built with a large, open courtyard, flanked by three levels of classrooms. It is the only all-girls public school in Santiago, named for a heroine of the early-nineteenth-century Chilean independence movement, the woman who fashioned the Chilean flag. The school is the first high school for girls in Chile, established in 1894, shortly after the Chilean civil war that ousted the president, Jose Manuel Balmaceda, and initiated a period of broader representation and human rights. At the entrance to the school, a white plaque bears the names of graduates who are among the "disappeared" – ten Liceo 1 students who vanished from the streets of Santiago during the Pinochet regime. Their death dates are all recorded between 1974 and 1977, though the bodies have never been recovered.

There is no heat or air conditioning in Liceo 1. Students wear their coats in the winter and bear the very hot summer as best they can, while still following the school dress code: navy skirt, white shirt, and a cotton overcoat or "lab jacket" that marks Liceo 1 students on the sidewalks and subways around the school. "The private schools have heat and air conditioning," Mauricio says, as one of a thousand examples of how privilege operates in the country. Entering the high gate of the school each morning, one is greeted by the principal, the assistant principal, and two secretaries, who stand in a receiving line, smiling at the students as they enter. In all, there are 120 teachers in Javiera Carrera, which averages about 170 students per teacher. Of them, Mauricio estimates, forty are male; he is the only man in the English department.

The current educational system in Chile, its structure, and financing still bear the stamp of the Pinochet regime. The Chilean Constitution, reframed by Pinochet in 1980, established a "free market" model for schooling inspired by the theories of the neoliberal economist Milton Friedman. Under Pinochet, traditional public schools were largely dismantled and replaced by a modified voucher system wherein schools would have to compete with one another for students. School funding became based on attendance on the days of government inspections, a system that inspired paranoia in staff and ultimately seemed to reinforce inequalities.[2] Today, schools in Chile fall into three categories. First, there are private schools, tuition-based and primarily reserved for the children of the elite. Then, there are public "subsidized schools," schools that receive subsidies from the government but that also charge mandatory tuition to students to supplement expenses. These represent the majority of schools in the country. Finally, there are traditional public schools. These schools are completely free, though they are allowed to ask parents for a nominal additional fee (*financiamiento compartido*) that they are not obliged to pay. According to recent statistics, only 37 percent of the schools in Chile are true public schools; the rest are private schools or subsidized schools with required fees.[3] Ironically, Mauricio says, subsidized schools are most often utilized by poor families who believe their children will get a better education from these schools than from regular public schools, where fees are not required. From Mauricio's perspective, this is absolutely not true. "Poor people are persuaded to send their kids to subsidized schools because of the uniform, because the school is clean. They're clean because they use their resources for unimportant things. But the standards are not so good." Salaries are lower in subsidized schools, there is no tenure, and students perform worse on objective measures – largely because these schools are run like private businesses, with those in charge pocketing the school funds, unchecked. Mauricio says that teachers are often let go after two years, replaced by younger and less-expensive recruits. Subsidized schools can fire teachers who attend protest marches; they don't pay their teachers on time.

Protest marches often target subsidized schools as symbols of the exploitation and corruption rampant in the education system. In 2011, nationwide protests erupted across Chile, and students occupied schools from June to January. Mauricio didn't work the entire second semester, though luckily, he was paid. Did the students achieve any of their demands? I ask. "Not a thing," says Mauricio.

From Mauricio's perspective, one of the more damaging reforms that persists since the Pinochet regime is the decentralization of funding for schools. As it stands now, school funds are dispersed from the central government to the local city halls, which control how the money gets spent. Each city hall sets its own standards for salaries and other school expenses. This shift from state to local authority has created serious inequities in the system, he says. Though funding is supposed to be the same in each district, in reality, schools are vulnerable to the whims of the city hall systems. There is a minimum of funding mandated by the state; beyond that, local bureaucrats can allocate funds as they see fit, and some schools suffer under the system. Indeed, funding differences can be considerable. Liceo 1, with a generous city hall, receives almost 30 percent more in funding than other schools in the area. These kinds of discrepancies happen often, Mauricio says, and schools and teachers are powerless to do anything about it.

The move toward budget decentralization meant that many of the longtime incentives for teacher improvement (salary hikes for additional degrees, for example) were removed. Teachers who were due these funds at the time that the reforms were first instituted ended up stuck in a decades-long fight for lost compensation. "The government said, 'okay, don't worry. We will give you that money very soon.' Then time went by, and nothing happened. Most of the teachers have died waiting for the money, which is called here *deuda histórica* (historical debt)." Mauricio explains that, though the current administration is more progressive in its policies, no government wants to pay out the many millions of pesos to this elderly cohort that has little political power. "You can see them at the strikes with their white hair," says Mauricio, "holding up protest signs, still calling for their stolen funds." While these poor teachers struggle, he says, the wealthy thrive. They send their children to the schools near the mountains, on the outskirts of town, where buildings are lavishly appointed and teachers are well paid. Mauricio says that people who live in those regions tend to be right wing. "They are not supportive of the unions. You can ask them," he says. "They will not be embarrassed to tell you."

***

Unlike most of his colleagues, Mauricio had an unusually easy time getting his first position, a fact he attributes partly to good grades and largely to luck. "When I finished the university, I decided to move to Santiago, because Valdivia was a very small town with few schools, very few positions," he explains. "This was 1998, and I needed to work not only for me, but also for my family that was depending on my income. One of my professors advised me, 'okay, why don't you leave your resume at the Santiago city halls?' So that's what I did. It was a lucky day." Almost immediately, the human resources department called Mauricio and told him about a retirement that had just taken place at Liceo 1. The need was urgent, they said; it was already the second week of the semester. Mauricio was interviewed immediately. "I remember that I was received by one of the assistant principals. She looked at me and said, 'You are so young' . . . and I was! I remember her face," Mauricio laughs, mimicking the look of incredulity he encountered. "Then, because they needed a teacher, she said, 'Okay, we'll see.' . . . I've been teaching at the school ever since."

The match of teacher and school was a good one. Mauricio fit in immediately and enjoyed the work. Several years into his work, however, his temporary position was reclassified as a tenured post. In order to stay on, he would need to compete for that permanent position with candidates from around the country, since these tenured positions in Chile are open to anyone with three years of full-time teaching experience. Mauricio says that the position was advertised in *El Mercurio*, the national paper. He still vividly remembers the formal interview that followed his application – the first such interview he had ever done. "There was one representative from the Ministry of Education, one representative of the city hall, one representative of the teachers' union, a teacher of English, of course, and the principal of the school; four people there," he says. Mauricio spoke about his commitment to teaching, his philosophy of education, his love of English. "They told me afterwards that mine was the best interview." From that point on, Mauricio kept winning awards: in 2007, he received a national Teacher of the Year award that was presented to him in a lavish ceremony by Chilean President Michelle Bachelet. Only two years after that, Mauricio's colleagues voted him Teacher of the Year in his own school. Then, he also won the citywide award. "There's nothing left but a global award," he laughs. All of this early success led to offers that would have taken him out of the classroom. He describes, for example, a 2004 invitation from the Chinese government to work at a Chinese television station in Beijing. "They were looking for someone who could speak Spanish and English – to help with their programming." Mauricio considered it very briefly. But the salary they offered was so low, he says, "I would have returned poorer than when I left."

As a veteran teacher, Mauricio has gained real flexibility in the way he organizes his weekly schedule. He now teaches three days a week, on Tuesdays, Wednesdays, and Thursdays, and then grades papers on Mondays and Fridays. Given his enormous enrollments, this structure works best for him. Grading days are mostly uninterrupted, and Mauricio can work in the teachers' room, the library, or even at home. The downside of this schedule is that midweeks are crammed with teaching from morning to evening. At Javiera Carrera, there are eight forty-minute periods in a day. On Tuesdays through Thursdays, Mauricio teaches all eight of those periods, with two fifteen-minute breaks, one in the morning and one in the afternoon. It is an extra challenge, with 200 students, to learn everybody's name, let alone to get to know their private interests or problems. Students understand this, he says, and they forgive their teachers for it. Sheer numbers also end up dictating the contours of the curriculum. Mauricio spends most of this time on reading, grammar, and listening skills. Writing necessarily takes a second place in the curriculum, as Mauricio and his colleagues grapple with the huge volume of papers.

Mauricio's first stop on a typical Tuesday is in the massive, open teachers' room on the first floor. The space, the size of a small auditorium, is laid out with round work tables and small lockers in which teachers stow books and personal belongings. Behind the locker area is a smaller space with some old stuffed chairs; the walls here are lined with photographs of distinguished alumnae of Javiera Carrera, which include the current Chilean president herself, Michelle Bachelet. Teachers come and go, greeting one another, stowing books and papers in their lockers. Mauricio introduces me to one of his friends, an English teacher, Sandra, who, at sixty-two, will be retiring at the end of the year. "Thank God," she says. She has a bad back, Mauricio says. "It is grueling work, hard on the body." In retirement, without 200 papers to grade, Sandra plans to return to her first love, music. She plays the guitar and loves the folk music of Chile. Finally, she'll have time to do these things, she says. Sandra is taking advantage of a new government incentive for older teachers to retire, a one-time payment of 21 million pesos, plus pension. From Mauricio's perspective, the incentive is very worthwhile and won't last long. Each time a new administration comes in, at four-year intervals, teachers need to renegotiate salaries and pensions, he says, and there is no guarantee that such a generous deal will come around again.

In the Chilean system, students stay together in one classroom all day, and teachers move from room to room. Before each of his classes, Mauricio picks up a large green ledger book from the office and brings it into his classroom. There, he records both attendance and grades. At the end of each class, the book is returned to the office so that the next teacher, teaching that particular group, can pick up the ledger and record his or her grades. There is a lot of walking throughout the day, from classroom to classroom, office to office. Teachers lug large canvas bags from place to place; stopping to chat with colleagues on stairwells and in the open hallways.

Mauricio's first-period class is in the "modern" part of the building, an annex built in the 1960s and aging in the particular way that modern buildings do. Water seems to be leaking through the metal window frames, and the cement exterior walls are stained. It is late April, and Mauricio's classroom is chilly; one of the dark-blue curtains is falling off its rod, the Formica floor has seen better days. There is a ceiling-mounted projector and screen, a series of large fans, a white board, and cabinets, some broken from their hinges, lining the back wall.

The class begins at 8 a.m., but because of the city's unpredictable transportation system, Mauricio says, students are allowed to arrive ten or fifteen minutes late. Because Liceo 1 admits students through competitive testing, many live fairly far away and must travel for up to an hour each morning. At the start of class, there are forty students present. As the session progresses, half a dozen more trickle in, quickly pulling out their workbooks, heads lowered. Twenty-two double desks fill the space from front to back.

"Now, misses . . . we begin!" he calls out. "Good morning, students!"

"Good morning, teacher!" they sing back in unison.

Mauricio starts the class by asking for volunteers to fill in answers to grammar questions he has put up on the board. "Don't worry. Don't worry," he says, over and over. "Don't be afraid to get it wrong." He selects two volunteers to approach the board and write their answers underneath his chalked questions.

"First one," Mauricio says, "yes or no? . . . . No." He points to a student's incorrect solution – "Frank asked to Ellen when the party begun" – erases it, and writes the proper response. "Past perfect," he says as he writes, "Begun or began?" The class calls out the answer and he writes it as they bend to correct their own papers.

After correcting both sentences on the board, he distributes a Xeroxed worksheet and reviews the instruction with the students, asking them to work alone or in pairs, to use their books, and consult him if they have any questions. Forty-six heads bend to the task. Several minutes pass.

"So any questions, misses?" Mauricio circulates around the class as the students work, consulting a bright, soft-colored textbook with explanatory exercises. After ten more minutes, a soft rumble of voices begins.

"Questions, doubts, problems?"

At twenty minutes, the conversation level rises, signaling that students are finished.

"Hurry up," says Mauricio, "it's almost time to be done."

The thrust of the next exercise is to convert spoken dialogue into "reported dialogue." The worksheet, drawn from an Internet resource, documents a two-way conversation between the fictional "Liz" and "Ian" about the use of invisible ink. The students must convert the worksheet's "conversation" into an "objective report" of the conversation, as if they were journalists. The worksheet begins with an example:

Sample – Liz: "What is invisible ink?"

Answer – "Liz asked Ian what invisible ink is."

Everyone gets to work, and the room is silent. Mauricio moves up and down the aisles, looking over the shoulders of his students.

"Any questions? Any problems?" he says. Then, "Hurry, misses, only ten minutes left."

This work, Mauricio tells me, is review for next week's test on the unit. Mauricio has designed his classes around month-long units in which two weeks are devoted to the introduction and practice of new material, then a week of review, and finally an examination. Everyone approaches the material differently, he says, but faculty share and support each other. Given the large class sizes, much of the period is spent on deskwork, with students collaborating on worksheets that Mauricio has created from textbooks, Internet sources, or his own imagination. Mauricio and his colleagues send their materials each evening to the school's official Xeroxer. Then, when he arrives at school the next morning, he picks up the giant packets of Xeroxed materials for the day's classes. It's an efficient system for the teachers, and one that spares them long lines waiting for a machine. It also spares students the burdensome cost of textbooks, which are not provided by the school itself.

Ninety percent of Mauricio's curriculum is grammar and reading comprehension, with little classroom time devoted to literary analysis or discussion. Students are sometimes assigned reading at home, Mauricio says, but the focus is only on comprehension, because it is this that the examinations will measure. Mauricio says he is keenly aware that this emphasis on mechanics puts his students at a disadvantage compared with their wealthy counterparts. Private schools, according to Mauricio, don't use the ministry's curriculum because they find it too basic. These affluent schools create their own curricula and scope and sequence, often based on what is being done in the United States or in other affluent countries. It is another example of the uneven distribution of cultural capital and a strategy for maintaining the status quo. Mauricio says he would love to do other things with his class: break them into small groups, engage in conversation, and do group projects. But the massive class sizes are daunting, and it would be cumbersome and impractical to try moving desks around. The best he can do to vary the tedium of direct instruction is to have students go up to the board to write their answers. This is a strategy he uses often, and students seem willing to make public mistakes without embarrassment.

At the end of the class, Mauricio calls two girls up to the front, and they write their responses beneath his written prompts. Again, both answers are incorrect, and Mauricio again solicits the class to correct them.

"Present perfect, past perfect. 'She said she *had drawn* . . . ' Remember, if you change one tense, you change all of them. *Had* done. Past perfect. *Had* been . . . "

Minutes before the end of class, Mauricio takes roll call (a strategy he uses to record all the late arrivers). He calls out the names, and each student in turn responds with a formal acknowledgment: "Present, teacher." All forty-five students are present and accounted for.

***

Between classes, Mauricio introduces me to Anna, the union representative for Javiera Carerra. She is a warm, open-faced woman who has spent more than two decades in the school. When I explain my research to her, Anna replied that the schools in Chile "are going downhill." She, like Mauricio, has taught through numerous political administrations and has developed a kind of resigned and bemused perspective that seems common in veteran activists. The classes are too large, she says, the workload is impossible, the resources get smaller and smaller. Mauricio encourages me to describe to her the draconian cuts I saw in the Athens schools, the strikes and protests there, and the erosion of standards. Anna shakes her head, smiles ruefully, and shrugs with resignation. "Nothing surprises me," she says.

Mauricio's second class is in the "old building," the original structure built in 1894. Here, the architecture is very pleasing, with long cool corridors and higher ceilings, wooden moldings and floors. The air smells of damp stone and paper. In his classroom, Mauricio again distributes Xeroxed sheets for review. The work is the same: seat-work done alone or in pairs, punctuated by board-work and recitation. Here again, forty-five students fill the classroom, leaving no seat free. Again, the students listen compliantly, bend to the task, and volunteer when called on to bring their work to the board. By the end of this second class, I have begun to feel the massive nature of the job, the weight of so many students whose futures rest in the hands of their overworked teacher. Fourth and fifth periods bring more groups of forty or forty-five. Mauricio again reviews grammar; again fills in his roster book with grades and attendance notations, again coaxes and praises his quiet and tractable students. Suddenly, in the middle of his sixth class, the silence is interrupted by protesters outside the window. Several hundred teenage boys are marching past the school, demonstrating for lower university fees and changes in the curriculum. At one point in their passing, the class collectively draws in its breath. Some of the protesters have called out a curse word to the girls inside. No one speaks, and the shock of the vulgarity hangs palpably in the air. "I think maybe they did this because they want you to join them outside," he says. Then: "Chop! Chop! Ten minutes," and everyone gets back to work. Even under these circumstances, there is no disruption, no insubordination, no off-task behavior. Mauricio leaves the room for several minutes to track down an aspirin. While he is gone, there is not a peep. "You see," he says, when he returns, "they are such good students. They work even without their teacher."

Mauricio takes me through the library, a pleasant two-level room that sits centrally between the old and new parts of the school. "We don't have a lot of books," he says, "and no English books at all." On multiple occasions, Mauricio has bemoaned the fact that books, in Chile, are extraordinarily expensive, since most published books for sale in the country are printed elsewhere. What's more, the city halls and Ministry of Education provide no resources for the acquisition of books. It is up to the individual school to decide what little discretionary funding to reroute toward their purchase, a decision that is hard to justify when there are so many other more pressing needs. Most of the books in the library are very old, hard-bound volumes that look as though they have been on the shelves, unused, for decades. There are four or five computers, some old, some newer, in an area separated by shelves. The Internet is out on this day, so no one sits at the terminals. Half a dozen students occupy the long wooden tables, doing homework.

Despite these resource limitations, Javiera Carrera is ranked high among public schools. As the only competitive-entrance, all-girls public school in Santiago, it draws a special population of bright students who have made a conscious decision to study in a single-sex environment. Mauricio says that parents choose Javiera Carrera for a range of reasons. Some merely perceive the school as a safer alternative to coed education, but many others see it as a place that encourages female empowerment. Given their academic focus, Mauricio reckons that almost all of his students will be attending college. The fact that the president attended the school also lends it prestige.

On their way out, Mauricio calls six students up to the front of the room and asks them to stay after to speak to me about their aspirations. They are among the strongest English students in Mauricio's third-year class, all serious-faced young girls with dark hair drawn back in braids and pony-tails. We begin, as I have done in other classes, by asking if any of them hope to become teachers. Five of the six say no, immediately. The sixth smiles guiltily and says, "Perhaps, if nothing else works out for me." We all laugh. "Why don't you want to teach?" I ask. There's a long silence: "The work is too hard," one volunteers. "Hard in what way?" I say. "The motivation," says the same girl. "The students aren't interested, and they are rude and loud. Not in this school, but in most others." We talk about the professions they hope to pursue. Most list professions in the sciences: engineers, biologists, doctors. These are professions that bring substantial salaries and that are respected. "As long as I am going to this school [a school with an entrance exam], I might as well try for a top profession," says one of the students. "Teachers are the very bottom of the university classes. Anyone can get a degree in teaching. It is the least competitive subject." The students tell me that, from their perspective, there are many "lazy, ignorant teachers," teachers who just come into the class, tell kids to open the book, and then zone out. "They hate teaching," says one girl. "They hate kids!" says another. "Less so in this school," says the girl who will consider teaching. "Here, it's fifty-fifty." "Mr. Ramirez is great," one says. "He will work with you until you understand. But honestly, it is hard to learn to speak English with forty-five students in the room. We can learn to read or to write. But we cannot learn to speak. And because there is no English exam for entrance into the university, there is less incentive to work on English than other subjects."

I ask the students what their parents feel about the teachers. "The same as we do. In their day, it was harder to become a teacher," someone says. "My grandmother is a teacher, and my sister is studying to be a teacher. My sister says the other students in her class are very poor students. My grandmother says that in her day, they were the very best." I'm reminded of what Mauricio has told me about the plethora of universities established under Pinochet, and the expansion of programs in pedagogy – the fact that there are so many people graduating with degrees in education, and no jobs. "I want to live a good life, to travel, to support a family. I can't do that as a teacher," concludes one of my interviewees. "My parents would be disappointed if that was all I became."

Once every two weeks, Mauricio takes each of his classes to the computer lab, where they work on software programs designed to reinforce their grammar and expose them to American-accented spoken English. The lab was built in 2005, and though there are forty-five computers for his forty-five students, only thirty-seven of them are working. Out-of-order signs have been placed over the monitors, and students double up when they have to. The class loves the Internet, they say, but that, too, was not working on the day I tried to get online in the library. The computer teacher is a first-year recruit whose goal is to be an English teacher. She tells me she will spend one year monitoring the computers, and then she can hopefully be assigned to a regular teaching program. "Next year when I'm a regular teacher," she says, "I'll get pregnant and start my life."

Throughout the day, Mauricio is free to come and go as he pleases from the school building. When he leaves the school during a free period, he signs out with an electric fingerprint machine. The machine was installed last year, "not to keep tabs on teachers," he assures me, but rather to confirm if they are in the building should a problem occur. Mauricio repeats this distinction to me several times. The sign-in and sign-out are not punitive measures to control teachers. They are implemented to protect teachers, "should something happen." This seems like an interesting psychological vestige of the recent past, when people did indeed disappear.

HAVES AND HAVE-NOTS

One evening, Mauricio and I have dinner with a former student of mine who is now principal of the international school in Santiago. Like many educators in the international school world, Kevin and his family have moved from one international school to another. His previous posting was in Beijing; he has signed on for a two-year stint in Chile, and will soon be moving on to another country.

At dinner, we are joined by Kevin's wife, Ann, and also the headmaster of the school and his wife. The HOS, the acronym by which he is addressed, was a former faculty member from a top U.S. university's school of management; he has taken the post in an effort to help the school boost enrollment and update its programs. Mauricio has explained to me that the school is the most exclusive in Santiago, located in the "rich area" outside the city center. Kevin's apartment is a beautiful, spacious retreat, high above the city. Like many of the apartment buildings in this affluent neighborhood, the picture windows offer spectacular views of downtown. Modern and graciously furnished, the apartment could be located in any major city of the world.

Our conversation at dinner underscores the differences between the world of Liceo 1 Javiera Carrera and the world of the affluent private schools. There is talk of "project-based learning," of "design thinking," of "cutting-edge pedagogies" and how to integrate them into the curriculum without sacrificing rigor. Kevin says that at least 40 percent of his students are native-born Chileans; the rest are from other countries. But the Chileans who enroll their children in the school tend to be the most affluent, the least likely to need financial aid. As the children of the elite, many will go on to universities outside the country, including the Ivy League. Graduates from the international school are well positioned for Ivy League colleges, the HOS says, because top American schools, intent on diversity, are interested in students from Chile, a country that is often underrepresented in their institutions. Teachers, I'm told, are also drawn from elite American schools. The head of school spoke excitedly about a new hire for next year: a young woman who had graduated from Yale and the Iowa Writers Workshop. "She is exactly the kind of teacher we look for," he says. Toward the end of our dinner, Mauricio mentions that I have asked to be taken to the protest march the following day, and we speak about the students' demands. The conversation turns to the subject of teachers' salaries. At the international school, Chilean teachers make less money than foreign teachers, and I question the justice of this. "It's just," the HOS says, "because they are still making more than they would in a regular Chilean school." Mauricio and I talk about this later. "How would he feel if he was paid less in a school with endless resources?" he asks. The class system is deeply entrenched.

PROTESTS AND STRIKES, REDUX

Thursday, there is a planned, city-wide student strike scheduled for 10:30 in the morning. Javiera Carerra students have been given permission to participate if they bring a note from their parents. The school, in other words, is tacitly endorsing their attendance at the protest. Mauricio and I also plan to attend the demonstration, and he tells the teachers this when we arrive in the teachers' room in the morning. "Be careful of the tear gas," a math teacher says. Today's protest is sponsored by students; the teachers' protest happened last week. "Too bad you missed that one," Mauricio says.

At 10:30, most of the school leaves for the demonstration, crowding around the Xerox printer to get their permission e-mails run off. In Mauricio's first-year class, only fourteen students remain, and the calm, quiet mood is palpably different, warm and informal. He continues the review as he did in other classes, but now each student has a chance to speak, and after several minutes, the class engages in a discussion about the differences between Spanish and English verb tenses. There is some laughter at the illogic of English grammar, and the mood in the room turns light – lighter than I have seen before. "Imagine if all the classes were like this," Mauricio says to me. And then again for the students to hear: "You see, with a small class I can help each student. We could even talk. I don't do this with forty-five." The students nod, gravely.

During lunch, Mauricio and I make our way down to the area near the Parliament building, the Palace de la Moneda, past the neoclassical, art deco, and neo-Gothic buildings that line the avenues of the old city. The seat of government is located in a grand white-marble building, visible from a distance, where thousands of students and teachers have gathered. Indeed, the streets are swarming with people, many holding signs calling for budgetary and curricular reforms, for the closing of subsidized schools, for a more equitable examination system. Young men sell buttons at the side of the road, reading "No Hay Futuro Sin Educacion: Publica, Gratuita, y de Calidad!" (There's No Future Without Education: Public, Free, and High Quality). Their complaints are the ones I have been hearing about all week: the lack of promised reform since the fall of Pinochet, the city hall system, the expense of the university, the tremendous segregation between rich and poor schools. Most politicians now support the continued fees charged by the high schools, says Mauricio, and the irony is that they themselves studied free, in a time before Pinochet.

The atmosphere is almost festive, but for the dour soldiers lining the streets, all armed with machine guns. Mauricio points out a group of white-haired protestors chanting in unison. "Those are the retired teachers who never received their wages," Mauricio says. "They're here at every protest. We all know they will never get their money." He warns me not to wander to the end of the march, since tear gas is invariably used at that point. Some of the students like to taunt the police, Mauricio explains, and it always ends up in some kind of violent confrontation. As we walk, former students greet Mauricio from the thick of the crowd; a contingent of girls from Liceo 1 pass by cheering at the sight of their teacher. "Teacher! Teacher!" they cry, and Mauricio waves from the sidewalk. The demonstration continues for several hours, only to be repeated the following week and the one after that.

Salaries for Chilean teachers are an ongoing issue of concern. They are very low and getting lower, relative to the rising cost of living. Losses against inflation have occurred over the course of decades, and most teachers speak about this with a mixture of anger and resignation. Mauricio is lucky because of the generosity of his particular city hall. As a veteran teacher, he earns 935,000 pesos, or $1,300 a month. He also earns a supplement from being selected as City Teacher of the Year (*asignacion de excelencia pedagógica*) in 2007. The honor gave him an additional 500,000 pesos a year, paid out in two parts, fall and spring. He will receive this supplement for the next ten years. Finally, Mauricio supplements his public school salary by teaching an English class for adults at the local university every Monday and Wednesday evening. It is an easy class to teach, he says, because the group is small and the students are motivated. The work keeps him connected to the university in a way that might prove useful at some future point, he says. Full-time university teaching is a long-term goal. Mauricio's salary allows him certain luxuries that other teachers can't afford. He loves to travel, for example, and every year, since he began working at Liceo 1, he has used his winter vacation to explore another international city. As a single man on a strict budget, he has been able to visit Hungary, Austria, Peru, Great Britain, Switzerland, Spain, Italy, Greece, Croatia, France, Czechoslovakia, the Netherlands, Germany, and Belgium.

Still, as everyone reminds me, most teachers with comparable experience earn considerably less. Mauricio says that the starting salary for the average teacher is about 500,000 pesos a month, or $720. Unions, according to Mauricio, have had little success making headway on the issues of salaries and resources. Their impotence in forcing change has made the union unpopular with some teachers. Though he himself is a member, not all public school teachers have chosen to join. For most who don't join, their reasons are financial and not political: 5 percent of a teacher's salary is withdrawn for dues, and many teachers who are just scraping by cannot afford that fee. Still, Mauricio feels strongly that union membership is necessary. Successful or not, unions try hard to negotiate fair salaries each year. "They defend you. If you have a problem, they are with you. If you have an issue with your principal or the city hall, they are there. When we are fighting for an increase in our salary, they are there." But Mauricio doesn't judge those who can't afford to join.

Mauricio has a deep commitment to equity and social justice, and speaks often about politics, the injustices of class, and the tyrannies wrought in the name of religion. For example, divorce in Chile was not legalized until 2004, he says. The resistance from conservative factions was full of dire warnings that preyed on the worst fears of the poor: "The family is going to disappear!" he says, mimicking the hysteria that preceded the vote. "Abortion, of course, is against the law, in every circumstance. Pinochet, before leaving office, passed a law outlawing abortion, even when the pregnancy threatened the health and life of the mother. 'It's an act of God,' say the conservatives. Still they have debated this since 1992," Mauricio says. As we walk downtown together, a group of bedraggled men and women chant against homosexuality, holding signs in a small park near the Parliament. "Nut cases. Crazies," says Mauricio. "Everyone knows these are insane people." Still, it is rattling.

Mauricio sees the rise of the right as an imminent danger to his country. Sebastian Pinera, Chile's previous right-wing president, is hoping to come back into office, he says, and if that bid is successful, he will eliminate all the progressive programs that Bachelet has tried to implement. Mauricio returns to this threat again and again: The conservative forces are dead set on undermining all the enlightened policies. "They discuss and discuss in order to postpone a vote for implementation," a kind of stonewalling strategy that has so far allowed few reforms to pass. Conservative dirty tricks have persisted, he says, since the time of Pinochet. The most damaging was a change in voting policy that continues to allow conservative politicians to stall legislation that would help the poor. In a Pinochet-era strategy designed to maintain conservative control, all political challengers have to get double the votes of incumbents in order to win their elections. The Bachelet administration is trying to change the system, but nothing has passed so far.

Mauricio's dramatic descriptions of the "two Santiagos" – one rich and one poor – seem borne out in our meeting with the head of the private school. The people who live in the rich areas, Mauricio says, never go downtown. They stay in their own area, go to their own schools, shop in the lovely malls that ring the center section of the city. "Did you notice that the HOS doesn't know the downtown area – the names of the streets, the location of the school?" he says. In a large demonstration against abortion a month ago, Mauricio says, conservative forces shipped in protesters from other parts of the city. "Wealthy blonds were brought in with their maids," Mauricio says. He could tell, he said, because the maids were wearing their aprons.

The injustices of class prejudice touch on many aspects of his life. Most of his friends, he says, are not schoolteachers, because teachers have neither the time nor the discretionary income to socialize, travel, or go to the cinema or restaurants. He is keenly aware of the differences between his own experiences at Liceo 1 and those of his colleagues in other schools. "In some schools, you have very difficult discipline problems, and teachers are alone; they don't have support." Resources, too, are very limited. "Basic things like paper," he says, "are in short supply." In order to receive resources like laptops and DVD players, schools must compete with other schools, submitting applications for improvement projects. Javiera Carerra's status as a test-enrolled school – and the alma mater of the president – puts it at an advantage. Some schools get nothing. It isn't a fair system, says Mauricio, "but fairness has never driven the decisions of people in power."

In the winter term after my visit, Mauricio writes to say that the school is once again closed down because of student strikes. Recently, protests have turned violent as police fired tear gas and students set fires to cars and to trash cans. He has no idea how long it will last, but several weeks have already passed with no change in the status of negotiations between the students and the city. From the outside, student complaints seem ironic. The current education minister, Nicolas Eyzaguirre, has been trying to enact a progressive agenda that would close down many of the pay-for-service schools created under Pinochet and address the practice of requesting copayments in public schools. Eyzaguirre has pledged to reform the system so that, by 2017, "Ninety-three percent of elementary and secondary schools would be free." For this, he has been attacked from both the left and the right. Both claim he is trying to eliminate choice.

Elsewhere, there are other forms of protest. To bring attention to rising student loan debt, an artist named Francisco Tapia, or "Papas Fritas" (French fries), confessed to burning $500 million in student loan documents after stealing them from the Universidad del Mar in Santiago, during a student takeover of the campus. "It's over; it's finished," Tapia says in a video, posted on YouTube. "You don't have to pay another peso. I am just like you, living a shitty life, and I live it day by day – this is my act of love for you." In a sequence of events that seemed to underscore the absurdity of Chilean politics, the ashes from Tapia's student loan documents were then put on display at the Centro Cultural Gabriela Mistral, the national cultural center in the Santiago. Soon after, police collected the ashes as evidence to investigate the theft of university property. To complicate matters further, Chile's Education Ministry has now shut down the university for financial irregularities, and, according to the *Santiago Times*, a court has ruled that the university will have to individually sue each student whose promissory note was burned, in order to continue to collect on the student loan debt. Tapia, says the paper, may also face jail time. [4]

Mauricio has returned to Valdivia to wait out the strike and get a bit of rest and relaxation.

7

The United States: Diversity and a Passion for Leadership

Windsor High School is situated in the oldest incorporated town in Connecticut, a town with a rich history as birthplace to Revolutionary War heroes and as an Underground Railroad stop. Driving through the quaint downtown area, one passes beautiful old clapboard houses with historic plaques on them reading 1740, 1780; then, farther out, elegant nineteenth-century estates, modern manicured McMansions, and the Loomis Chaffee School, a private boarding school with a yearly tuition that rivals an Ivy League university. The town center is a broad, green expanse, almost laughably genteel, a caricature of the affluent, sleepy New England towns depicted in Norman Rockwell paintings.

Windsor High School stands in dramatic contrast to its town. A sprawling brick structure built in the 1970s, the high school is as lively and diverse as the town is quiet and homogeneous. Activist Jonathan Kozol has excoriated policy-makers for using the word "diversity" to describe many urban and semi-urban American schools. Diversity, he argued, has become a euphemism for institutions with demographics that are 90+ percent black and Hispanic.[1] At Windsor High School, however, the term "diversity" is not a misnomer. The school is truly integrated, a model of ethnic and cultural blending that seems increasingly rare in institutions so close to major urban centers. Because the district for Windsor is wide, including racially mixed, working-class neighborhoods that skim the outskirts of Hartford, 70 percent of students are nonwhite, including a wide range of immigrant students from Asia, South America, and the Caribbean. Among those students classified as "black," the diversity is dramatic. There are African immigrants, children from Jamaica and the Dominican Republic, and African Americans whose families have lived in the district for generations.

Windsor High tries to provide something for everyone. Besides the school's English as a Second Language class, there is a range of supports for a large special needs population. There are vocational programs, school-to-work programs, and programs for high-achieving students, including a program linked to the University of Connecticut that affords college credit to high school classes. Though Windsor is a middle-class school, there are substantial numbers of students on free lunches, and the number of upper-middle-class children is shrinking. Windsor's affluent families (and there are a significant number of them) often send their children to Loomis Chaffee. "The only rich families who use the public school," notes one longtime resident of the community, "are the ones who want to make a political point"; that is, families who are willing to sacrifice the resource advantages of a Loomis for the "real-world" diversity of Windsor High. "But there are fewer of those kinds of parents around in the past few years," he says, "because that kind of idealism isn't really 'in' right now."

With the exodus of the affluent from Windsor High School, poor families from Hartford have moved in to fill the vacant slots. There is a perception among teachers that some families use the residency addresses of aunts, cousins, and other family members to allow students to enroll in the Windsor district, a huge step up from the worst of the Hartford schools. True or not, many freshman arrive at the high school poorly prepared – both academically and behaviorally. According to teachers, these "outsiders" tend to pull down scores and add to disruption, which in turn drives more middle-class families out of the school. It is, they say, a vicious cycle.

The diversity of the school and its efforts to be everything to everyone can create its own set of problems. Windsor has been dogged by low scores on the Connecticut Academic Performance Test, the high-stakes test that measures basic proficiency among graduates. These scores have been a source of ongoing tension between the school and the community, and a source of angst for teachers who are invariably blamed when the numbers dip below state averages. As in most districts where scores are low, the causes are complex. But certainly diversity is a factor: teachers and administrators at Windsor point to the number of special needs and second-language learners who are compelled to take the test. Itinerant leadership may also play a role: for a period in the 1990s and early 2000s, there were five different principals in the school, each staying long enough to try his or her hand at raising scores. Recently, leadership has been more stable, and scores are improving. Still, the district has a long way to go to catch up with more affluent areas just north of the town.

TEACHING THE MOST CHALLENGING STUDENTS

It is an early fall day at Windsor High. At the sound of the first warning bell, Bonnie Fineman emerges from her office with an armful of papers and a small cart on which she carries the paraphernalia she will use in her classes. Bonnie is a thirty-seven-year-old English teacher at Windsor, currently serving as the department chair. She is wearing her usual preppy uniform: a pink Oxford shirt, a pair of black trousers, and a pullover sweater. Her hair is cut in a short bob, a schoolboy's cut. She has an athletic look about her, strong, immaculate, and spare.

Bonnie's first class of the day is a ninth-grade "college-level class," a euphemism at Windsor High for classes with students reading years below grade level. Earlier, Bonnie has spoken to me about the class, saying it is one of the most challenging she has taught in all her years in the profession. Some students, she says, are reading on the fourth-grade level; all are reading below average; and many have emotional or behavioral problems that cause constant disruption.

Bonnie tells me she is "really stressed out" this morning; two of the main roads she takes to school were closed, making her morning commute twice as long as usual and delaying the elaborate daily preparations she makes before this first class. On a typical day, Bonnie arrives at 6:30, a full hour before the start of school. Now it is 7:10, and she is just starting to arrange the room for her first-period lesson. Like all her lesson plans, this one is built on an extensive sequence of activities, using a range of materials. She has set up various "stations" around the room, with blank poster paper affixed to the walls and desk clusters around those stations. She has also set up a SMART Board with the intention of highlighting a page from the text. Though she is famous in the department for her tech-savvy skills, today the projector is not cooperating.

"You good with computers, David?" One boy has entered the classroom early, and Bonnie calls to him from the back of room. "Can you get this to play? If you could, that would be amazing."

David strolls up to the computer and fiddles with it as other students slowly arrive, pushing dreamily through the door and moving around the room. Bonnie greets each one, looking up from her preparations. Each gets a personal comment.

"What? You've got a Cape Cod sweatshirt! Wow, that's awesome. That really takes me back ... "

"Hi, Pablo. Are you feeling better today?"

Two more students enter, one singing falsetto. "Wow, that's some voice you have!" Bonnie says. "What's that song?" No one responds to her greetings.

Students begin to take their seats, kicking book bags under their desks, some spreading their long adolescent torsos across the desks, as if stretching out for a nap.

The public address system erupts in a static-y warning: "School begins in two minutes. Please turn off all electronics." Students take this as a prompt to check their e-mail and do a bit of last-minute texting.

At the sound of the buzzer, eleven students are seated throughout the room, six boys and five girls. Several more saunter in after the bell, including Bella, the special needs aide, hired by the district to help support Bonnie's work with the most troubled students. Bella circumnavigates the room slowly and then settles into a seat near the front.

The class is behind in its work because Bonnie had been out the week before with a bad virus. Flat on her back with a fever and migraine headaches, she tells me she constantly worried about the time away; would the substitute be able to control the class? Would any work get done? A colleague tells me later that Bonnie fought against the virus for days, showing up sick and in pain until it was clear that her presence was doing no one any good. She took two days off, then passed the virus on to her partner Danie, who is now out from work this week.

"Did you get these journals when I was sick?" Bonnie asks the class, holding up a white and black composition book. The class looks up, slowly raising their heads like sea turtles, but no one speaks. "I see that [the substitute] didn't ask you to put your names on them. Please do put your names on these now." She distributes the journals to the students, moving around the room to hand them out one by one. "Ken, do you have a pen or a pencil? We're going to watch a video clip. Anybody need a pen? Juan, you want to put your name on that? You need a pen? I've got an extra pencil here. Yes, you do need to write your name." Much of Bonnie's time is taken up repeating the same instructions again and again, as if battering a fist against the stubborn distraction of the class. She does this without any sign of annoyance or fatigue. "You'll be needing to put your names on these journals," she says again. "Anyone need a pen?"

"The focus of our class today," she says, pointing to the objectives written in block letters on the board, "is 'How do characters become who they are?'" Underneath, she has listed the three hoped-for goals for the ninety-minute session:

1. Understand that – just like people – characters have traits that make them who they are.
2. Write about your character and how you got that way.
3. Read about Spear and determine his character by finding description in the text that reveals his identity.

Bonnie has chosen to begin the lesson with a trailer from the television show *Veronica Mars*, a series that she thinks will appeal to these fifteen-year-olds, since its heroine is a teenage detective.

"Watch this very short video," she says, "and then let's talk about the things that make Veronica Mars who she is." The trailer speaks explicitly to Veronica's past: the mysterious death of her best friend, the firing of her father, a former sheriff. The class watches the brief video with varying degrees of interest. At the end, Bonnie claps her hands together. "So!" she says, "what were some of the things that shaped the character of Veronica?" A long silence follows. "She had a friend who died," says a boy in a Kanye West T-shirt. "Good, Shane, good start," says Bonnie. "Did you catch any other details? Something about her dad?"

Little by little, she coaxes details from the class. Every answer, no matter how truncated or concrete, is praised and repeated, extended and connected. "The dad lost his job; how might that make you feel?" The class is silent, and several boys have turned away toward the door.

"Let's listen again and think really carefully," Bonnie says. "I want to see if you can come up with three more details about who she is. You have to be a little more alert. It's the same thing we need to do when we are reading." She plays the five-minute clip again. This time, several students are able to repeat some of the facts stated in the video.

"Okay," Bonnie says after more tugging. "We're trying to unwrap the character by picking up on little details. That's basically what we are going to do today, using you as the subject. So open up to the first page of the journal . . . If it was you and not Veronica Mars, what would the narrator be saying about you? Who are you, and how did you get that way? This is free-writing," she reminds them, "I don't care about the spelling or grammar. No wrong answers here. Eight minutes of writing. I'm going to set a timer for you."

The students look off dreamily or start to write a little. One boy turns in his seat and stares at the bookcase. Bonnie moves around the classroom, leaning over the journals of one student after another. "I'm so impressed with your writing," she says to a student who has stood up to stretch. "Keep going . . . Eight minutes, guys. We're shooting for eight minutes of writing. I'm impressed with the effort I'm seeing."

Bella leaves the room.

The timer bings, and Bonnie begins the arduous process of coaxing students to share what they have written.

"I saw some of you wrote down stuff like 'I'm an athlete.'" "I've noticed, Shane, you're diligent about schoolwork." "Anybody have an event that made them who they are?"

One boy says softly that his little brother died. Another volunteers that his parents are from Jamaica, that they speak patois. Bonnie follows every comment with an expression of interest and gratitude. "Wow," she says, again and again, "thanks for sharing that."

The third part of the lesson is to turn the same strategies of analysis used for the video and the free-writing to the text of a story that has been projected onto the whiteboard in front of the classroom. Students in low-level classes often have difficulty completing homework, so assigned novels and short stories are read in the class itself, often at a very slow pace, so that one text may take months to complete.

"Read along either here or on the sheet on your desk," she says and proceeds to read through the projected page slowly and with some feeling. As she reads, she stops again and again, encouraging the students to note telling details.

"Here's a clue," she points to the projected text and notes a phrase embedded in one of the sentences: "'Like the natural politician he was . . . ' What kinds of traits does a 'natural politician' have? We're looking for clues like this."

A girl with elaborate cornrows leans over to her friend and asks her what a politician is.

"You can do this," Bonnie says to the class, reading aloud another line from the story. "'Spear noticed a white girl sitting in the front row.' What does this tell you about Spear?" A mumbled response comes from the front row, and Bonnie leaps on it. "Good! He's aware of people, and maybe what about people? Maybe race? Maybe he's sensitive to race?"

This close reading and prodding for responses goes on for another ten minutes. Then, Bonnie moves to part three of her choreographed lesson, small-group work. She has affixed different colors of poster paper on walls and windows around the classroom, and has stationed desk groups around each sheet. Student are asked to read through several pages and use highlighters to underline suggestive details in the text that might point to key traits in the main character. "I want at least one detail per page, minimum," she says.

The students turn to the task, and Bonnie begins to move around the room again, praising, pointing to clues, listening attentively. The repetitive instructions begin again. "So what are you doing, Matt? What are we looking for? Who is going to read aloud? What page are we supposed to be on? What are we looking for? Who needs a pen? What's our focus today? So how does that paragraph tell you something about what Spear is about? Who needs a pen?"

Gradually, the groups begin to focus. "If his father gave anti-white speeches, what does that tell us about Spear?" Some students begin to list one or two observations on the poster paper. But others have grown restless. We are one hour into the ninety-minute class, and two boys are out of their seats wandering around the perimeter of the room. Several more are looking at calculators.

"Don't just highlight anything," Bonnie says to a boy who is using his highlighter to cover the page in yellow lines.

The story, by Julius Lester, is about race hatred and reconciliation, and Bonnie must work carefully, she says, to bring these issues to light without sounding pedantic or sanctimonious, while encouraging students to see their own lives and experiences in the text. Bonnie walks over to one of the desk groups near the back of the room. Two of the four students have stood up and are wandering around the classroom. She turns her focus to the remaining two seated students. "Look," she says, "Marco found a good line here." She reads what he has highlighted: "'Spear suddenly found himself groping for words ... '" Bonnie looks up from the book at the two students, who are momentarily attentive. "Who is he unaccustomed to speaking to?" she asks.

"Girls," says Marco.

"What kind of girls?" Bonnie presses him.

"White," says Marco.

"You got it," says Bonnie. "As a black person, he is not used to speaking to white people ... Now, give me just one more example before the end of class. Ninja," she says to the second boy, now with his head on the desk, "do you know what I want you to do? Can you be the scribe for your group? Can you – "

The buzzer signaling the end of class interrupts her sentence, and the students are on their feet. Bonnie shifts gears: "Nice job today. Nice job," she says, as the students push past her with their bulky backpacks. "Nice job, Wayne," she says. "Call my mom," says Wayne, whose mother has been called three times for problem behavior. Tell her I'm doing good." "I tried," she says, as Wayne walks past her. "She doesn't call me back."

As the last of the students exits the room, I feel myself relax. Just *watching* Bonnie move from group to group, cajoling, praising, admonishing, trying to yank engagement – or at least compliance – out of the group has left me covered in sweat.

***

Though Windsor High School is an integrated school, low-level classes are dominated by minority students, a fact that the administration has recently tried hard to address. In 2012–2013, a controversial episode occurred when a consultant was brought to the school to assess the reasons for the racial disparity between upper- and lower-level classes and to uncover other forms of "white privilege" barring equity in the school. The consultant caused tremendous tension and a good deal of unwanted publicity when he submitted a report accusing teachers of racism. Already perceiving themselves as overwhelmed by the complexity of their work, faculty expressed outrage at the findings, especially when it was discovered that the consultant had received an exorbitant fee for his work. Teachers claimed that the researcher entered the study with a priori conclusions, that he asked leading questions, and that he seemed to have little understanding of what it was like to teach in a real classroom. Soon after, the contract with the consultant was terminated, but the episode left a bitter taste in the mouths of many teachers.

Other strategies for integrating classes have worked better. In 2009, for example, an organization called Project Opening Doors, funded by the Gates Foundation, included Windsor High School in a broad-ranging experiment to increase the number of minority students in Advanced Placement classes. Students who agreed to enroll in AP classes were paid to take and pass the exam, with higher rewards going to higher scores. A student who received a passing grade of 3 on an AP test would receive $100 for each test he or she took. A grade of 4 brought $200, and a grade of 5 brought $300. Students who took five AP tests could conceivably earn $1,500 for simply working hard and studying. Teachers, too, were paid for their results, earning merit fees for every student who passed the test.

Though some felt that the whole strategy was distasteful – paying students to study had always seemed the last frontier in the pursuit of motivation – and the union was uneasy with what amounted to merit pay, the program achieved impressive results. Bonnie says that, since Project Opening Doors, "enrollment in AP classes has quadrupled, and classes are now dramatically more integrated." "I started teaching AP ten years ago with nine white girls," says a fellow AP teacher. "Now, we have three sections of seniors and three sections of juniors – and the classes are much more mixed in terms of gender and race." The monetary compensation part of the program, however, was eliminated two years ago, when the local district failed to raise matching funds for the work. It is not clear yet how this will affect either enrollments or pass rates on the tests.

***

Bonnie Fineman grew up in Hamden, Connecticut, just outside New Haven, the younger of two sisters in a family of educators. Bonnie's mother was a reading teacher, and her father was a professor of psychology at Southern Connecticut State University. Teaching was a constant topic of conversation at home. "Every evening, we had dinner together, and all of the conversations were around school. All of the conversations. We almost never talked about anything else." Bonnie remembers constant stories about the challenges of teaching, "the rants about education, and students." Her parents' anecdotes, told with humor and drama, were always entertaining, and they created a sense, from an early age, of school as a world where interesting things happen, for better or worse.

Like many children of teachers, Bonnie herself was a model student, well rounded and fully engaged. Though she loved many sports, volleyball was her favorite, and she played throughout high school. Her second love was English. One of the most important influences in Bonnie's life was an English teacher, Risa Nitkin, whom she encountered during her junior year in high school. Nitkin, Bonnie says, taught her how to write. "She wouldn't let anything get by. She was critical . . . extremely supportive, but critical, and I trusted her. She used questioning a lot. She would ask a critical thinking question and have us go back in the text to really justify our answers. It was more like a seminar-style class. Very high level and challenging."

Once Bonnie got to college, at Rutgers University in New Jersey, she saw the payoff from Nitkin's efforts. "Right away, my composition professor in my freshman year said, 'You're one of the best writers that we have had as a freshman. You must have had really good training.'" The praise had its impact almost immediately. Bonnie decided to major in English. The reaction at home was more circumspect. "My father asked, 'What are you going to do with that?'" Bonnie remembers. "That was his first question: 'What on earth are you going to do with that?' and I said, 'I don't know, maybe go into law . . . ' And then it just kind of dawned on me that I wanted to go into the field of teaching."

Having made that decision, Bonnie started going back to her mother's school, East Rock School in New Haven, observing her, this time with new eyes. She had, in her mother, another ideal role model. Susan Fineman had been named Teacher of the Year in New Haven, and her skill and loving affect had given her, even then, a kind of fame in the city. Former students would stop her on the street, and Susan would respond with warmth and uncanny recollections. "She'd say, 'Ah, how is your father?' She remembers every student." Observing her mother's impact on children's lives: "It just became clear to me: yes, this is what I am going to do."

From the moment she decided to teach, Bonnie also returned to memories of Risa Nitkin. She recites a litany of traits she has tried to emulate over the years: "Trying to have some humor in [my classes] and trying to make connections for students; also that idea of being critical without being judgmental of student work, not accepting poor writing or poor work, but working with the students. I can remember staying after school with [Nitkin], and we would work for an hour on a paragraph. Just one paragraph. And that's sort of my motto with students, that the work's never done, you can always revise, I'll always stay after with you ... That's how she was with me."

The decision to teach meant that Bonnie would need to go back to school. She enrolled in a master's in English program at Southern Connecticut State University, the school at which her father taught. That program carried with it the necessary coursework for obtaining a teaching license, including the requisite student teaching class. Once again, Bonnie was lucky. Her teaching placement at Wilbur Cross High School in New Haven was with a cooperating teacher, Deborah Hare, who served as a third key role model. Hare was a published writer, whose book *Homeboys* documented her work as a teacher in the New Haven schools. "I learned so much from her about how to be a teacher," Bonnie says. "She was very active in the community, she knew all the families, she was close with all the kids, and everything was about forming 'a community of learners.' It was all about getting to know the students on all levels. Getting to know who they really were. Acknowledging all of the unique things about her students. And I just saw her doing that, and that ended up becoming something that I really cherished in the classroom."

Bonnie says that student teaching was by far the best part of her teacher preparation experience, but that the internship was far too short. Her placement, from October to December of that year, hardly served to prepare her for her first real class. Even today, years later, Bonnie remembers it as a flaw in teacher preparation. Students enter into their lifelong

work with such minimal experience in front of a class, making the first
years of teaching unnecessarily difficult.

Bonnie's first year was indeed difficult. She applied mid-year for an
opening at Warren G. Harding High School in Bridgeport, a position she
had heard about through a friend of her mother's. The school had been
mired in political turmoil; the principal had been asked to leave. There
were student protests. "When I called the principal before beginning, he
said, 'It's going to be tough,' but I wanted to save the world, so
I went there."

Bonnie arrived at Harding in January, already the fifth English teacher
hired that year. She says:

> It was very challenging; the principal was gone soon after I arrived.
> They had basically removed all the administrators from every building,
> and they were bringing in this superstar superintendent from New York
> City, who always walked around with an entourage; she was pretty
> strange. I had two classes of seniors, and I had special [high-stakes] test
> preparation classes with ninth- and tenth-graders, and for them the last
> thing they wanted to do was go to school. There were cars getting stolen
> out of the parking lot; I had a desk thrown over at me one time because
> I had to assign homework over a weekend; someone running outside a
> window, police chasing them. I mean this was typical. Students rolling
> joints in study halls. I'm not making it up. And I just said, "I would love
> to stay here, but I can't without leadership."

Bonnie started looking for another job. She and a friend attended a
Connecticut teacher job fair, a massive event with representatives from
some of the state's most affluent districts: Greenwich, Wilton, New
Canaan. She ended up being interviewed by Shelton, a small, conservative,
and homogeneous district in southern Connecticut. The offer came almost
at once, accompanied by an invitation to coach the boys' volleyball team, a
thrilling proposition for someone who loved sports as much as literature.
"It was an amazing experience on the coaching end," Bonnie remembers.
"An incredible, life-changing experience." The teaching, however, was not
as appealing. "There was no diversity there. It's very provincial. No one
goes anywhere. Most of my students had never even stepped foot out of
Shelton. Even if I took the students on field trips or tried to introduce them
to different authors or different perspectives, [the students were still difficult to reach], because of their community, or how they grew up, or their
parents." The sense of entitlement created barriers that were more
daunting than poverty. "Eventually, I said, 'I want to go somewhere where

I can be recognized for my teaching, so I can really make that the biggest part of my life.'"

Her next stop was a job in a very different community – the working-class and ethnically diverse town of East Hartford. Bonnie looks back fondly on her brief time in East Hartford. "It was a wonderful school," she says. "I would have happily sent my own children there if I had children then." But by this point, Bonnie could feel that her interests and ambitions were changing. She had begun to think about ways to engage her natural leadership skills. During the evenings, she had enrolled in a program for school administrators and received her certificate. The program's internship placement had been at Windsor High School, and through it she had come to meet the principal and some of the other English teachers in the school. When a position of English chair at Windsor High School became available, Bonnie applied for it with mixed feelings. "I felt I had to make the move," she says, "but it was with regret. The transition was difficult. I still think about East Hartford with great warmth."

Because the pay scale in East Hartford was considerably higher than in Windsor, moving meant a sizable salary cut. What's more, as half-time teacher, half-time department chair, she works harder now than she ever has before. One of the unexpected challenges for Bonnie has been separating the teaching part of her job from the administrative part. Teaching has always been an intense and all-consuming activity for her, and it takes work to bring her full self to her morning classes, knowing that bureaucratic obligations await her after classes are over.

Good time management and long, long hours characterize Bonnie's day at Windsor High. By 9:00, she has finished teaching her two classes. Then she turns to her work as chair. She is also charged with the supervision of eighteen teachers, work made doubly complicated given new regulations that require vast amounts of paperwork and documentation in the service of "accountability." "There's just a ton of paperwork," Bonnie explains. "It's always hard trying to manage all the different forms and things that need to be done on the computer. The time I really like is the time I spend with individual teachers on goal setting, giving feedback, giving more feedback. Sometimes I feel that valuable work takes a back seat because the amount of paperwork ... checklists and forms." Bonnie estimates that the documentation takes up to eight to ten hours per teacher per year; for a staff of eighteen, that is 200 hours of work.

Adding to the difficulty of the job is the fact that, when she first arrived, she inherited a curricula that was, at best, chaotic. "All different kinds of curricula had been written in different formats, housed in different areas. I couldn't even ascertain where we were. I decided to just start over and tried to use what we had and draw from it, but it took more than 300 hours a course to write a good quality curriculum document ... and then multiply that times seven courses that we wrote ... the teachers and I." Bonnie says that if you look at her schedule, you would see that some days she has three meetings happening at the same time. "Building-level meetings, district-level meetings, Board of Ed meetings at night to present curriculum or data ... and being in classrooms from anywhere between twenty minutes to sixty minutes of observing teachers, which is really the best part, but it's not as often as I want to because of all the other duties."

TEACHING THE STRONGEST STUDENTS

Bonnie's second class of the day is a section of ninth grade "high honors." She praised this group to me the day before, saying how warmly she feels toward the students, and how attentive and kind they are. Still, she says, there are challenges. Most middle school students, even the brightest, still have difficulty with analytical thinking and don't know how to develop a thesis statement. "They are very plot oriented." Bonnie's goal with this group has been to push them toward critical thinking, toward argument and a higher kind of engagement with the text.

The students are reading *To Kill a Mockingbird* and gradually "working up" to a writing prompt that will end as a critical essay.

"Good morning, let's get ourselves ready!" She claps her hands, smiling and looking around the room. "Let's everyone get out their sticky notes so you can mark passages that are interesting or important." The sixteen students, seven black, seven white, one Hispanic, and one Asian, move immediately to gather their materials and open their books. One student asks if she can resubmit a paper that received a lower grade.

"Good question, Asia." Bonnie turns to the full class. "I will always take work back with changes. Why wouldn't I want you to make it better? If I give you feedback and you answer that, you'll get five bonus points."

She has put the organizing question for the day up on blackboard: "Scout: who she is and what has made her who she is?"

In many ways, the format of this class is the same as that for the low-level class – close reading of a selected passage from the book, highlighting key sections, extracting details through close observation of the text. But here, the friendly atmosphere and sense of student engagement is wholly different. Bonnie begins by asking students to brainstorm ideas about the text and the character. Even among the brightest ninth-graders in the school, extracting analytical details is a slow and difficult process. She gives an example, noting how a remark made by Scout suggests she doesn't like school. Then comes the pressing for critical analysis: "Why doesn't she like school? What is her teacher like? What does that teacher seem to represent? How might not liking school shape someone's personality?" As she speaks, she reminds students again and again that this or that sentence or word is important. "Write that in the margins," she says. "Put a sticky note near that phrase."

She moves the class into the next stage of the lesson, small-group work. They are to review several pages and then consult with one another, sharing examples of telling details that speak to Scout's character. The students are grouped into a rough semicircle. Bonnie moves around the classroom as they work silently.

"You want to have some strategies to bring back to the class. I would make sure you have some details to bring to your partners when we are ready to discuss." "Destiny, you're on to something here. Now, you and your partner need to find more examples of things that describe Scout's character." "Good work so far. Now you have to dig more; it's below the surface."

Bonnie squats down to speak to another pair of students, a boy and a girl who have been skirting the delicate topic of racism: "Why is it so unusual that her dad would treat people like that? Be honest. It's the South ... What is Scout starting to notice about the town and the people around her?"

Finally, a student breaks through with the answer Bonnie is hoping for. "Yes!" Bonnie explodes. "Jem and Scout are learning to treat people as equals, which is unusual in Alabama at that time. The first time I taught this book," Bonnie tells the class, "I realized at the end that the students thought that Scout and her dad were black. I totally messed up. They didn't realize that they were a white family in the South."

The second part of the class is focused on getting students to write an introductory paragraph to an essay on *To Kill A Mockingbird*. Drawing a rough picture of a house on the blackboard, she goes through what is clearly a familiar exercise. "A house has to have a sidewalk that leads up to something." She draws the sidewalk. "That's your hook. Then there's the front door: the main idea, your interpretation of something. And then there's the doorknob: the way in. That's the preview of what will happen in the paper." It's a bit of a stretch, but students seem deeply engrossed in this exercise. Two boys draw houses in their notebooks.

The class goes to work, in groups of two, and Bonnie roams from student pair to student pair. She praises and pushes, praises and pushes. "Good start," she says, again and again. "I love that, because we didn't talk about that. She *is* a curious child. So where do you think that comes from? Excellent. I like when I go to groups and there are new ideas. That makes me happy."

After eight or nine minutes, Bonnie shifts gears again. "Let's review the study questions," she says. Notebooks come out compliantly, and Bonnie moves the class through the questions they have prepared in advance. Even among this high honors class, there is clearly a vast range of abilities. Some students ask questions that suggest they have barely understood the plot of the story; others offer observations that are sophisticated and sensitive. One can already see the future academic stars, the small band of elite students who graduate from Windsor each year with Merit Scholarships and full tuition fellowships. One of these students, a spindly, bespectacled boy named Dave, raises his hand to offer an insight about Scout's treatment of Boo Radley. Bonnie has been talking about how the town is afraid of change, afraid of difference. "Maybe," he says, his voice still high as a young child's, "Scout is frightened by Boo Radley not only because he's different, but because she's different, too. Maybe she sees herself in him, and it makes her uncomfortable."

"Wow, Dave," says Bonnie. "That's a really great insight."

Bonnie says she sees a clear line of connection between teaching and coaching. "A lot of the things that I prided myself on as an athlete and then a coach are exactly the same things that ended up becoming important to me as a teacher. I started to see the similarities early on and realized, 'Why don't I just run my classroom the same way I would run my team?' Everything that I really learned about, how to lead ... It all came from coaching ... seeing the coaches that I really admired as a player, so I started trying to emulate them, and trying to emulate them, first in my own coaching and then in my classroom." For Bonnie, that means trying to create, in every class, the coherence and interdependency of a team effort. Like a coach, Bonnie says, she is constantly trying to "create high expectations for my classroom, make sure I'm measuring [the students] all the time just like I am on the court, using statistics, making sure I provide praise for the people that are working really hard and showing success, teamwork, collaboration."

***

Bonnie met her future spouse, Danielle Toto, in 2004. Danie, a military veteran, had just returned from a tour of duty in Iraq. "I still had a tan," Danie smiles, relating the circumstances of their first encounter at a bar. Bonnie was working at Shelton at the time, and beginning to feel the deep sense of disconnection there that would lead to her eventual resignation. She was impressed with Danie, a real estate agent, from the moment they met – her calm demeanor, her sense of discipline and integrity. Danie, too, was impressed. After their meeting, the two began instant messaging one another. "It wasn't until we started communicating via IM," Danie laughs, "that I was like, 'Oh! This person actually has a brain, and they're articulate, and they know how to spell!'" she laughs. "So, what attracted me to her was the intelligence." At the time, Bonnie knew that she had to keep her relationship with Danie a secret from her colleagues at Shelton. "I had nobody at the job who knew that we were together," Bonnie remembers. "Or rather, I'm sure they knew, but I didn't talk to them about it . . . It was extremely uncomfortable."

"You determined, right off the bat," Danie adds, "that 'I am not going in to the next job with people not knowing about my relationship.' She had made that decision to draw the line."

In 2006, the year of Danie and Bonnie's civil union, Bonnie took the position in East Hartford, a community that was far more welcoming. From the start, she made sure that she was honest with colleagues about who she was. It was deeply freeing. "At Shelton, I could never go to a football game with Danie . . . could never say 'This is my partner' or 'This is my girlfriend.' At East Hartford, if someone said 'Oh, tell me about yourself,' you could." The same is true at Windsor.

Danie is a small-boned, slim woman with a serious face and a boyish haircut. She has the perfect posture and self-contained aspect of someone trained into fierce self-discipline. Real estate, Danie says, is a job that draws on her skills as a listener, a problem solver, and a behind-the-scenes support person. She sees herself as possessing traits complementary to Bonnie's, and from Danie's long description of their differences, it is clear they have spent a good deal of time analyzing and parsing their own personalities, and thinking about how work and home life intersect. "Bonnie's a workaholic," Danie begins, "so part of my job as her spouse is to try and recenter her back into being able to say no. She has a hard time saying no. As a department chair," Danie says, "you need to be able to close the door and get your work done. Bonnie has an open-door policy, and anyone at any moment can interrupt her. But then she is stressed at home, going, 'I have a million things to do.' I tell her: You need to be able to close the door and say, 'This is *me* time.' She has a really hard time doing that."

There are other differences between Bonnie and Danie that make for a strong bond. "Bonnie would rather be in charge," Danie says, "and I would rather not be in charge ... I would rather be the foot soldier than the sergeant." Bonnie can also be pulled in many directions at once, Danie says, while she is less flexible: "Having control of my day, having control of who I'm with and what I'm doing is important." Danie sees her role as a partner as protecting Bonnie from her own good nature, her tendency to be everything to everyone.

When I ask Danie what she admires most about Bonnie, she lists four things: first, her work ethic. "Bonnie gets up every day at 5:20, no matter what. She could be sick, she could have gotten one hour of sleep; it doesn't matter, she gets up." Second, her generosity: "She never goes anywhere empty handed." And third, her amazing memory: "She remembers being like an eight-month-old," Danie laughs. "It's incredible ... She remembers the craziest things."

"Except to put the wash into the dryer," Bonnie laughs.

Finally, Danie says she admires Bonnie's natural leadership qualities: her desire to take the reins, to be a role model, to nurture. It is these qualities that drove Bonnie into coaching, then into administration, and more recently into motherhood; Bonnie and Danie have taken in two foster children and thrived on the experience. "Our first foster daughter arrived when she was sixteen years old," Bonnie says, "after being in dozens of foster and group homes." Bonnie and Danie parented this young woman until college, watching with deep pleasure when she graduated last year from the University of Hartford. The second foster child arrived several years later, when the girl's former foster family turned out "not to be a good fit." "She stayed with us for respite care. We had her at our home on weekends, during vacations and holidays, or, basically, at her request." This second young woman also thrived under Bonnie and Danie's care; she will be graduating Eastern Connecticut University this May with a BA in women's studies.

"Both girls contributed to our lives in very powerful ways," Bonnie says. "I think we learned how challenging it can be to be parents! I actually found teaching *much* easier than parenting. There's so much to consider, as a parent and a spouse. Danie and I had to learn to create a united front about our expectations. It was a tremendous amount of responsibility to provide support, guidance, and structure to two children who had been repeatedly mistreated by other adults, including their own parents. It has been rewarding to see them grow into mindful, thoughtful, and reflective adults." Attending the older girl's graduation was deeply moving. "She had great obstacles, but completed her degree with a very respectable grade point average. It was amazing seeing her walk across the stage. It's humbling when she tells us, 'You taught me that,' or 'I do this because you showed me why it is important.'" Bonnie summarizes the experience with typical clarity. "For me," she says, "being a foster parent allowed me to evaluate my own values and my own ethical code, so that I had a better foundation to be a good person to others."

Perhaps because she has thought so much about parenting, Bonnie is attuned to the needs of her students' parents. She has created a system for communicating with parents that allows for ongoing, open-ended communication – something she feels is critical to the work. "It's all about how aggressive you are at keeping parents involved," she says. "What I typically do is make a list of all of the parents, and I e-mail all of the parents weekly to tell them what we are doing in class, give them examples, give them links. I write: 'Hello parents, here's what we're working on, here are some resources. Check the website I just uploaded this thing.'"

A DEBATE BETWEEN COLLEAGUES

One winter afternoon, Bonnie sits down with Sam, another veteran teacher in her department, to talk about their different views of the field. Sam has been at Windsor for twenty-three years and teaches both low-level classes and AP classes, though his specialty, he would assert, is working with the stronger students. He and Bonnie are close friends, but they share different views on the school and the profession.

Bonnie starts by complaining that the school – most schools – are too focused on meeting the needs of faculty and administrators, at the expense of students. "There are so many issues, political issues, issues of logistics," she says. "It's such a tough profession, it's so emotionally and physically draining that the focus ends up being on the adults when it really should be on the students – on everything that we can do for the students to help them to be successful."

"I see the problem being the opposite," Sam says. "We are so concerned with student self-esteem and student feelings that we create a kind of anti-adult atmosphere in the school. Unlike you, my sense is that teachers are a very low priority in decision-making. No one ever asks, 'How will this impact teachers? Or how can we make this school a place where adults want to work over the long haul?'"

"I don't want to discount the importance of the adults being happy and feeling supported," Bonnie says, "but poor decisions get made by adults – whether they are administrators, whether they are teachers – because it's just easier to do something that way; instead of really thinking about the students. Here's an example. I try to work after school with students, every day. But you cannot work with a student after school at all, in any effective way, because announcements would come over the loud speaker about every minute, from the time that the after-school sessions would begin until the buses arrive. Why? Because it was too much to have adults walk up to find students that they are looking for, or too much to write parents and say, 'Parents, guardians, if you need to contact the child, please use a cell phone, so we don't have to interrupt instruction.' That's what I mean by adult centered."

"I'd call that policy of interrupting our work anything but teacher-centered," Sam says. "It undermines your authority and your effectiveness when you are constantly interrupted. It devalues the work of teachers, and suggests that some minor student or parent issue, some announcement about a football game or a missing form, is more important that the serious work being done by the teacher. Schools need to respect teachers' expertise. The endless paperwork we have as teachers, the uploading of grades and other data that takes huge amounts of time. In a school that was teacher-centered, that kind of mechanical recordkeeping would be seen as a terrible waste of talent. Doctors don't spend hours on billing and uploading patient information. They hire other people to do that work so that doctors can practice medicine."

The subject turns to ability grouping. Bonnie is a fierce defender of mixed grouping; Sam is not. "I've been in those types of schools that are highly, highly tracked, like four or five levels," says Bonnie. "I've always felt that the classroom environment is much richer and much more collaborative and inviting when you have all different kinds of students in there. With good planning, it can be done, and it can be done well, and it's not insulting to them. I understand that there are students who could potentially, as people say, 'bring the rest of the group down,' but if you manage the classroom well, it shouldn't be a problem. If you plan well, it shouldn't be a problem. Frankly, I find it very insulting to students when we say, 'Oh, you're all the students who are scoring really low, so you're not capable of working with other students who may be are scoring higher on things.' I think they can, and I think that they can contribute in valuable ways, whether it's their own experiences, or maybe they'll have an 'aha!' moment and be able to contribute in other ways. But I find it insulting, I think it is very difficult to get those groups motivated, because they know, they're very aware of why they're in there. I think there is good evidence that they can learn from each other. Students who are very capable are going to continue to be very capable. You can enrich the classroom in other ways for them, but there are lots of methods that you can use to have lots of different students working together."

"I wouldn't be able to teach if the classes weren't tracked," says Sam. "While I appreciate everything you say about the benefits of heterogeneous grouping, your comments seem very idealistic to me. There are students who, even with great coaxing, simply do not want to work hard. There is no question in my mind that those students compromise the quality of a class. It's painful for me to watch how they undermine the energy and enthusiasm of those who want to work. While I agree that there is an imperfect mechanism for placing students in levels, I disagree that levels be erased. Base the levels on motivation. Say, 'Anyone can take an honors class if they are willing to work hard, regardless of test scores or earlier measures.' I could accept that. My success with AP is based on that premise. Many of the students whom I encouraged to take AP were ones with incredibly low PSAT scores – like 300, 350 in English. But if they are motivated, fine. If they stop being motivated, please then leave. Don't drag us all down with your negative attitude."

"I think that schools in general have a hard time dealing with behavior problems because they are so complex," Bonnie says. "It's really hard sometimes to figure out what the root of it is. Is it academics? Is it things going on at home? It could be so many different things. It's just very complicated to deal with behavioral problems and to have the supports in place – enough support and enough variety of support – to really help students who are having behavioral problems. I do think, though, and I can see it in my colleagues' classrooms, if you have an engaging class and you have a really interesting lesson, then those behavioral issues tend to diminish, or at least they are a lot less as opposed to a lesson that's not really very engaging. So, that's sort of the first course of action for behavior. But it's this whole line, do we punish a student and say, 'You're not behaving, so now you can't be in the classroom'? which in some cases is what they want (they're trying to avoid learning). The whole climate of the school can set a tone. If a parent walked into the building and visually saw the low-level classes, I could imagine why it would be perceived as racist. We have such a diverse school, and yet my entire college-level class (the lowest level), every single student in there is African American. Every single student. And one Hispanic boy. So, if a parent peeked into a classroom, that's what it looks like. And why is that happening? It could be academic; it could be behavioral. But if its academic, then we are really doing something wrong because there is no way that the black students should all be in the lower level classes. And if it's behavioral, we have to figure that out too. Teachers and administrators, we're doing something wrong."

"Whenever I speak to you, I feel very old-fashioned," Sam says. "I really appreciate what you're saying, and I believe deeply in diversity. Excellence means diversity. But I don't think I should have to fight to keep students engaged and attentive. To me, a great class is a great literary discussion. It's about the poem, the text. It's about teaching kids to derive meaning and pleasure from literature, to turn them into lifelong readers, literate human beings. I think that between the memos and forms, the technology expectations, the behavior problems in the lower-level classes, and the bad press calling Windsor teachers 'racist,' all teachers are at great risk of burnout. I'm a veteran teacher with almost thirty-five years in the profession – so I am, to some extent, protected by my own savvy, by my ability to look at things with a detached eye. But a new teacher coming in, fresh out of school, might well find the job completely overwhelming."

"I'm more hopeful than you," smiles Bonnie, "that a new generation of teachers will be able to find the balance. I'm optimistic about that. I'm optimistic, in general."

***

In the fall of 2014, Bonnie accepted a position as a district coordinator for language arts, K–12, a position that dramatically increases her salary but means she will no longer teach. The decision was difficult for her, but the offer seemed to fast-track a goal that had been emerging for some time: an ambition to lead and a desire to fix things in a bigger way. "Honestly, I saw it as my opportunity to try to improve instruction across the district," she says, "and so, even though it's going to be a challenge because I will miss teaching, for me, the more important factor was, 'What can I do to impact education on a larger scale? And what can I do to have more impact?'"

Down the road, Bonnie thinks she might like to become a principal and, perhaps, teach some courses at the local university for student teachers. She is keenly interested in teacher education, too, and has many ideas about how her own training could have been improved and how she could make it better for other new teachers entering the field. But for the meantime, she says, "I'm passionate about this school system, about the kids, about the incredible power of diversity. And I believe I can have an impact on making things better." Bonnie admits that the downside, of course, is that a passionate teacher, with ambition to lead, has nowhere to go but outside the classroom.

8

Conclusion: The Teacher in Comparative Perspective

Seven countries, seven high school teachers. What can be learned from looking at these seven lives, both individually and in comparison to one another? In certain basic ways, all seven of the teachers profiled here have much in common: all are performing recognizably similar work. They go to school each day. They receive payment for their labor. They teach in classrooms with desks and chairs. Though some of their schools are unheated while others are beautifully appointed, though some are lecturers while others see their role as facilitators of student-centered pedagogies, they all speak about their teaching in similar ways. All seven feel their work is important, and all seven would choose teaching again, despite the hardships and deprivations that often accompany their labor.

Apart from these fundamental similarities, however, the lives of teachers differed dramatically across this study. Salaries varied widely, relative to both the standard of living and the wages of other professions. Cultural perceptions of teaching itself also differed widely. As I will discuss, this study underscores the extent to which different countries perceive the profession differently. These differences are not all measured in compensation or resources, and some are difficult to measure empirically. But conversations with practitioners in each country make clear an ineffable *felt sense* of high or low value by the society. And in every case, that sense of cultural value, the "status" of teaching, had an impact on how the teacher perceived his or her work.

Studying the lives of teachers also led me to certain core understandings about the nature of good teaching, worldwide. The first is that the people charged with teaching children must be both intelligent and well educated. As I will discuss in more detail, countries differed considerably in their expectations for the intellectual quality of their teachers. Teacher education also varied widely from one country to another. Perhaps it is no surprise that in those places where entry was selective and training was rigorous, teaching as a profession was respected and students performed well on international measures of knowledge and skills. The second understanding is equally important: once hired, retaining good teachers requires that schools be places where smart individuals are willing to work over the course of decades, that schools be clean and safe, that administrators afford practitioners a modicum of power and authority over their practice, that salaries be high enough to allow teachers some leisure to think and grow. As I will argue, in every country, wealthy or poor, implementing these reforms is not beyond the realm of possibility. In many cases – following the lead of those places where teaching is a thriving occupation – such reforms would simply mean shifting priorities and redistributing existing resources, changing the language we use to speak about teachers and the kind of authority over their practice we are willing to afford them.

THE VARIOUS MEANINGS OF PRESTIGE

One of the most dramatic differences across these seven countries concerns the level of social prestige afforded to the work of teachers. Sociologists, both in the United States and abroad, have long grappled with the question of professional status and the elusive traits that define prestige within a given culture or a given profession. Research on teaching underscores those differences and complications. Cultures nurture lessons in citizenry that run so deep it is sometimes difficult to distinguish learned traits and beliefs from nature itself. Many Asian countries, for example, place a deep cultural value on their senior citizens. Notions of privacy and private property differ from culture to culture. When dramatic cultural changes do occur, as they did in Finland with regard to the teaching profession, the transformation seems almost magical, prompting other cultures to assume that those reforms cannot be replicated in their own countries. At the end of this chapter, I will speak about this idea of cultural transformation, considering some earlier movements such as environmentalism that gradually gained traction, prompting lasting changes in attitudes and behaviors.

In considering the global differences in teacher prestige, I begin with a list of qualities that economists and social scientists have used to define occupational status. In his essay "Class, Status and Party," Max Weber defined status as grounded in three essential factors: *property, political power,* and *prestige.* Property is wealth, the possession of material assets. Power is the ability to do what one wants and to impose one's will on others, notably through political influence. Prestige, he argued, can be granted without wealth or property, through the stature associated with possessing special knowledge.[1] For teachers in America, Weber's categories have some obvious corollaries. Property for teachers might refer to the special material benefits of the work, tenure and guaranteed pensions being the most explicitly positive forms of status. Political power, in the case of teachers, might be seen to most clearly derive from union membership and the lobbying arm of the profession, arguably a historically potent force for teachers.

Weber's definition of prestige, however, linked as it is to "specialized knowledge," has long eluded the American teacher. This is true for a number of reasons. The first concerns our culture's attitude toward children and their relative place in the social hierarchy. The second has to do with the historical place of book-learning within the culture. Of the two forms of specialized knowledge associated with teaching (work with children/work with books), it is the reverence for the book, I would argue, that has been crucial to a culture's respect for the profession. In America, work associated with children has historically garnered low pay and low status, most dramatically so in those jobs where it is accompanied by the perception of no necessary attendant book-learning: nannies and child care workers in the United States earn less than locker room attendants, pedicurists, and housecleaners.[2] Early childhood education has long struggled for legitimacy and even a modicum of respect within a larger profession that itself struggles for prestige.

The low status of teaching in America can be traced, however, not only to these attitudes about children, but also to our attitudes about book-learning. Richard Hofstadter, in his *Anti-intellectualism in American Life* (1966), authored one of the earlier surveys of this phenomenon, laying out the historical roots of America's resistance to the book. American democracy evolved, he argued, in a way that served to undercut the value of intellectualism. Utilitarianism, evangelical Protestantism, and capitalism all devalued bookishness and celebrated traits of character that precluded deep learning.[3] We see evidence of this anti-intellectual impulse in the earliest nineteenth-century popular culture, and even in the choice of heroic figures – the Paul Bunyons and Horatio Algers – that the culture chose to glorify. That suspicion of book-learning persists today, deeply engrained in the American character and leaving the country susceptible, some have argued, to demagoguery.[4]

Around the world, there is no equivalent to this American suspicion of book-learning. Indeed, in a country such as France, the historically high status of teachers may be connected to that culture's long-standing view of itself as a nation of readers, a country that has valued debate and intellectual engagement as a core value. In Eastern European countries, especially before the fall of communism, teachers were venerated for their learning. In developing countries in Africa and Asia, education alone has marked individuals as worthy of status, regardless of their income. India, which is itself in the process of changing, has long held the intellectual and spiritual wisdom of teachers as a marker for status. Sociologists have noted that the attitudes, values, and expectations associated with the teacher in India are embodied by the word "guru," a 2,500-year-old Sanskrit term with a broad spectrum of meanings – from teacher to spiritual guide to mentor. At the basis of all these terms is the notion of deep learning.

As globalization flattens differences, Western capitalist values seem to seep into every country, undercutting the intellectual reputation of teaching. This is happening on a number of fronts. Teacher education across the world is, with only a few exceptions, being watered down or altogether eliminated, reinforcing the notion that scholarship is not crucial to the work of teaching. Fewer students than ever are interested in majoring in the humanities, reinforcing the low-level skills of those who choose to teach in those areas. Students majoring in science, technology, engineering, and mathematics (STEM) fields, a burgeoning cohort, are even less likely to choose teaching. In Azerbaijan and Chile, I was hard-pressed to find a single young science lover who would even consider a career in the field. Economics, engineering, technology work, and other STEM fields have held almost universal interest for young people. In emerging economies, where money, understandably, is a primary first concern, low wages and low prestige are fatal disincentives.

For the first time in decades, the subject of teacher shortages has reemerged in the news. In the last year, American newspapers have been filled with articles warning of new and massive vacancies around the country. Unfriendly teacher policies in states like Kansas and Wisconsin have meant an exodus of professionals from those states.[5] In August 2015, a *New York Times* story, entitled "Why Teachers Can't Hotfoot It out of Kansas Fast Enough," laid out in microcosm the ongoing dilemma for American education. According to the article, Kansas is facing "a substantial shortage expected only to get much worse." Pay for Kansas teachers is lower than the pay in all but seven states ("though not by much in most of them."), job protections have been cut by lawmakers, collective bargaining has been reduced, schools are chronically underfunded, and several of the largest districts have been given permission to hire unlicensed teachers. Days later, another statistic came out of California, stating that districts there have to fill 21,500 classroom positions statewide, while the state is issuing fewer than 15,000 new teaching credentials a year. In all states, veteran teachers who waited for the economy to recover before leaving their positions are now exiting in large numbers. At the same time, fewer students are willing to enroll in certification programs. In states like California and Indiana, dramatic reductions in enrollments for teacher licensure programs signal the beginning of an ongoing problem.[6]

Internationally, the problem is even more acute. Projections made by the U.N. Millennium Project identified recent teacher shortages as one of the primary stumbling blocks in attaining the goal of universal primary education. Teacher shortages have emerged in every area of the globe, from Western Europe to Sub-Saharan Africa. The cause for these shortages differs from country to country. In Arab states and in Africa, the paucity of educated young people, the sociocultural impediments to female employment, unstable policies for improving teacher education, and declining salaries are major contributing factors. In Western Europe and South and Western Asia, the reasons for teacher shortages are like those in the United States: impending surges in retirements, unattractive working conditions, low professional appeal, and low compensation.[7] In 2012, a UNESCO study reported that in the next year, 1.7 million new teaching posts would be open worldwide, and many countries would not come close to meeting those needs.[8]

What, then, can countries do to reinvigorate interest in the field? What traits and practices seem to correct some of the deep problems and prejudices associated with the profession? In the following pages, I identify three aspects of the profession that seem to impact prestige and status in the most overt ways. These include (1) the relative ease or difficulty of professional entry, (2) the question of salary, and (3) the kind of authority invested in the teacher by the culture in which he or she is practicing. Together, these traits of teaching seem to correlate with the quality of those who choose the profession and the capacity of schools to retain those people over time.

DIFFICULT PROFESSIONAL ENTRY AND THE STATUS OF TEACHER EDUCATION

Unsurprisingly, in all seven countries I visited, the prestige of teaching correlated with the competitiveness of obtaining a position as a teacher and the rigor of preparation. Where teaching was most venerated – in Finland and Taiwan – open positions were scarce and highly coveted. Turnover was rare; entry was difficult. These were also countries where teacher education – the gateway into teaching – was considered serious work, where apprenticeships were long, and where faculty spoke about their training as demanding and intellectually rigorous.

As it does with so many other aspects of the profession, the United States falls in the middle of the pack worldwide, in terms of the rigor of teacher preparation and professional entry. In terms of teacher training, our country has historically set a fairly low bar. Entrance into teacher preparation programs is easy, and consequently, the quality of those enrolling in such programs tends to be low, relative to other undergraduate majors and graduate programs. It is hard to say which came first in the United States – low quality or low prestige – but a historical consideration of the study of education suggests that, from the start, the discipline had a difficult time situating itself in the nineteenth- and twentieth-century academy. As a latecomer to the standard fields studied in higher education, teacher education was considered the poor cousin of all academic departments. Arguably the first interdisciplinary field, education lacked the focused, specialized, and rarified traits of most disciplines. Here was a course of study that included psychology, sociology, philosophy, and history. Because the field, from the start, was so radically interdisciplinary, it left itself open to critics who argued that there was no discrete and undisputed body of knowledge necessary for the practice of teaching, a fact that has made the field vulnerable to accusations of charlatanism. To this day, many of the most prestigious colleges and universities in America either do not have a department of education at all or, if they do, do not allow their students to major in that subject. This includes some of the country's most famous women's colleges where teacher training, in the mid-twentieth century, was seen to undermine efforts to present themselves as equal to elite men's colleges. At Smith College, for example, teacher education has held an uneasy place in the curriculum, moving from the department of philosophy to psychology to its own discrete department only after World War II, when coursework could focus on statistics, measurement, and testing. Indeed, today's aspiring teachers at Smith, as in all Massachusetts colleges and universities, are prohibited from majoring in education. A statewide law to this effect was intended to raise the intellectual preparation of incoming teachers. Preliminary certification in Massachusetts, sufficient to assume a full-time classroom position, is possible with nothing but a general test of content knowledge.[9]

Stanford professor Linda Darling-Hammond has written extensively on the causes and effects of this low status of teacher preparation. A fierce advocate of professional training, Darling-Hammond has argued for the exceptional complexity of the work. The long list of necessary skills and understandings, wrote Darling-Hammond, includes:

> ... how people learn and how to teach effectively, including aspects of pedagogical content knowledge that incorporate language, culture, and community contexts for learning. Teachers also need to understand the person, the spirit, of every child and find a way to nurture that spirit. And they need the skills to construct and manage classroom activities efficiently, communicate well, use technology, and reflect on their practice to learn from and improve it continually ... Teachers need not only to be able to keep order and provide useful information to students but also to be increasingly effective in enabling a diverse group of students to learn ever more complex material. In previous decades, they were expected to prepare only a small minority for ambitious intellectual work, whereas they are now expected to prepare virtually all students for higher order thinking and performance skills once reserved to only a few.[10]

Compounding that difficult set of required stills is the demographic complexity of the classroom. In the United States, 21 percent of public school children live in poverty; 35 percent have diagnosed learning issues; over 9 percent are designated as English language learners, and over 49 percent are members of a racial or ethnic "minority," many of them recent immigrants from cultures that teachers need to understand.[11] The haphazard preparation of many teachers, Darling-Hammond argued, is not evidence that teacher education is not necessary. On the contrary, the constant criticism of teachers suggests that preparation needs to be improved. Darling-Hammond pointed to these expectations for knowledge as evidence that teacher education is crucial and that it requires a level of rigor that is equivalent to the preparation required of other professions, like lawyers and doctors. Indeed, Darling-Hammond's recommendations for reforming teacher education sound a good deal like medical school training. Like medical education, teacher preparation should require a difficult and highly competitive application process, including interviews; classes that offer training in the specialized skills and knowledge of the profession, combining conventional classroom work with "rotations" into real-life settings; and professional development schools staffed with master teachers who can articulate their craft to novices. Like medical education, teacher education should draw on a changing body of knowledge, developed from ongoing research, increasingly sophisticated, and quickly integrated into the curriculum. Today, medical education requires a thorough and exhausting education for a field that cannot be entered into on whim and one that dissuades attrition, if only because of the monetary and time investment the student has made. While teacher education may necessarily be shorter and less costly, it should be no less rigorous and intellectually challenging.

Looking globally, then, it is not surprising that in countries where teaching is a prestigious occupation, entry into teacher education programs is difficult. Finland famously claims that it is harder to get into a teacher training program than it is to get into medical school. Finland selects candidates from the very top of their graduating classes, then requires rigorous and intellectually difficult preparation, including the requirement of a research-based master's degree and extended fieldwork. Taiwan similarly sorts its candidates, accepting only 15 percent of applicants and then requiring complicated career trajectories into full-time employment.

In countries such as France and Chile, recent reforms have moved in an opposite direction, making professional entry easier and more streamlined. In Chile, a long-standing, five-year program for teacher licensure has now been replaced with a standard four-year bachelor's degree. In France, teachers can now be assigned classes outside their area of expertise. Both Mauricio and Laurence noted these changes as symptomatic of a general devaluing of the profession, a sense that the trait of specialized knowledge necessary for professional status was eroding. Perhaps the most dramatic example of easy entry was Vasso's experience in Greece, where she and her colleagues received only minimal preparation, virtually no internship experience, and a system of job placement that was haphazard at best.

Without changes in the real and perceived rigor of teacher education, the field has made itself vulnerable to criticism on several fronts. First, there is the sense that teaching is easy work, that anyone can do it, and that, therefore, it is due little respect or support. Second, there is the assumption that the field can be saved by short-term alternative programs designed to drop smart young people into classrooms and then lift them out again in two or three years. The burgeoning of these easy-entry programs, starting the 1990s, has done a great disservice to the profession worldwide. In such low esteem is teacher education that programs such as Teach for America (TFA) advertise informally that students already certified are less likely to be chosen. Whether true or not, at Smith word has circulated that a student's chances of being selected for TFA improve if she has no coursework in education whatsoever.

In most countries I visited, the content and curriculum of teacher pedagogy coursework was criticized. A majority of the teachers with whom

I spoke could not recall the details of what they learned, referring vaguely to some concepts in psychology and methods. Finland and Taiwan were exceptions. Annukka could explain in great detail the work she had done in preparation for teaching, and her interest in the art and science of pedagogy was reinforced by the fact that she herself was charged with generating curricula and writing textbooks. The knowledge gained in her teacher education classes, in other words, was used by Annukka in her daily work. It had become a key part of what allowed her to perform effectively. Teachers in Annukka's school sat together and spoke about their daily strategies for covering the material. They collaborated in generating content for classes and made constant connections between what they had taught and how students responded to the material. Teacher education was crucial, in other words, to a teacher's survival in the field. Lessons learned in the university became a scaffold for solving new problems.

Though Feng-juan in Taiwan tended to work in greater isolation than Annukka in Finland, she, too, spoke with respect and good feeling about her preparation. Feng-juan came into the field just as teacher education was changing in Taiwan. A new Teacher Education Act, after the fall of the Nationalist regime,[12] expanded the number of schools with teacher preparation programs while still managing to retain the best students and faculty that had given these institutions historical clout. Taiwan scholars attributed the high standards to a kind of cause and effect: "The ability of these programs to admit academically able students has made it possible to attract scholars from prestigious universities to become teacher educators at the university level. These faculty are in general able to provide quality teacher training for their students and to advance academic research in the field of education."[13]

In France, a different kind of teacher preparation was one factor influencing the historical prestige of high school teaching. There, high school teachers have needed exceptionally thorough subject knowledge in order to qualify for a place in a French *lycée*. If pedagogy was not stressed, knowledge in the field was crucial. Still, today, all French high school teachers must pass the challenging CAPES (*certificat d'aptitude au professorat de l'enseignement du second degré*) exam.[14] Job placement in France is then based on a point system, in which experience and success gradually accrue on a teacher's way to the more coveted geographic regions, such as Paris. Because of Laurence's particular placement in the *classes préparatoires*, her preparation was especially rigorous. Such teachers are required to pass a second exam, called the *agrégation*. First introduced in 1766, the *"agre"* is notoriously difficult, reserved for "the crème de la crème" of French teaching candidates. Open only to applicants holding master's degrees or above, the *agrégation* takes a full additional year of preparation at the university. The exam generally consists of a preliminary written part where most candidates are eliminated, followed by an oral part where the candidate must demonstrate the ability to prepare and give lessons on just about any topic within the scope of the discipline. A description of the exam from the French Ministry of Education offers the following details:

> In most disciplines, the lessons expected extend well above the secondary education level; indeed, the candidate may even have to present a lesson appropriate for the 2nd, 3rd or even 4th years of specialized studies at university . . . The *agrégation* is also used as an unofficial national ranking system for students, giving a fair comparison between students of different universities. This is especially true in the humanities, where the *agrégation* is highly selective and demonstrates erudition of the candidate. The students of the *écoles normales supérieures* often give up an entire year of their student life to prepare for any potential question. Generally, less than 10 percent of those taking the exam actually pass.[15]

The teachers with whom I spoke at Jean Jaurès worried aloud that the recent loosening of entrance requirements for teacher education programs was impacting the prestige of the profession. Those changes sound familiar to American teachers, focused as they are on addressing "student needs" and a call for equity. Instituted by the French Minister of Education Luc Ferry in 2004, the new program has called for a focus "on simple priorities, such as preventing illiteracy" rather than what Ferry called the "accumulation of diverse concerns of varying importance" that "too often destroy the efficiency of training."[16] Words like "efficiency" and a general questioning of the value of rigorous intellectual training have caused alarm among Laurence's colleagues. They point to recent articles in the French press noting that fewer students are taking the CAPES and *agrégation* exams, and that, as a result, regional districts are filling vacancies by recruiting outside staff and then paying them less than regular teacher salaries. French teachers feared that this was the first step on a slippery slope of lower standards, to American-like policies of alternative certification and privatization.

COMPETITIVE SALARIES

No one goes into teaching to be rich. Still, huge differences emerged in the wages of teachers, relative to the cost of living, across the seven countries in this study. Countries with the highest relative wages – Finland, Taiwan,

France, and the United States – have lifted the profession into the middle class. In Finland and Taiwan, teachers' salaries were equivalent to those of other white-collar professionals. Countries with the lowest wages – Azerbaijan, Chile, and Greece – were, predictably, those where education is most problematic. As a consequence, lifestyles differed widely. Annukka owned a second home and collected shoes, while Vasso could barely make her monthly rent, and Gulnaz held three jobs to support her family. Though Mauricio has managed to travel the world, he lives alone, on a shoe-string budget, works two jobs, and gets critical, supplemental income for a variety of ancillary responsibilities and awards.

For centuries, teacher pay has been a sticking point for American communities. Low pay has dogged recruiting since the earliest schools were formed in the United States, and it is universally blamed for the exodus of men from the field once industrialization opened new avenues for employment. In the early nineteenth century, school terms were short, allowing white male teachers to do the work of the classroom as one of many jobs. This changed by the turn of the twentieth century, when educational bureaucratization required new teacher degrees and licenses, making a once-informal system no longer worth the trouble. A 1920 essay in the *American School Board Journal* described the problem clearly: "The requirements of training for the artisan have increased hardly at all in 75 years; the requirements for the man city teacher have increased many fold. The reward of the teacher has advanced, however, at about the same rate as the reward of the artisan. Relatively, the position of the teacher is much less desirable."[17]

Dan Lortie's 1975 sociological study of the profession uncovered other interesting and telling things about the mostly female American teacher workforce he studied. He found, for example, that psychological rewards were the primary source of motivation for teachers and that the reliance on psychological rewards increases the longer the teacher remains in the field. This is true, undoubtedly, for reasons that have to do with the structure of the profession itself. As Lortie and others have pointed out, teaching was and remains one profession that is both "unstaged" in terms of mobility and "front-loaded" in terms of salary and remuneration. As an unstaged profession, new teachers, arriving in their classrooms for the first time, are charged with exactly the same tasks as those who have been working for thirty years. The only way to vary those tasks – five classes a day, two to three preparations – is to leave classroom teaching altogether; in other words, the only promotion available to teachers is to become administrators. The front-loading of salaries is another entrenched trait of the profession that has its roots in the historically transient nature of the work. Since the feminization of the field, teaching was long perceived as a short-term commitment, a way station for women before marriage and child-rearing. For those unfortunate enough to remain in the field over time – spinsters and widows – the assumption was that few incentives were necessary to keep them there. The fact that they remained meant they had no better options. So it is that teachers' salaries, though never really competitive with other white-collar professions, are more competitive at the starting point or low end of the scale. Salary increments decrease over time, so that the average American teacher merely doubles her salary over the span of a thirty-five to forty-year career – compared with much more dramatic increases for other white-collar work.[18]

In general, across the globe, teachers' salaries are low in comparison to other workers, let alone educated workers. Though the cost of living obviously differs from one country to another, in most countries, teachers earn well below the average national salary.[19] Finland, Japan, and Singapore teachers earn the highest salaries; Chile and Greece are among the lowest. Still, salaries today are apparently less potent a factor in determining student interest in teaching than they once were. Young people are susceptible to other incentives, to the conditions of the workplace, hours of work, length of vacations, and other such ancillary benefits that teaching could potentially offer to families. Studies show that given a choice, many young people around the world would forgo higher salaries for improved working conditions and other perks associated with prestige jobs.[20] If authority and prestige were present as incentives, the fact of receiving merely a middle-class wage would not thwart a country's best candidates from spending their lives in classrooms.

AUTHORITY, INSIDE AND OUTSIDE THE CLASSROOM

The concept of authority, as it exists in the world's classrooms, is also complicated and variable. In the abstract and ideally, the teacher's role should carry a good measure of professional authority, sufficient to impress parents and to gain compliance from students. But from where does that authority derive? In the countries I visited, a key factor determining status was the degree of authority afforded the classroom teacher, both in the school and in the community. Authority was expressed differently from place to place, and perceptions of authority differed from one individual to another.

Weber distinguished authority from coercion (or pure force) by outlining three categories of "legitimate domination" of an individual over a group: *traditional, legal-rational,* and *charismatic.*[21] Traditional authority is based on established beliefs and deeply ingrained traditions. An example of this might be the authority of a father, priest, or rabbi. Legal-rational authority is authority whose legitimacy comes from the rules that govern an individual's appointment to an office. Police officers and corporate presidents hold legal-rational authority in their positions. Charismatic authority was defined by Weber as "resting on devotion to the exceptional sanctity, heroism or exemplary character." An example of this might be a rock star, a revered athlete, or a guru. Though the position of teacher in the United States has always been culturally fraught, nineteenth- and early-twentieth-century pedagogues still wielded some degree of traditional and legal-rational authority over their students. Literature, memoirs, and journalistic recollections of American classrooms often showed teachers as paternalistic figures or switch-wielding policemen, who, in either case, inspired tractability and compliance.[22] In American schools, however, traditional and legal-rational authority all but disappeared in the second half of the twentieth century. The antiwar and counterculture movements of the 1960s and 1970s began a process that gradually wrested power away from adults. Timothy Leary's famous dictum to "Question Authority!" has been emblazoned on bumper stickers and T-shirts ever since, reflecting a deep-seated skepticism of both intellectual and bureaucratic authority that has marked the last years of the twentieth century and first years of the twenty-first. Wikipedia, crowd-sourcing, YouTube, reality television, and other forms of knowledge-gathering and entertainment are predicated on subverting the myths of authority. Millennials, those born after 1980, are essentially "digital natives," for whom information is accessible without the conduit of adult authority. What remains, noted the historian Gerald Grant, is only the tentative power that comes from charismatic authority. Student compliance is predicated on the teacher's ability to win over the class, to charm them or impress them by the force of personality.[23] This wholesale shift away from the teacher's traditional or legal-rational authority makes the job much more difficult, both in practical terms and in terms of personal ego. Young people, especially those engaging in short-term programs like TFA, enter the profession ready to engage their classes based on passion and personality, only to find out how little their students find them charming. Without the successful exertion of charismatic authority, the work becomes stressful and humiliating. There is no sense of impotence quite like that of a teacher who has lost control of his or her classroom.

Historically, other countries have suffered less from this ambivalent relationship of teacher to authority. In Taiwan, as in many Asian countries, teacher authority has been deeply embedded in historical and cultural norms. But its own recent history of colonialization and domination has ironically reinforced those traits. As others have noted, Taiwan's traditional and legal-rational respect for the teacher comes from a constellation of factors related to its ancient and recent history, much of it under the subjugation of others. From China, under whose rule Taiwan lived since the late seventeenth century, Taiwan appropriated the notion of teacher as both *jingshi* (learned scholar) and *renshi* (moral figure). During the period of colonial subjugation by Japan (1895–1945), the status and authority of the teacher was reified. Japan had an enormous influence on Taiwanese society, much of it in ways that Taiwanese themselves acknowledge to be positive. Massive building projects and urban renewal transformed Taiwan under Japanese rule. In education, teacher status was reinforced, since the Japanese tradition of respect for the pedagogue, the *sensei*, was as powerful as that of the Chinese. What's more, as colonizers, Japanese teachers were perceived as educationally and culturally elite, a stereotype that added to the prestige of the role. Finally, under the Nationalist regime of the KMT (1949–1993), teacher status was again reinforced as teachers became the crucial players in maintaining the legitimacy of the state.[24]

In France, Laurence's authority over her *classes préparatoires* seemed to derive less from cultural and social imperatives than from the sense of her possessing something that her students genuinely needed: information and skills necessary to pass the arduous *concours externe* exam and fulfill their career ambitions. While teacher status in France has declined, as it has in other Western European countries, in the rarified atmosphere of the *classe prépas*, I perceived an almost Asian respect for Laurence. The belief that the teacher possesses something that the students want and need represents a kind of authority that sociologists don't discuss in terms of the teaching profession. I see this as another category of power altogether, apart from the three defined by Weber. Here, it is a material authority, one that derives from the power of the teacher to offer or withhold critical information that can lead to material benefit. In no class as much as the *classe préparatoire* is this one-to-one correspondence between teacher and examination so direct and palpable. With the test serving not only as the singular route into the Grandes Écoles, but from there into a life of wealth and power, there was no ambivalence about the importance of the teacher. While her interactions may have been informal and friendly, her authority was absolute and her status was high.

This theory about the relation of authority to status is made complicated in the case of Greece, a country undergoing seismic changes. From
the perspective of an outsider looking in, Vasso's classes showed her little
respect. They talked to one another as she taught. They wrote on the desks
in full view of their teacher, and in general seemed to flout her authority.
Yet Vasso felt herself respected by her students, never once complaining
about their behavior or bemoaning the fact that she wielded so little overt
power in her own classroom. Vasso's refusal to chastise her distracted
students, her suppression of her own traditional or legal-rational authority
over them, ultimately emerged for me as a kind of political act. Given the
dire circumstances in which she was working and her own slashed salary,
I came to read her attitude as a kind of unspoken form of revolt: "Of course
my students are misbehaving," her actions said. "They are being exploited
and oppressed by a corrupt government that has allowed its people to
starve. Of course they defaced their desks and the walls of their school; this
is a rational response to oppression." Conventional student/teacher
authority had given way to a shared form of daily protest: All of them –
students, teachers, and administrators – were in the morass together.
Students, powerless to vote or voice their frustration in other ways, chose
vandalism and classroom disengagement as their form of push-back;
Vasso's form of protest was to let them do it, and also to vote "no" on
austerity in the 2015 elections in Greece, even if it meant leaving the
European Union ("I would rather be a poor person than a slave," she
said). The educational philosopher Doris Santoro would have described
Vasso's behavior as an example of what she called the "Cassandra effect," a
kind of "moral madness" that arises when teachers are required to engage
in practices, whether pedagogical or curricular, that they believe are
immoral or unethical.[25] This realization about the power of anarchy as a
form of protest reminded me of the urban classrooms described by counterculture theorists during the period of the Vietnam War. Jonathan
Kozol's description of his classes in *Death at an Early Age*, for example,
emerges as an interesting parallel. Confronted by a political agenda larger
than his teaching – the social neglect of the urban poor, the corruptions of
government – Kozol described his laxity and conscious subversion of rules
in his own classroom. In a famous sequence from that book, Kozol
ruminated on the ways in which his fellow teachers continued to teach,
unquestioningly, in the squalid conditions of their inner-city classrooms. "I
had a hard time with the problem of being honest," he wrote, "of confront-
ing openly the extent to which I was compromised by going along with
things that were abhorrent, and by accepting as moderately reasonable or

unavoidably troublesome things which, if they were inflicted on children of my own, I would have condemned savagely." [26]

True teacher authority, then, seems to derive from two places. First, it derives from without, where cultures respect the work of teachers and schools, and place value – whether abstract or concrete – on scholarship; and second, from within, where teachers in turn respect the systems that hired them, choosing to endorse the values of that culture, internalizing and promoting them.

CHANGING THE METAPHORS FOR TEACHING

A popular website for teachers, called TeachHUB.com, recently featured an article entitled "Back to School Prep Guide: Eight Metaphors for a Teacher." The list included terms like Coach, Juggler, Gardener, Tour Guide, and 9-1-1 Dispatcher. These terms are very far from the "moral scholar" and "learned figure" that the Taiwanese word for teacher implies. Though American teachers may well juggle and coach, these metaphors make light of the harder work of the ideal teacher, to pass on culture, knowledge, and values in an inspiring and meaningful way.[27]

Teacher metaphors matter. Perhaps the most potent and lasting of the metaphors for teaching in America has been the trope of "public servant," with an emphasis on "servant." In the Introduction to this book, I presented a teacher's contract from 1932 that laid out, in the most dramatic terms, how teaching was long seen as a form of worldly sacrifice, a secular kind of monastic service. This attitude may have been expressed more explicitly in certain parts of the country, but was nonetheless endemic. The expectation that teaching was service became the prevailing metaphor from the earliest recruiting of female teachers into the field. Catherine Beecher, quoted in the Introduction for her messianic views of teachers' roles in the culture, laid the groundwork for the popularizing of the trope of service. In her essay "Remedy for the Wrongs of Women," Beecher began her entreaty to educated women by refusing to describe the deplorable conditions of schools: "I dare not do it," she said, rather coyly. "It would be so revolting, so disgraceful, so heart-rending, so incredible, that in the first place, I should not be believed; and in the next place, such an outcry of odium and indignation would be aroused as would impede efforts to remedy the evil of it."[28] Beecher reinforced her argument by suggesting that inborn characteristics of self-effacement and service orientation ideally position women for the role of savior.

By the mid-nineteenth century, Beecher had succeeded in recruiting an army of women into the field. Educated women from the Northeast became the self-sacrificing saviors of godless cowboys in the Wild West and of oppressed former slaves in the South. Letters and journals of these teachers documented how explicitly their mission to teach was aligned with saving souls.[29] Charlotte Forten, a black, Philadelphia-educated teacher in the Sea Islands of South Carolina, concluded a journal entry in 1864 with an assertion of her sense of religious mission: "My heart sings a song of thanksgiving at the thought that even I am permitted to do something for a long-abused race, and aid in promoting a higher, holier and happier life on the Sea Islands" (p. 130).[30]

These perceptions of teaching as monastic service created huge barriers to change. When men began to reenter the field in the 1960s and 1970s – some out of counterculture idealism, but many to avoid service in the Vietnam War – their more aggressive efforts to build up salaries or reform pension benefits were met with widespread community hostility. Lortie wrote of this period that towns and cities replaced comfortable feelings of what he called "ritual pity" with a new stereotype of teachers as activists. Teachers who fought for their rights, engaging in collective bargaining for things as basic as a lunch break or a $200 raise, lost community support. They were no longer saints and martyrs but blue-collar workers, chastised for laziness and selfishness.[31] "[Before collective bargaining] it was conventional to lament their low pay and refer to them as 'dedicated' workers who gave more than they received," wrote Lortie. "But such relationships undergo change when teachers assert their collective power."[32] The rise of union activism and the strikes of the mid-1960s and 1970s effectively changed the American metaphor for teachers, introducing a new series of stereotypes, including those that ridiculed teacher education and suggested that teachers, especially male teachers, were those who failed at other occupations. George Bernard Shaw's famous dictum, "Those who can't do, teach" is part of the American vernacular. "Those who can't teach, teach teachers," is a latter-day addition to that motto, which has always seemed more troubling than funny to me.

Given all this, it is not surprising, then, that those who do make teaching a lifelong career tend to rank psychological or intrinsic rewards as primary. Surveys of teacher attitudes, conducted by the National Educational Association since 1967, have invariably ranked student motivation and indifference as the first source of teacher dissatisfaction. If professional satisfaction is largely predicated on the pleasures of serving, then a lack of student responsiveness must necessarily be a source of great heartbreak and dissatisfaction.[33]

WHAT THE PHILOSOPHERS SAY

American's greatest educational philosopher, John Dewey, was curiously silent on the issue of service as a motivation for teaching. As a vocal advocate of teachers' rights, however, Dewey pointed to the ironic contradiction that the very teachers who were charged with teaching children about democracy were themselves subordinated in a decidedly undemocratic system of school governance.[34] Dewey's vision about good teaching, however, did call for an intellectual rigor and subject expertise that is often overlooked in discussions about progressive pedagogy. In writing about the teacher's need for intellectual preparation in his subject, Dewey wrote: "[Subject knowledge] should be abundant to the point of overflow ... [and] it must be accompanied by a genuine enthusiasm for the subject that will communicate itself contagiously to pupils."[35] As Dewey described them, the very best teachers are not self-effacing facilitators but intellectual leaders. Indeed, we tend to think of Dewey, the father of progressive education, primarily as an advocate of child-centeredness. But anyone who has actually read his work knows that the philosopher scorned the notion of child-centeredness for its own sake. Indeed, he wrote against the excesses of child-centeredness in terms of its impact not on the student but on the teacher:

> The old type of instruction tended to treat the teacher as a dictatorial ruler. The new type sometimes treats the teacher as a negligible factor, almost as an evil ... though a necessary one. In reality, the teacher is an intellectual leader of a social group. She is leader not in virtue of official position, but because of wider and deeper knowledge and matured experience. The supposition that the principle of freedom confers liberty upon the pupils but that the teacher is outside its range and must abdicate all leadership, is merely silly.[36]

By reminding his audience of the important intellectual role of the teacher, Dewey described a kind of work that puts the adult in the forefront rather than subordinating her, that underscores her leadership position, not the service role that is so often associated with progressive education. Dewey's ideal was for teacher-scholars whose knowledge of a subject is so profound that it frees them to focus simultaneously on all the complexities of the learner – cognitive, psychosocial, and emotional. As he described it, teaching is a profoundly multidimensional job, requiring a vast, refined skill set.

Dewey's picture of the ideal teacher never gained much traction, either during his lifetime or after his death. Instead, as I describe above, service and sacrifice continued to represent the ideal throughout the twentieth century. Perhaps the most explicit scholarly writing on the teacher's self-sacrificing role can be found in the work of the contemporary and widely read philosopher Nel Noddings. Noddings dramatically placed sacrifice in the forefront as key to good teaching. Indeed, her very argument – that teaching calls on an all-consuming caring from the practitioner – harkens back to the trope of sacrifice from earlier in the twentieth century. In her book *Caring: A Feminine Approach to Ethics and Moral Education* (1984, 2003), Noddings described the classroom as a place where there are two ethical entities: the students, whom she dubs the "cared-for," and the teacher, the "one-caring." In this much-quoted book, Noddings described the ideal stance of the teacher as one in which the individual student, at the moment of interaction, must "fill the firmament" of the teacher's consciousness. Anything less than this, any self-serving motivation on the part of the teacher, is not only suspect in the abstract but actively forces the student to compromise his or her ethical ideal. In other words, the student who must compete for the teacher's respect, or the student who acts out of a desire to impress the teacher, becomes ethically corrupted in the process. Embedded in this philosophical formula – as old as the feminization of the profession – are the seeds of professional burnout. Indeed, Noddings concluded her essay this way:

> What the cared-for contributes to the relation [between teacher and student] is a responsiveness that completes the caring. This responsiveness need not take the form of gratitude or even of direct acknowledgement. Rather, the cared for shows either in direct response to the one-caring or in spontaneous delight and happy growth before her eyes that the caring has been received. The caring is completed when the cared for receives the caring. He may respond by free, vigorous, and happy immersion in his projects (toward which the one-caring has directed her own energy also), and the one-caring, seeing this, knows that the relation has been completed in the cared-for.[37]

Noddings described the rewards of teaching as the selfless pleasure of watching students learn and grow, an expectation that has long set teachers up for disappointment and burnout. This kind of reward is difficult to sustain and control: students don't always respond to teacher caring. Often, in fact, they actively reject it. Through no fault of the passionate and idealistic teacher, students sometimes subvert, insult, and disrupt. We know this is true because of the high rate of teacher attrition – between 40 and 50 percent within the first five years – that still dogs the profession in America.[38] This is a number that has remained fairly constant in the last thirty years and one that is higher than any other profession. Though research into this attrition shows a variety of reasons for teachers leaving, the majority points to a sense of being overwhelmed by the demands of the job and a sense of their inadequacy in the face of job expectations. When the ideal of the work calls for complete self-abnegation, it is hard to imagine how anyone would be expected to stay for more than five years.

The feminist psychologist Valerie Walkerdine has noted that child-centered pedagogy has, ironically, undermined the status of teaching. Students are no longer subject to the imperious pedagogue, but the price of their autonomy is borne by the teacher. This form of self-erasure – being fully there for the Other (recognizing each student's individual needs, and rejoicing in the student's unfolding development) sets up as its alternative self-absorption or self-promotion. Linked with the overwhelmingly feminine nature of the teaching workforce, the trope of self-sacrifice takes on a troubling dimension: "good" student-centered teachers, she wrote, like "good" women, create learning environments predicated on their invisible labor.[39]

This metaphor of service seems to have historically played a lesser role in other countries. As I discussed earlier, Asian countries saw teachers as wise men, not public servants, an attitude that reinforced the privilege of those lucky enough to study with them. Spiritual mentors and role models, surrogate parents, rabbis, gurus. These are metaphors that have historically accompanied the role of teacher in Eastern Europe, Japan, China, and parts of Africa. When I asked veteran teachers in France and Germany to use metaphors for the way they perceived their own favorite teachers, the terms never suggested the notion of service: "role model," "genius," "task-master," "sage." Many others, however, including those who contributed chapters to this volume, have seen a change in the profession over the last twenty years. Perhaps the most blatant evidence of the change is visible in the expansion of TFA to encompass at least thirty-five other countries, including China, India, Israel, Japan, Germany, and even Sweden. The popularity of such programs, sold to idealistic young people with the same message of service and self-sacrifice that fueled the American program, signals a sea-change in global attitudes about teaching, a sense that the American metaphor has prevailed.

TEACHER-CENTERED SCHOOLS

One of the most interesting and surprising outcomes of my work across seven cultures was in noting that the two most highly ranked countries on the PISA scale had systems of education that were almost antithetical to one another. The Finland education system was overwhelmingly concerned with student collaboration and creativity, choice, and freedom. Emotional and psychological concerns were front and center in teaching and learning. The Department of Pastoral Care attended to the students' affective needs. At Annukka's school, students worried about their teachers' moods and personal lives; teacher/student soccer games cemented warm feelings; and a general sense of familiarity and friendship percolated throughout the school. In Taiwan, things couldn't have been more different. Curricula were traditional and strictly parsed in predetermined units of study; students sat in strict rows and listened mostly to lectures presented by teachers who stood on elevated platforms. Classes were large and largely anonymous. In one class I observed, Feng-juan called on students by pulling a stick from a large bowl and reciting a number. Given such dramatic differences, how do we explain the success of both these countries on objective measures of student performance? How could two such opposing pedagogies produce similar forms of success?

I would argue that the key factor that links both these countries is the way that both cultures value the work of the teacher and transmit that message to children. But what can be transported? In a recent article in the *Washington Post*, Finnish educational scholar Pasi Sahlberg wrote a sobering assessment of what would happen if "Finland's great teachers taught in U.S. schools."[40] Burdened by teacher-effectiveness measures, by standardized testing, and the kind of teacher isolation characteristic of American schools, Finnish teachers would quickly burn out or simply fade into mediocrity. The system would drag them down. Similarly, most American teachers, transferred to Finnish schools, would become good teachers. The system would prop them up. It is tempting to argue that the single most important factor in improving quality in education is teachers, but Sahlberg rightly pointed out that this commonly articulated truism fails to take into account the full picture of what makes for a successful school. Great teachers survive only when conditions allow them to be great. That means that the schools themselves must be intelligently run, that principals and other administrators must understand and support good teaching, and that students must behave and act respectfully. Stated in my own terms, I would say that schools must be "teacher centered." By teacher centered, I am referring not to a preference for frontal pedagogy or old-fashioned notions of teaching and learning but to policies and attitudes that incentivize strong student interest in joining the profession of teaching and that support their practice once they are hired. Ironically, Finland, the most student-centered school I visited, was also the most teacher centered. Teachers controlled what they taught and when they taught. Their class-rooms were clean, well lit, and well ventilated. Teachers were served tasty, simple food in the dining room and were treated with courtesy and respect by their students. Principals were there to make things easier for the teachers, whether that meant fielding encounters with difficult parents or serving us coffee when we sat in the teachers' room.

Today, much of this does not happen in American schools or in those schools I visited where teaching was not seen as desirable work. Take curricula, for example. In America, the fact that the majority of teachers feel that high-stakes tests are pedagogically unsound has had no impact on educational policy.[41] School reform efforts most frequently proceed des-pite, not because of, teacher input. When states impose new curricular mandates or introduce new statewide testing, teachers are viewed as a stumbling block to implementation. Administrators are charged with "getting the teachers on board," as if they are conscripts who might try to jump ship. One of the clichés of the profession is that teachers resist change, a statement that is often thrown around in schools and among policy-makers as if teacher recalcitrance was simply a knee-jerk and irrational response to reform. But why shouldn't teachers react this way? Any American teacher who has spent more than a decade in the profession has already intuited what school reformers haven't gleaned in a century of tinkering: that lasting and meaningful change doesn't come from fiat or simply from reforms to curriculum and pedagogy. If the teachers are respected and even venerated, the school will flourish. If they are not respected, if they are seen as merely recalcitrant civil servants, the school cannot thrive.

This argument is even borne out in corporate management theory. Education policy-makers in the United States have long been influenced by the models put forward by business and industry. In the 1980s, for example, corporate downsizing and bottom-line accountability inspired lasting education policy reforms in the area of testing and teacher account-ability. Cooperative learning and goals-based performance standards also have their roots in management theory. What, then, is the more recent thinking about corporate competitiveness and productivity? Many of the most influential books that have been published on this subject in the last ten years have shifted their primary focus away from concerns about markets and economies of scale. Instead, employee morale has become a central priority. Jeffrey Pfeffer, professor of organizational behavior at

Stanford, reflected this shift in the field when he argued that a loyal, intelligent workforce is the key to corporate competitiveness – even more important than protected or regulated markets. Companies that fail to nurture their workers, Pfeffer said, are essentially "leaving money on the table."[42] These lessons have been embraced by some of the world's most successful companies, including Apple, Proctor & Gamble, and Starbucks, all of which instituted new policies that protect and reward employees at the short-term expense of the bottom line.[43] When workers are disgruntled, distracted, or poorly trained, no brilliant strategy for expanding market share will compensate for that liability. Why should it be any different in schools?

As teachers worldwide continue to age and then retire, schools will be faced with two very different challenges. First, they will have to attract excellent new people into the field. Second, they will have to figure out ways to help large numbers of older teachers stay invested and committed to their work. Every country I visited will be encountering the problem of incentives. In the face of globalization, what can teaching offer a high-achieving college student to lure him or her away from business and industry, medicine, law, or high-tech work? Obviously, schools in capitalist countries will never be able to compete in terms of salary and other material benefits. But teaching holds a natural attraction to idealistic and passionate young people, as evidenced by the success of the global Teach for All movement. In my own school, an elite liberal college that once produced large numbers of public school recruits, introductory education classes boast some of the largest enrollments in the school. Students sign up in droves for courses on educational psychology and child development. However, too many students are chased away from the field after their initial prepracticum observations in urban schools or even in our local suburban high schools. What they see when visiting schools is demoralizing to them. Teachers work in isolation, and they work with too many students. They rarely interact with other faculty members, except over rushed lunches. They teach from books they sometimes do not like themselves and that – to judge by their condition – seem to have been used by generations of students. By the time Smith students become seniors, less than a handful each year are interested in becoming certified to teach high school, to devoting their whole lives to the work. Certainly, the same is true in other countries. Students in Greece, a country that once boasted a high level of prestige for teaching, now see angry, demoralized teachers working under difficult conditions. Students in Chile see huge classes; in Azerbaijan, they see a squalid school building and a country that cannot pay its teachers a living wage. If schools around the world are to attract a new generation of educated teachers, they need to address the conditions of teaching, and do it quickly.

In terms of the burgeoning ranks of veteran teachers, the problem is even more complex. If good new teachers are hard to attract, it is even harder to reenergize those who have been victims of the system for decades. Some of these teachers, especially those in their forties and fifties, have almost half a career ahead of them. With salaries front-loaded and no vertical advancement in the field, such teachers have little incentive to grow. Their cynicism and exhaustion infect their classes. Good teaching (as any good teacher will tell you) is not only about content and curriculum. It is also about the intersection between that content and the person teaching it. For better or worse, teachers teach themselves – their value system and their sense of the world. School reformers in the United States have long worried about what should be taught, how, when, and with what materials. And yet, to a great extent, teachers are the curriculum: affect, attitude, and persona may well have a more powerful impact on classes than do the books they use or the pedagogical techniques they employ. From what I have seen, the same is true around the world.

In a famous 1932 essay entitled "Dare the Schools Build a New Social Order?," the scholar George Counts accused the public schools of sharing in the blame for the economic catastrophe that had befallen the country. By failing to instill (he used the word "impose") democratic values in young people for generations, a creeping corporate greed had gradually taken over our politics and economy. Schools must embrace their power, Counts argued. Profound changes in attitude can be brought about through schooling, but only if teachers remain free from the pressures that undercut their essential, democratic mission. I thought about Counts's essay often during my visits to schools around the world. How free was each school to "build," if not a new social order, then a free-thinking and principled student body? How free were teachers to use their intelligence and passion, unconstrained by nationalistic agendas or the interests of corporations? In virtually every country I visited (even Finland, where some teachers complained of a creeping new focus on bottom-line accountability), the gradual loss of teacher power and authority seems to loom as an unsettling threat to the culture.[44]

This shifting attitude toward the teacher worldwide seems to have a corollary in contemporary ecological criticism. Scholars have referred to the gradual destruction of the environment as "slow violence," violence that has occurred quietly and incrementally, over decades, often out of sight of the most affluent nations. Only now, when the climate crisis is impossible to ignore, have we finally begun to acknowledge the problem and take action.[45] "Slow violence," I contend, is an apt term for the conditions of teaching across the planet. Since the turn of the last century, there has been a steady, unprecedented eroding of teacher authority and power, and a profound shift in the way teaching is perceived. In the last decade, that shift has escalated with the near-universal advent of technology, the globalization of testing, and the attrition of the world's most educated young people from the field.

Yoking the teacher crisis with the environmental one makes sense for many reasons. The two are inextricably linked. If the ecological crisis was human-made, brought on by ignorance, corruption, and indifference, the solution is also human-made, built from new generations of environmentally conscious people designing new planet-saving technologies, living mindfully and ethically. The only way to create those future citizens is with great teachers doing their work in schools that understand the critical value of their mission: producing ethical scientists, politicians who refuse to dump their waste in poor countries, and a population of individuals who would never think to throw away, rather than recycle, a soda can. This same conceit applies to all the most urgent issues of our time: to poverty, radical fundamentalism, and racism. If the teachers don't have the skill and intelligence to change the hearts and minds of young people, who will? It is time to understand that teachers, more than any other group, are the healing white blood cells of the planet, the last line of defense against whatever future challenges we, the human race, are destined to confront.

9

Teachers in Their Own Words

FATIMA BENSALI ABUBAKAR, THE PHILIPPINES

Teaching in the Philippines is viewed, in theory, as a noble profession. Its nobility lies in the fact that it is seen as the mother of all professions. Indeed, all professionals emerge as a result of the unwavering commitment and dedication of a good teacher, who molds the behaviors, attitudes, and skills of the students. And to mold students is to mold society.

In practice, however, teaching is seen as a low-prestige course of study. Many of those who are now in the teaching profession only became a teacher by chance or by accident. I remember when I graduated from high school in 1978, I wanted to be a nurse. But because the local university did not offer nursing courses, I ended up enrolling in a teacher education course. My parents were very conservative and didn't want to send me (being a girl) to university in a big city. Most of those who landed in the teacher education course were the sons and daughters of poor parents who could not afford to send their children to medical schools and other more prestigious programs.

In the past, a license was not required for entering the teaching profession. Renewals were done informally. The process became difficult and complicated when the Professional Regulatory Commission (PRC) in the Philippines decided to include teaching in its new licensing programs. This was in the late 1990s. Since then, all graduates of teacher education courses are required to pass the Licensure Examination for Teachers (LET) before they can be hired to teach in public schools. Those who don't pass can still be hired in regions – far-flung areas – where no one else is willing to work.

After I graduated in 1983 with a degree in education, I got a teaching job in Basilan, a remote area of the country. I accepted the job, notwithstanding the risk I would have to face in an area where most students (because poverty had postponed their education) were far older than I, and where most were members of the Moro National Liberation Front (MNLF), the secessionist group engaged in armed struggle against the government, fighting for the independence of the Bangsa Moro homeland. Before the advent of Western colonization, the Bangsa Moro homeland had an independent, powerful government, known as the Sulu Sultanate.

I remember having a student in a third-year class in Tipo-Tipo, Basilan. I was twenty-three years old then, and he was thirty-four. It was a bit terrifying for me at first, looking at him and his companions carrying high-powered firearms in class. But he was such a fine, cultured man, as I came to know later. Gradually, I became accustomed to looking at the students in their military uniforms in the class. In later years, I learned he studied law and became the vice mayor of Tipo-Tipo.

Working in far-flung rural areas was very difficult. I was then a young mother of three. My husband used to drive me to the bus terminal at 4:30 a. m. every Monday. After almost an hour's travel, the bus would arrive in Lamitan. Then we, the passengers bound for Tipo-Tipo, had to disembark and transfer to a passengers' jeep. After nearly two hours, I reached my station.

Teaching was a challenge. In the first place, I had to assimilate to the tribal culture, which was different from the culture I knew. Added to this was a seemingly hostile environment, due to the threat of violent encounters of feuding clans. My concern at that time was my life and my safety. I felt I was not safe in school, because I would always imagine imminent encounters with the lawless elements or with the military, since the school was located near the highway where military units were always passing.

I tried my best to be an effective teacher. I tried to project myself as elegant and smart. My students were mostly "special learners" in the sense that the majority were adults, though it was not formally an adult class. I was ashamed to be absent from my classes, because I knew the students expected so much from me and respected me both as an educated woman and as the wife of an eloquent and admired preacher.

After a time, I moved with my children nearer the location of my assignment to avoid tardiness. Besides being dangerous, the commute had become very costly. My husband visited us every weekend, since he had to stay in the capital town of Isabela. It was very difficult for a family to live separately, but we both needed to work. I tried to find a way to be transferred. I regretted having accepted the assignment. Then, there was a shoot-out in the village market. It happened about 100 meters from where I was staying with my children. The violence was the result of ongoing family feuds, feuds that were rampant among the warring clans in the province. In that shootout, one person was killed. A few days later, I requested a transfer to the town school. In my mind, if I were not granted a transfer, I would have had to resign because I was placing myself and my children in jeopardy if I stayed on.

Fortunately, by February 1986, I was transferred to the island annex of the biggest secondary school in the province, situated in Isabela. I now commuted by motorboat. In that island annex school, I had to teach four different subject areas, since there were only three of us with one volunteer to teach first- through fourth-year classes. Having four preparations in lesson planning was very difficult, but it was better than where I had been previously, since it was very peaceful on the island. By June of that same year, I was recalled to the main campus to become a fourth-year advisor. I felt better, since I only had two preparations with six classes, and this had been the load for a regular teacher; the advisory class made it a total of seven classes a day. The atmosphere in the town school was very different from that of the rural school where I had been, in terms of facilities, class sizes, instructional materials, and supervision. Supervision was very rigid and strict, and teachers had to be prepared to show their lesson plans at any time.

When, after thirteen years, I became the department head, I tried to be more flexible. But I reminded teachers to always be ready with their lesson plans with appropriate visual aids and to employ interesting strategies to draw more students' participation. I advised them to instill, not only in their students but in themselves as well, the value of and love for reading. If they hope to be respected by their students, teachers must be well informed and knowledgeable. Indeed, it is obvious that you cannot give what you do not have. It is a bit alarming if teachers are just a step ahead of their high school students, and this sometimes happens. In fact, the results of the test administered by the National English Proficiency Program (NEPP) to elementary teachers in English showed that teachers' level of proficiency is just equivalent to the grade six level. I wonder what would be the results in the secondary schools had those teachers been tested. This finding affected the higher institutions' decision to offer better teacher education programs. Still, the higher institutions blame the elementary and high school system for the teachers' poor performance on the exams. The fault is at every level.

I have known much violence in my life. One of my students was murdered in school, a terrible event that occurred during a passing period between his previous class and mine. I had to face an investigation because

I was the advisor of the class. Twenty years ago, my husband was also the victim of violence. He was murdered on December 4, 1995. I was left a young widow at 33, with nine children and a single teaching job to support them.

Two years later, I was promoted to lead the Department of Values Education, a title that made me sound like a preacher – my husband's vocation. I have tried, since then, to teach universal values of love and peace, regardless of tribal affiliations. My goal was to safeguard my dignity as a model in the community, a woman of values and virtues, especially after I became a widow. After three years of leading the department, I was again promoted to a higher post as education supervisor in Values Education. In this job, my reach is even broader. I can supervise and monitor instruction in every district, and have an impact on more people than ever before.

In general, the plight of teachers today is not much different than it was many years ago when I began. Lawlessness and violence persist, only they come now with different names and faces. History keeps on repeating itself. Violence and corruption are difficult to combat in a third-world country like ours, continuously impoverishing the nation but enriching the fortunate few. Confucius, the great teacher and philosopher, said, "In a nation that is well-governed, poverty is something to be ashamed of; in a nation badly governed, wealth is something to be ashamed of."

ANA PAULA DE ARAÚJO, BRAZIL

For as long as I can remember, I have always felt in my soul the great desire to teach. When I was a little girl, I used to play the teacher with my brothers and friends. And when they got tired of being my pupils, I would create an imaginary world in which I would teach my dolls. Since the awareness of my vocation came early in my life, I decided to enroll after high school in a three-year course through which I'd be prepared to teach literacy skills to children. Besides the classes at the university, whose focus was on grammar, I also went to a private language course in order to become more fluent in English. At this school, I started teaching English as a Foreign Language, based on a communicative teaching approach. This is the work I continue to do.

In many emerging nations like Brazil, countries that have a multiethnic and multicultural population and severe shortages in human and economic resources available for education, English language learning has been seen, up to very recently, as a luxury for the upper classes. However, starting about twenty years ago, the need for qualified workers in industry and the demands made on individuals by globalization have led the Brazilian political and educational establishments to reintroduce foreign languages into the curriculum. Because foreign languages had been practically banned from the public school system for the previous thirty-five years, language teachers had to rebuild the profession and also deal with problems such as overcrowded classrooms full of unmotivated pupils, and with a general lack of resources.

Fortunately for me, I have suffered less from these difficulties than have other teachers. This is because for the last fourteen years I have worked as an educator and researcher at the Federal Center for Technological Education of Pelotas (CEFET-RS), a Brazilian public education institution that offers secondary education (high school and technical, professional, and college-level courses). It also offers engineering and technological degree courses. Besides these courses, my institution has instituted postgraduate-level programs – distance learning and training courses, consultants, scientific-technological exchange, and other programs that have given us a reputation for excellence. In comparison to many other schools in Brazil, my institution is lucky to have high-quality human resources as well as materials and support provided by the federal government.

I have always tried to give my students the opportunity to learn not only the grammar rules of a language but also the culture and history of countries where it is spoken. Although English is spoken in many places, I have tended to focus on America, since we share a common continent, and because we are increasingly linked in economic, political, and social ways.

Although I teach a range of students, I want to focus here on some important pedagogical experiences I have had with one specific group of youth and adults who had been excluded from the formal school system for some time. Generally, these people were pushed to quit school to start working hard in order to help their families survive. Before they quit altogether, many had educational difficulties. Working with such individuals has been an ongoing challenge for me. The students in this special three-year program are taught basic high school subjects (e.g., math, physics, chemistry, history, geography, Portuguese, English, and so on), as well as specific technical subjects that allow them to get certification as a technician in the area of computer assembly and maintenance. Since most of these students work full time (morning and afternoon), school time starts for them at 6 a.m. and finishes at 11 p.m., Monday to Friday. So, it's not hard to figure out how tired they are when they get in the classroom. One of my roles as their teacher is to literally and figuratively "wake them up." That is, to wake them up to a new world of possibilities.

Although Brazilian authorities, including Ministry of Education officials, know that the ability to comprehend, read, and write in a foreign language has become a basic requirement for a healthy economy, there has not been any official language teaching policy in the national curriculum. The only thing that has been determined is that a foreign language is an obligatory curricular component in our schools, which, in order not to break the law, have offered their students the average of one 50-minute foreign language class (usually English) per week. I wonder whether it's possible to learn any foreign language by being exposed to it in such a short period of time. What's more, most teachers present foreign language instruction in a very fragmented way, ignoring the context for learning grammar and spending no time on conversation and use. As a consequence, many students simply fail to learn.

In my institution, especially in the program for youth and adults, we try to give students the opportunity to experience meaningful learning. Subjects are taught in an interdisciplinary way through pedagogical projects that are designed by us, with the purpose of having students articulate the diverse areas of knowledge to better perform problem-solving tasks. That is certainly not easy to put in practice. Teaching and learning a foreign language is something complex because of all the variables involved in the process. I would say that it's even more complex when we talk about those of our students who have just restarted the process of formal learning after a long period out of school. If there is any degree of veracity to the concept that the optimal time to start learning a foreign language is when the individual is pretty young, my students are at a disadvantage in this respect. It may take longer (and it usually does) for them to learn and develop certain competencies, but this does not mean they won't succeed. Many times I have to slow down so that everybody in class can understand what's being taught. I use collaborative learning, and other techniques to help encourage those who have difficulty. Everyone I teach has a desire to learn.

The only real obstacle for my students is exhaustion. Not only do they come to me after a long day of labor, some of them come to class carrying an invisible burden of personal and emotional problems. Poverty is a pervasive problem for my students. The problems that come with deep poverty sometimes lead to absences. When those absences are recurrent, I ask the students to tell me why they are missing class. Many are visibly embarrassed. One student said, "I'm sorry, I couldn't come to school the other days because I didn't have money to buy the bus tickets." So many times, I've had to hold back tears while trying to help students find alternative ways to study or get to school. Other students speak to me about family issues, marital discord, the sickness of children, or violence within the home. When such problems become unbearable, students simply leave school. As a teacher, I often find myself acting as mother, psychologist, and best friend.

The news media and others often quote school dropout rates as an indication of the success or failure of our schools. I would say that the dropout rate in our program for youth and adults has gradually been decreasing, thanks to a set of individual and collective measures. It's been up to us, the teachers, to find pedagogical approaches that work best for our population of students. In order to do that, we get together once a week to discuss educational matters and design interdisciplinary projects. In our school, we are allowed time off from work to attend conferences and encouraged to take part in educational programs. Unfortunately, this is not common practice in most Brazilian schools, where teachers are not given any time or funding to invest in their continuing education.

In my opinion, Brazil should invest in better educational policies that would, among other things, provide teachers with benefits to make it possible for them to do research in their respective fields, as well as participate in professional development programs and activities. Teachers should definitely be much more involved in making educational policies.

VIKTOR KIRILLIN, SIBERIA

My homeland is called Yakutia, and its official name today is the Republic of Sakha (Yakutia). It is situated in the northeastern part of Russia, whose other name is Eastern Siberia. It is the biggest region in the country and is the treasure house of minerals and natural resources of Russia. It is the only region in the Russian north where the indigenous population has preserved its own language and culture and that retains its own theaters, museums, and high school institutions. It is a land with severe climate, where in winter it is minus 60 degrees C and often over 35 degrees C in summer. The people have become hardened for ages and have learned to survive in any condition.

Sakha-Yakutia is the only region in the country where the English language has been announced as the third state official language after the Sakha and Russian languages. This is because we recognize that English is the world's lingua franca, that it is important to learn it, and that every-body should know how to speak English, at least at the level of a beginner. Most of the workload in getting to that point lies with the teachers of English in the secondary schools, and we try to do our best in teaching this beautiful language, despite all the difficulties. In my opinion, we are presently surmounting the obstacles successfully.

In the former Soviet Union, the foreign language teachers were con-sidered to be the bearers of new ideas. During the Cold War, [teachers] were highly qualified masters and truly devoted to their jobs. It was a real challenge for them to work in the closed country without any target language environment, where English was thought to be a tongue of the world's capitalism, and so of the enemy. This was the so-called Stagnation Era in the USSR, in the 1970s and 1980s. The Afghanistan war, the inter-minable Communist Party and Komsomol Congresses, and the empty counters of the shops – those were our reality in those days. Never did we hear spoken any English nor any other foreign language except Yakut in the villages and Russian in the towns. The only good thing about that time was that there were no advertisements on television!

In those days, the educational materials available for foreign language teaching were called the "educative-methodical set" and consisted, in theory, of textbooks, teachers' books, and audio cassettes. But we were provided with the textbooks and sometimes with the teacher's books only. I don't know where the audio cassettes disappeared to, but I never saw them. So, the only person to whom the pupils were able to listen was me. And how could I speak good and normal English when I myself had been lacking any language practice?

There were some records, and sometimes I played them on a record player that I brought from home. The pupils listened to the artificial and wooden voices of the speakers, who were reading their dialogues and texts as if they were official reports: the newspapers told about the new Com-munist victories, the television and radio sets talked about the five-year economics plans and their achievements, and they often broadcasted classical music, operas, football games, etc. Everything was boring and dull from the children's perspective. Once, having caught the alienation and disinterest in my pupils' eyes, I gave up the idea of listening to the records. I thought it would be better to read aloud all the conversations and stories myself. I tried to change my voice any time I read the different roles, and it seemed the children became interested more than before.

Our schools were too poor. The only classrooms that were provided with special equipment were the rooms of physics, chemistry, geography, and biology. The Russian and Yakut classrooms were full of portraits, of course. Portraits were everywhere: famous writers, well-known scientists, cosmonauts, and afterwards, the Afghanistan war heroes. A very limited number of schools were provided with the language laboratory equipment, and all the teachers of foreign languages dreamed of having this in their schools. But the equipment was too bulky, and what was worse, inconvenient to use in the forty-five-minute period, meeting two times a week. I often saw how the teachers used their language laboratories: they usually operated them during what we called "demonstration lessons" at the start of a unit. The rest of the time, the expensive equipment was locked away, and soon became worthless. The pupils easily broke it, unscrewing the microphones and cutting off the wires. When my school was finally given the portable language laboratory equipment by the Ministry of Education, I used it only a couple of times. I was afraid it would be broken, and then, as I said, it was too inconvenient to use. Eventually, I took away my expensive microphones with their wires and hid them in the bookcase.

I tried to do my best in designing my classroom. The walls were drawn with colorful pictures relevant to Great Britain and the United States: the Tower of London, American cowboys and Indians with their famous feathers, etc. I thought the pupils should feel the air of English-speaking countries right after they had stepped into the English language's classroom. [At that time] in the Soviet Union, there was something called the Communist "contra propaganda," which meant [teachers should provide lessons] contrasting and setting off the Soviet and the Western styles of life. Certainly, our life was always much better than that of the capitalist countries. We teachers of foreign languages and especially of English stood always on the front line of the Communist propaganda, because we were the most responsible for the rising generation, and the Communist district committee strictly demanded that we teach only Communist ideas.

A funny recollection has come to my mind. Once, in the 1980s, another command was received from the Party: to strengthen the contra propaganda among schoolchildren with the help of the English language. I thought for a while and decided to make a wall sheet. In those times, there were few magazines, and the *Ogoniok* ("A Little Flame") was the only one with colorful pictures in it. I cut out some pictures of children and put them all on the board with two headings in English: "Our Childhood" and "Their Childhood." It was too easy to guess that under the heading "Our Childhood," I had glued the colored bright portraits of the happily smiling, blue-eyed, rosy-cheeked Russian boys and girls, and under "Their Childhood," photos of famished and exhausted black children toiling in the coal mines. Today, I laugh recollecting the subject of the posters. At the time, I really believed it was true.

Today, in Sakha-Yakutia, it is much easier and more interesting to teach English and any other foreign languages. If the English teachers used to complain about the absence of special or authentic teaching materials, the lack of textbooks, or something else, there is no reason for complaints today. I think the only thing to complain about is the teacher's own laziness or idleness. Of course, we don't have the advantage of hearing English around here, but we can use video materials, CDs, audio cassettes, and web resources as well. Our Internet is slow, but it is better to have it than nothing.

Until recently, the Russian secondary schools prepared their graduating seniors for either oral or written types of degree examinations, and institutes of higher education admitted the students through conducting the same type of examination. Today, there is a "unitary Russian state examination," a test where the students do the written tests only. This kind of exam is one of a great number of innovations and reforms being conducted now in Russia. They say it is taken from the West-European and American experiences, and so we "are coming nearer to the civilized world" and don't need to complain. There are still opponents among the higher education teachers and professors who say that our former Soviet system of examinations was the better one to measure students' knowledge thoroughly. All the teachers of English in my area think that the Russian state exams are too complicated in their form and structure. They seem to be assigned for the college/university students who study English language skills with career intentions, or for those who live somewhere in the highly developed countries of Western Europe, where there are many opportunities to learn English. Nonetheless, the machine of government has started to reform the secondary school educational system. The school libraries are now provided with all the needed textbooks; rather, I should say "they try to provide," because the most of the textbooks are getting older quickly and becoming out of date. The Ministry of Education keeps recommending new textbooks that offer new and better methodologies, but the schools can't afford to get them because of the permanent lack of money.

JEANNETTE HARKER, SOUTH AFRICA

I finished my last year of school in 1985. It was a year of racial riots and uprising all over the country. Many of my classmates followed their hearts and pursued "liberation before education." I, being a young mixed-race girl, raised in a strict Christian home according to even stricter moral values, did not have that freedom of choice.

At the time, the only fully paid scholarships available for university students were in the teaching profession. Only the very rich and extraordinarily gifted among us were even considered for study in any other field. Even though I nurtured dreams of being a very successful and rich executive, I had to face reality. My parents would never be able to afford tuition fees at a university. The only option left to me was to pursue a bachelor's degree in languages and psychology, after which I could complete a teaching diploma to secure a position as secondary teacher at a school designated for "colored" children only.

I performed reasonably well at school and therefore could apply to the universities in the Western Cape. Acceptances were based on June examination results of one's final school year. All the student unions were involved in boycotts and riots against the apartheid regime of the time, protesting against the very low quality of teaching. My nervous parents issued me an ultimatum. I could study at the University of Stellenbosch (a very prestigious, all-white Afrikaner university that would allow thirteen students of color on their campus for the first time in 1986) or stay at home and find a job. I chose to become one of the very first students of color to study for a bachelor's degree; I did this amidst a sea of thirteen thousand hostile white students, who made it blatantly clear on many public occasions that I was not welcome. It was a harrowing, humiliating experience.

I completed a three-year degree program to graduate with a bachelor of arts in languages. During my first year, I had to take five first-year subjects (all full-term, year-long subjects), then narrow them down to three "specialized subjects" in my second year and choose two majors in my final year. After the degree, I still had to complete a one-year compulsory teaching diploma in higher education, which covered material in my major as well as the study of pedagogy and methodology for secondary school teaching. Much to the surprise of my colleagues, I was able to study the same materials, compete on the same level, and achieve the same grades as the white students.

Once I had my teaching diploma, I also had to take a language proficiency test that tested your ability to teach in either English or Afrikaans, the two official languages of the time. I tested proficient for both (my majors were English and Afrikaans) and applied for a position at the school I had once attended as a high school student. During my internship at the school, the principal had approached me with an offer to stay and teach, and I had accepted. I was very fortunate to walk into a permanent position at the school. Some qualified teachers had to substitute for years before a position was offered to them, or a vacancy was published in the Government Gazette. I realize today that it had to do with the prestige and recognition that came with just being a student at Stellenbosch. Many doors would be opened to me because of that.

In 1991, I started teaching English to grades 8 to 12 at my alma mater. I loved the children and their endless enthusiasm. I felt especially good about the fact that I was an English teacher, a subject that could open endless possibilities to them in the larger world. Teaching became a passion, not a job. I voluntarily joined in extracurricular activities and helped out with "spring schools" (during the one-week spring holidays, schools usually have preparatory examination classes for grade 12 learners in all subjects, to prepare learners for the final external examination in the fourth term) and extra classes. I also became very involved with the provincial sports organizations – all work for which I received no additional compensation.

We teachers were very respected people in the communities at the time and received respectable salaries, although not comparable, of course, to what professionals in the private sector earned. This remains true today. But back then, I worried little about money; I was young, single, and had an adventurous spirit. Teaching teenagers seemed like a dream come true.

The head of our English department decided that each teacher should teach only one grade and then follow that cohort of students to the next grade and the next, until graduation. He reasoned that in this way, teachers would come to know the learners so well that success for all was inevitable. The workload, however, made teaching even the most familiar students very challenging. Each teacher was responsible for six to seven classes of about thirty to forty students. Each of us taught forty-one out of forty-nine periods per seven-day cycle, with each period lasting forty to fifty minutes.

Typical of nonwhite schools at the time, my alma mater had seen better days. Here, as elsewhere, there were no enclosed hallways or well-equipped libraries; there were no computer centers or sports facilities. Most sports training occurred outside, where the schools could find any open space that could be used as a "court." Supplies were meager, and even basic resources were limited. Under the circumstances, however, we managed quite well, committing ourselves to the students and trying to work within the limitations that seemed then like a fact of life.

After seven years of teaching secondary school English, I moved to Worcester, a town about 300 kilometers away. I had fallen in love with an architectural designer who lived in this new city, and we felt it would be easier for me to move than it would be for him. Teachers were more mobile than other professions. I assumed I would find work. It was 1997, seven years after Nelson Mandela was freed from prison, and three years after he became the first president of a new "rainbow" nation. Despite the transition of power, however, schools were still segregated in many ways. Parents who could afford it would enter their children into the formerly white schools because they had better facilities, reputations, and general resources. Poor black and "colored" schools remained poor, though now these schools were labeled "previously disadvantaged," as if the problem were wholly in the past.

In this period of national transformation, the education system necessarily had to be reformed. The extraordinary inequalities created by apartheid somehow needed to be eradicated. To begin to accomplish this, Curriculum 2005 was founded, a new national curriculum for all schools, irrespective of race, creed, or color. But while children were theoretically allowed to attend any school of their choice, integration did not immediately occur. Teachers in previously all-white schools remained where they were. Teachers at previously black schools (colored as well) did the same.

In my desperation to move to another town to be with the love of my life, I literally closed my eyes, prayed to God, and did the unimaginable at the time. I applied for a teaching position at an all-white school, a prestigious Afrikaans boarding school. I was aware that the government had to intervene at some point to integrate the staffs of schools, and I hoped for some divine intervention. Because I had studied at the same institution as did several of the school's administrators, I was pronounced "good enough" to teach at this school. The new school administration did make it very clear, however, that I could be "returned to my previous position, if circumstances required it." I discovered years later that management was under immense pressure from the local government to appoint a teacher "of color." Because of this affirmative action, and seeing that I was the only person "of color" who was crazy enough to apply for the position, I was appointed.

I was petrified. More than once, even before I took up my position at the school, I fantasized about running away. Once there, many students made it very clear that I didn't belong. Students were blatantly rude and disrespectful during my classes. I stood my ground and dealt with it as best I could. Children are just children. Once they realized I meant business and knew my "business," they accepted me as a person, and we worked together. The teachers were more discreet in their prejudices. In the staff room, they were very friendly and welcoming, but they remained aloof and distant. No effort was made to make me feel more at ease or to socialize with me on a more familiar footing.

I taught English, grades 8 to 12, to white Afrikaner Boerseuns – rural boys, whose fathers had huge farming empires, where the only "people of color" they made contact with were the laborers on their farms, whom they regarded as inferior or even subhuman. To compound the difficulty, these boys, together with their parents, regarded English as a foreign language. After the English Boer War, the language came to be perceived as the "language of the Antichrist." In this regard, my color worked to my advantage at the school: English was more acceptable to them when it was spoken by a black woman, who was already an outsider and "different."

In terms of resources, the school had everything! There were workshops for woodwork, welding, engineering, and many other fields. The school had more than twenty rugby teams, each team with its own sponsors and administrators. There were numerous tennis courts, a huge swimming pool, rugby stadiums, cricket pitches, athletics fields. The school even had a target shooting range (with rifles supplied). It had four boarding houses, each with its own cafeteria; each house had its own colors, rituals, and committees, etc. There was great school pride. At my new school, I did not have to worry about paying for paper and copies out of my own pocket.

For as long as I taught at the school (eight years), I remained the only black teacher on staff. Many new additions were made to the staff after 1997, but the only people of color remaining at the school besides myself were the tea lady, gardeners, and caretakers. The administration at the school made it quite clear they were concerned about black kids "taking over the school." They were always frightened of "black power" and of interference from educated black parents. They did whatever they could to keep the school unchanged. And they mainly succeeded – as do some schools today – because a school's governing body determines its language of teaching. As long as the language of teaching remained Afrikaans (home language), black children wouldn't be able attend because they spoke mainly Xhosa or English.

In recent years, however, some schools have begun to integrate. Former whites-only schools have now appointed teachers of color, but the process remains a slow one. I am continually and consciously trying to convince my teaching colleagues of color that they are able and qualified to apply to white schools as well, but many are just not up to the challenge. Without a critical mass of colleagues who are like themselves, the prospect of teaching in such a school seems daunting.

With the acceptance and implementation of our new constitution in 1994, corporal punishment was abolished in all schools, and teachers face losing their jobs if they are accused of touching students in any way. The school was renowned all over the country for how disciplined its students were and how politely they all behaved. It was important to the school to maintain that impression. Still, I have perceived that parents too easily and unashamedly shift the blame for unruly, lazy students onto the shoulders of teachers. Very often, they do so openly and publicly in front of their children and other students. They clearly align themselves with their children, against the authority of the teachers. This is a terrible practice that happens all over the country. The main reason why some students refuse to accept the authority of their teachers, or openly disrespect them, is to be laid squarely at the feet of parents. It is expected that teachers be counselors, friends, disciplinarians, and caretakers! No wonder, then, that so many of us become despondent.

Indeed, my worst moment of teaching occurred around the problem of discipline and parental lack of support. I have always been a very strict teacher; I have to be, in order for the boys to take me seriously. If they did not complete their assignments or homework, I became very upset and voiced my disappointment clearly. This one morning, a perennially lazy grade 12 boy had failed to complete his homework yet again. I always remonstrated the students at this school for having this wonderful opportunity at a quality education for which their parents pay so dearly (whereas others, who would be more appreciative of such an opportunity and would value and benefit from it so much more, do not have the faintest hope of ever graduating high school). I clearly remember how I explained to him that he was behaving like the Japanese kamikaze pilots during the World War, committing suicide to his own future by failing to complete assignments and refusing to do his homework (a bad comparison to make, I know). It irked me that such an obviously intelligent and gifted young man would throw his opportunities away like that!

The young man left the classroom immediately, went to his father at home, and told him that I was discriminating against him and speaking in a derogatory way about his religion by calling him a kamikaze. The next day, there was a terrible hush around the school, and everywhere I went, it felt as if they were talking about me or discussing something I should not know about. I was called into the principal's office, where I stood "on trial" alone, guilty without even the opportunity to plead innocence. Next to the principal were the two deputy principals, the student, and his father. The father stated their case, and I was asked to respond. The boy was Muslim and, seeing that they also had a form of "honorable suicide" in their religion or culture, they felt offended. Eventually, the boy and I apologized to one another and even developed a solid teacher–student relationship. What remained with me, though, was a bitter aftertaste. I had been motivated by good teacherly motives, wanting only what was best for him, and I had to endure the humiliation of having to account for my "abusive" actions. It demoralized and depressed me for some time after that. I dealt with it and got over it, though. I guess teaching is like that everywhere. You are a professional, and you may not allow personal problems to enter into your classroom. "The show must go on!"

Today, the demands on teachers are extreme: many teachers are faced with forty to fifty learners per class and teach around forty-five out of forty-nine periods per cycle. Language teachers work the hardest; all students in all the schools have to pass English as either a home language or "first additional" (second) language. They study language based on between four and six "outcomes," covering literature, language, writing, and speaking. From grades 10 through 12, students take grueling midyear and final exams. The examinations consist of three separate papers, each two to three hours long. They write a paper on literature, one on language use and structure, and one on writing of texts, creative, and functional (transactional) writing. Except for grade 12 finals, all the other papers and assignments are assessed by the teacher responsible for teaching that grade. For the teacher, this process takes a great deal of self-discipline, time, and energy, especially given the growing class sizes in most schools around the country.

After eight years, I left the school behind, knowing that I had been an excellent teacher, that I had used my time there to show my students and colleagues that people are the same, regardless of skin color. I knew that even if I did not succeed in changing mindsets, I succeeded in making them aware of the fact that all people should be treated with respect and dignity. I reveled in the fact that I did not have to outperform every teacher at the school any longer, just for some form of recognition. I was tired of having to prove myself time and time again. I was ready for change and up to new challenges.

Since 2005, I have given up classroom teaching and now serve as a curriculum developer, offering support to mostly secondary school teachers all over my district. I work with English teachers from twenty-seven high schools and about seventy primary schools, from grades 9 to 12. We have to meet at least three times per year, during which time we thrash out policies, exchange new ideas, and evaluate and monitor the standard of teaching. I love this job because I meet with all the teachers on a one-on-one basis whenever possible. I render support, provide a shoulder and an ear, and I team-teach, demonstrate, and conduct classes. I have learned so much from my colleagues, and I am humbled every day by the strides they make toward improving the future of South Africa.

We are growing teeth, we are rising up, we are free!

GABRIELA LASLAU, ROMANIA

What I am telling you now is not only my own experience; it comes from the collective memory, both written and unwritten, of my country, and from the experience, still alive, of some of the people I know – my parents, friends, and relatives.

Spiru Haret, a great Romanian mathematician and astronomer, the Minister of Education at the turn of the twentieth century, laid the foundations of the modern Romanian educational system, a system that emphasized modern languages, the sciences, and the humanities. In recognition of his merits, a crater on the Moon (the dark side of it!) was named after him.

After World War II, however, Romania came under the influence of the Soviet Union and became a Communist country. In 1948, by a simple decree, the educational structures institutionalized between the two world wars were smashed, and all religious or private schools became state schools. The same law emphasized the importance of the Russian language, which was to be taught at all levels, beginning with the fourth primary grade, with both French and Italian becoming now of secondary importance.

This is where my parents' memory starts: they remember how Communism was put into practice in its first years, and the terror that came with it. They both came from poor families with many children, and their parents had been trying all their lives to work the land they had and even buy some more (sacrificing sometimes their sons' and daughters' education). All of a sudden, everything they had striven to gather as property was swept away overnight and became "everybody's land." There was much pressure on them comply. Families were told that their children would be removed from school if their parents refused to turn over all their belongings (cattle, wagons, tools) to the government as "collective" property. Those who refused were beaten, imprisoned, or killed. Others who had no property became champions of the new system – activists of the new era. They went from door to door, promoting the new ideas. They were the first Communists, and they enjoyed benefiting from the common property to which they had contributed nothing. On a larger scale, this had happened everywhere, in the small and larger cities: factories, banks, the main utilities, everything became everybody's.

After this first stage was accomplished, the shapers of the new nation proceeded to transform or "recreate" people's "consciousness." With the idea of property destroyed (the great capitalists were already in jail), it was the turn of the intellectuals. Every form of opposition was severely punished. The Romanian prisons became concentration camps, not for ethnic reasons (the memory of Auschwitz was still fresh), but for spiritual ones. Priests, monks, writers who refused to acknowledge the advent of this new "heaven on earth" were tortured to death. The Romanian literature sadly undertook the task of recording the "glorious" revolution of this country: the transformation of villages from places of ignorance into havens of enlightened collective prosperity, the reconfiguration of cities through the construction of more and more factories and more and more blocks of flats to shelter the new workers (poor country people deprived of their land and any other means of subsistence), and the demolition of everything that could remind the people of the previous era. In Bucharest alone, dozens of historic monuments of culture, princely courts, old churches, and monasteries were destroyed and replaced by the horrific concrete structures that can still be seen today.

The same thing happened on a spiritual level; the historians and thinkers – the new ones – started reinterpreting and rewriting our history in such a way as to make it fit the new times, which came as a natural step in our evolution. So, if you looked at things attentively, most of our writers and thinkers in the past criticized the "putrid" bourgeois values and ideas, foreseeing the glorious Communist ones.

The Communist regime being sacrosanct, schools and teachers didn't focus on encouraging our critical thinking. It's dangerous to teach history or literature having one national textbook, with very few critical sources; oh, but we had Ceauşescu's inspiring texts, to which we always had to refer, no matter what the subject was. Still, I had great teachers, dedicated professionals who managed to do their jobs, distancing themselves from the moral prerequisites of the regime and never mentioning the victories of socialism or the comrade's brilliant strategies. I will never forget my French and English teachers in the secondary school or the history one in high school, who compensated for the huge amounts of intellectual garbage we had to swallow.

There is one more point I have to add here; it's the wooden language that was used (and still is, if you pay attention to the political discourse), a language you had to learn if you wanted to survive in those times, because it was the only one that could give shape to the spiritual realities of that era. There were people who were very good at it and could speak for hours about realities that didn't exist; I wasn't, so I couldn't.

Teaching in such conditions was relatively easy if you complied with the rules of the system and never questioned them, because the system took care of you. There were very few discipline problems in schools, so the teacher was the supreme authority, an institution in itself, because, by and large, nobody questioned his authority. The method applied was, in 90 percent of the cases, frontal teaching. The student emulated him and tried to reproduce the information received. Few were the subjects that allowed for variety, and these were mostly the modern languages, but, in general, just like now, everything depended on the teacher's ability and willingness to do more.

From September to November, high school and university students, soldiers, and prisoners "gladly and willingly" participated in the gathering of the crops. Without any tools or equipment, we picked apples, grapes, corn, and beetroot until our hands and feet became sore and blistered, because we had neither the training nor the experience to do it. Or, to make things worse, we were taken out of school again and trained to become future workers (usually technical jobs, requiring low qualification) by people who had no pedagogical preparation and came directly from factories. It is heartbreaking to think of the sheer waste of time and intellectual resources.

On the other hand, education at that time was a very serious process, and there was nothing to distract you from that. Due to the lack of entertainment facilities, we learned, learned, and learned (like the great Comrade Lenin had advised us to do). Everything hinged on the university exams. I had decided to study foreign languages, even though I knew this was a very competitive field. There were only nineteen vacancies for English students that year, and I succeeded in getting one. We had ten hours of courses and seminars every day, and only six on Saturdays. The focus in every class was on memorization, and never for a moment did I have the feeling that anyone cared that I had to improve any other part of my personality. There were no extracurricular activities, no student exchanges with other countries (even Communist ones), and no motivation, other than the intrinsic one, to improve our standards. I had only twenty lessons in pedagogy over the course of four years, and I could practice-teach only three times. When I eventually became a teacher, the only things I had to draw on were my own memories as a student and my common sense.

I was in my third year of university when the 1989 bloody Revolution occurred. It was like waking up for the first time in my life. The borders were opened, new TV channels appeared, books that had been forbidden were available again. There were new and different people, political dissidents, new leaders. It was chaos, but it was wonderful, because I could express my opinions loudly and clearly without fearing I could be reported to the Securitate.

In the last twenty-five years as a teacher, I have had the opportunity to read modern methodology books, attend conferences presented by native speakers, participate in workshops, see live demonstrations, discuss textbooks, and choose ones that suited me best. I have continued to evolve, and the Romanian students have evolved as well – moving from accepting the system submissively to expressing pertinent criticism. The entire system has developed. Private and religious education was reestablished; there are vocational, science, and arts schools, and within each of them, different profiles. There are dance and language schools. Indeed, there is too much change. Every new ministerial cabinet feels it is their duty to introduce something new, even if the change is only for the sake of the change (changing the number of years in each cycle, the names of the cycles, the types of exams necessary to go from one cycle to the other). Many of these changes have nothing to do with improving the quality of education.

Perhaps the saddest change that has happened is in the teacher's position in society. Under the Communist system, a teacher was seen as noble and respected, and she enjoyed the same appreciation as a good doctor or lawyer. Today, the Romanian teacher sits on the lowest step in the social ladder. This is because of two factors: the teacher's very low income and the lack of moral and spiritual values of society itself, where performance is judged according to the speed of financial accumulation, the faster the better. Our children are exposed daily to the images of the nouveaux riches, the overnight billionaires who, despite their very low schooling, express opinions, set trends, and shape consciousness. Every country has its "American dream"; if we describe it in terms of the Romanian reality, this would be to become the owner of the national football team or the president of a political party without having read more than two books in your whole life.

And still, the Romanian school has had and will always have graduates whose great talent and creativity make it famous in international competitions. Unfortunately, very few of these "gold medals" come back to their country to play an active part in its moral and economic recovery. They choose to have a better life somewhere else, and who can blame them for that?

RENATE EVJENTH, NORWAY

I have been a teacher in a Norwegian lower secondary school for the past five and a half years. I teach a school in a small rural area, approximately thirty kilometers southeast of Oslo. The school has about 420 students and forty staff members. The school itself was built in 1965 but was totally renovated in 2005. The renovation meant a lot, both to the students and the staff, and we now have an entirely different work environment from the one we had a few years back.

When I first came to Ås years ago, the school building was old and worn down in every sense of the word. The classrooms were smelly, the windows were leaking, and the toilets and wardrobes were in very bad shape. Now, the school building is entirely different, both on the inside and on the outside. The outside is covered in red brick, and the inside is totally rebuilt from head to toe, so to speak. The classrooms are fairly simple when it comes to decoration. The walls are all white, and there are no curtains. The students' desks and chairs are made out of thin pine and are neatly built with straight angles. An American friend of mine told me that the furniture looked "totally Ikea," although I know for a fact that all the furniture has been made by a Norwegian firm that specializes in office and school decoration. Physically, the classrooms are organized differently, according to what level and what suits each class the most. The teachers, who have the main responsibility for the class, have also the freedom to organize their classrooms the way they want. Mostly, classrooms are organized with students sitting together in pairs (or in threes). In some classes, the students are also placed alone.

The school teaches eighth- through tenth-grade grade students from the age of thirteen to the age of sixteen. Each grade level has approximately 140 students, and they are again divided into classes of thirty to forty-five students. Each grade level has a team of teacher, and each team has a team leader, who has the main responsibility for the teachers and the pedagogy, plus overseeing the daily need for substitute teachers and so on. Each class has two to three main teachers, who have daily responsibility for the students and who also have contact with the parents. Each teacher in Norwegian lower secondary school teaches two to five different subjects. I teach four different subjects: Norwegian, German, English, and food and health studies. The main teachers normally follow their students throughout their three years of lower secondary education, which means that we get to know our students fairly well.

Teachers who work in lower secondary education in Norway have different backgrounds, and their education can differ to some extent. There are, however, some basic criteria for people who want a career in education. When you have finished upper secondary education, you can apply to a college that offers teacher training. There are a number of teacher training colleges throughout Norway. To be accepted into these colleges, you have to have a certain level of academic achievement. It is a competitive degree program. When you have been accepted, you have a four-year education in front of you. These four years of education will enable you to teach students from first to tenth grades. Of course, the lower secondary schools prefer it if you have a specialization in the subject you will be teaching, and this is also something that has become obligatory for all new applicants who want to teach lower secondary school in Norway. You need at least to have studied the subject in question for one year (that means having at least sixty credits) to be able to get a teaching position in lower secondary school now. This rule was made effective on August 1, 2008.

When I went to teacher training college, I never felt that I got a clear sense of a teacher's everyday life in school. In Norway, you have to study four years to become a teacher. During these four years, you have some subjects that are required for all students, and then you have some subjects that you can choose among, according to your interests and your skills. Pedagogy was, of course, seen as the essential topic for aspiring teachers, and we had to have several weeks of actual training in different schools. We had to train both for elementary school (six- to twelve-year-olds) and lower secondary school (thirteen- to sixteen-year-olds). When we were in training, a group of four to five pre-service students would follow a single teacher throughout the day, taking on all the tasks of the teacher. It was an interesting and demanding time for us, and I remember that we worked hard during those weeks. But we all felt, of course, that our training was in a very unnatural environment. When one of us was student teaching, the rest of us, plus the teacher himself, was always present. That meant that a lot of the time, there were six adults in the classroom, something that never happens in ordinary classrooms throughout Norway.

I remember one training period where my group of five student teachers was to be trained in a small village school, a school with only thirty students in total. In small villages, there are still some of these small schools left. The school was divided into two main parts, where the first- to fourth-graders were taught as one group, and the fifth- to seventh-graders were taught as another group. This meant that there were several challenges for us. First of all, when all the adults were there, the students were close to being outnumbered. This was a very strange feeling, since most teachers in Norwegian schools find themselves in the opposite situation – wishing that the economy could allow smaller student groups and more teachers. Another big challenge in such a group is, of course, how to differentiate among the different age levels of the students and the different levels of learning abilities within the same age group. In our case, we had just one girl as the only fourth-grader in her school. She was perhaps lucky in many ways, having the possibility of getting a lot of attention from her teacher. On the other hand, she probably felt very alone, since she had no other classmates her own age, and often she was left to herself, doing individual study, as the teacher had to pay more attention to the first- and second-graders, since there were more of them and they were less independent and needed more help.

The summer after I finished my master's degree, I was offered the position I hold today. I was working as a temporary summer guide at the local museum in my home town. During my master's studies, I had started to change my mind about becoming a teacher. My friends in university felt the same way. Some of them wanted to continue studying, doing a doctoral degree; some wanted to go abroad, and some wanted to do a career in administration and management. I myself leaned toward the latter, and when my master's work was over, I started looking for administrative jobs. The only problem was that most companies were looking for people with experience in administration, and they were also looking for people with university degrees in management – not English literature and pedagogy. At a certain point, I figured out that, although I really didn't want to do it, if I were to find no job before fall came, I should really just face reality and apply for teaching jobs. As any other person, I had a huge student loan and other financial responsibilities, and these could not wait forever. Therefore, I just handed in a few applications for teaching jobs, just to have done it. I had been searching for jobs for a few months and gotten so many rejections that I was really relaxed about it and fairly certain that no one would hire a "rookie" teacher, anyway.

Then came the phone call. The principal of a lower secondary school had received my application and was offering me a temporary job for the coming school year. I had to teach not only English, but also Norwegian, religion, and social studies. "Was I up for that?" he asked. "Was I a sociable person with a good sense of humor? Was I bright and motivated?" I hung up, and, after only twenty minutes, the principal called me back and said that the job was mine if I wanted it. Two days later, I packed my bags and left for Ås.

The initial transition into teaching was tough. The school building itself was built in 1965, with 420 students and over forty teachers – quite big by

Norwegian standards. It was a huge challenge to be able to understand everything at first – the schedule, who does what when, who is who, and so on. My colleagues tried their best to welcome me, but entering a classroom for the first time was really scary! I had never been in a classroom as the single adult, being in charge of everything myself. Now, I was to teach 150 eighth-graders alone. That was an enormous number of names to learn in a short period of time, not to mention all the essays I was supposed to read and all the grades I was supposed to give. During teacher training practice, I always felt we got too little practice in evaluating students' performance, and this was also something I found particularly hard to do when I first arrived at Ås. Despite having lovely colleagues at the school, I still felt very much on my own. As a new teacher, you are expected to plan your lessons, teach them, and then evaluate both yourself and your students afterwards. At first, I had more than enough trying to keep my own head above water. I felt that I could just stay at work until the wee hours, because there was always something I had forgotten to plan or some essays I had not read yet. I remember I sometimes felt that I had no time for anything else besides my job, and that I really did not know whether I had chosen the right profession. The students were nice most of the time, but sometimes I felt that they were all against me, and that both they and I really just wanted me to leave the teaching career. Many mornings, I lay in my bed thinking I really did not want to go to work, and I really should just go to my principal and give him my letter of notice. I often called my mum back home and told her this, and she really encouraged me and told me things would get better and this was just a stage I had to go through.

And then they did get better. It happened in April of that year: the students with whom I had most of my classes started asking me whether I would stay on as their teacher next year. I told them that I did not know yet, but that I thought I might not, since I only had a temporary position. My principal had been quite sure when he told me that he could not promise me any position next year, since there would be no vacancies then. When I told this to my students, they got really sad and wondered if they could do anything to keep me there. I still remember the feeling it gave me when a bunch of thirteen- to fourteen-year-olds told me they really wanted me to be their teacher next year as well, and they would do almost anything to keep me there. I almost felt like crying, but of course, I had appearances to keep up, so I could not do that. Anyway, the students decided to write a letter to the principal saying that he had to let me continue as their teacher. If I left, they would just get an old, cranky woman who had no sense of humor and who would only punish them and be very strict. Then, they would not learn anything. They all signed this letter, and they gave it to me to give to my principal. Of course, I never gave this to him, but I still have that letter, and every time I read it, I get a huge smile on my face and a warm feeling inside. I will always keep this memory in my heart. That, and the big roar they made when their other teacher told them I was hired permanently and they would get me as their teacher the next year. They were so happy, and so was I.

I was so pleased to be this class's main teacher for the following two years. The day they graduated was a very sad day for many of them. Many of the girls were crying over not seeing me anymore, and some of the boys came up to me and told me how grateful they were to have had me as their teacher. I was not that sad there and then, because I had more than enough dealing with all the crying girls. It crept up on me when I got back home, and one of the girls had given me a letter to read. There, she told me that I was the one teacher she always had searched for and wanted as a little girl. I was like the big sister she never had, and she was so thankful for everything I had done for her. I cried that night, thinking of all the good times we had spent together. I found out how lucky I had been, meeting these wonderful kids, and that only by coincidence. I had not initially wanted to become a teacher, and the fact that I moved to Ås was just to have some kind of job to be able to pay my bills every month. Now, I understood that being a teacher was more than that. You get personally involved in your students' lives. You want the best for them, and you want them to do well in life. If they have worries, you have worries. If they are happy, you are happy.

The challenge of seeing to every student's needs at every moment is something I have brought with me into my everyday life as a teacher, too. I do not think that a single day goes by without my having the thought, "Did I manage to help Simon today, or did I fail again?" In the hectic, everyday life in my school, I feel that I never have enough time, and my students suffer from this. While in teacher training practice, I thought, "How can they do it?" and now, when I have been teaching for a few years myself, I still think the same: "How can I do it?" Being a teacher is so much more than learning your own subject well. There are so many other challenges in teaching that are equally important.

ABDULLAH ALI AL ASMARY, SAUDI ARABIA

On a hot day in August 1998, I was hurriedly interviewed by senior teachers at the Ministry of Education. At that time, English teachers were in great demand. I was convinced that day that I would be appointed in the capital, Riyadh, since I knew there had been a need for teachers there. Instead, I was assigned to a remote town 100 miles away, in the heart of the desert. I could not absorb what had happened and I began to contact anyone I could to reverse the decision and find me a position in Riyadh. Finally, I went to the Ministry of Education itself. "Nothing can be changed," they said. "Such decisions are made on the highest level and we can do nothing but obey." Okay, I said to myself. I was in desperate need of a job. I'll go and be there for a year, and then move on.

I was assigned to teach at a secondary school called Al Yammamah Intermediate and Secondary School. On my first day, I was summoned by the school headmaster who was keen to spoon-feed me on the latest ministerial regulations on matters of discipline, commitment, and the like. He then gave me my schedule: twenty periods each week; each period, forty-five minutes. I was also given the assignment to monitor students at rest time, attend morning assembly, and observe students while marching into class.

It was the first time I was to ever confront students face to face. I received my education at an arts college in the department of language and linguistics. Because of the sharp shortage of qualified English teachers, it was quite common to hire nonspecialist teachers to do teaching. English was among the school subjects that had been in a great demand.

The first class with the students was a disaster. After a few minutes, students started to misbehave. Lack of confidence and the lack of preparation crippled me throughout the year. Having early on lost control of the class, I began to act recklessly, shouting angrily at each minor infraction, and I complained to school officials about my students' misbehavior.

Soon a bitter confrontation with the deeply conservative school headmaster erupted. For him, good teaching meant a totally quiet class. We clashed over my performance and he cited another colleague's teaching as perfect, thorough, and exemplary. "A quiet class is concrete evidence that learning is taking place," he concluded. In defending my case, I argued that in a foreign language class skills are better developed by greater interaction between the class members. Cemetery-like silence is not my way of doing things in class. My remarks angered the headmaster, who, the very next day, summoned the district supervisor to attend and monitor my class and write a report on my performance. Ironically, I did well in class that day, and the students behaved themselves. After the class, the district supervisor hailed my performance, particularly my command of English. Not wanting me to get off the hook completely, though, he did criticize the way I held the piece of chalk between fingers which, as he concluded, could send a message to students that the teacher was promoting "smoking," which was clear to him since he himself was a smoker.

I was relieved by the visit and the report. I believed this could put an end to the confrontation with the headmaster. But nothing changed. My relationship with the students deteriorated. I came to see that my insistence on hard work from the students was violating their sense of what was expected of a teacher. Many of the students assumed they could get good marks, with little effort. My unwillingness to reward their laziness meant I would always be in conflict with them.

Luckily, after that first year, I was able to secure a position in Riyadh, at a better school.

The educational system in Saudi Arabia is centrally determined. The Ministry of Education, the governmental body responsible for running the public education for boys and girls, is responsible for recruiting and promoting teachers, designing textbooks, preparing and repairing school facilities. Each teacher is required to teach twenty-four periods each week. Each period is forty-five minutes. Besides his or her teaching duties, the teacher is also obliged to monitor students at rest time, oversee activities of a specific class, and, further, set and correct exam papers.

One of the hottest debates in our educational system nowadays is the fact that teachers are overloaded by duties that adversely affect their teaching performance. Many of us believe that these time-wasting activities should be assigned to a teaching assistant. This idea is not enthusiastically endorsed by educational policy-makers, who insist that such hiring would cripple the already troubled budget. In the past, teaching used to be one of the highest paying government jobs compared with many other jobs. A teacher with a master's degree was paid the equivalent of an assistant university professor. However, recently, many of these dream salaries were cut short.

It is no secret that the students' declining levels in English and declining performance in science-oriented subjects are of considerable concern. Business people usually complain that although students spend approximately six years in studying English, they cannot handle a job that requires a modest level of fluency. The Ministry of Education has conducted a nation-wide survey to study the source of the problem. The survey results were published and revealed that the blame should shared by students, teachers, and the curriculum. Certainly, in terms of teachers, not all are academically qualified to teach at schools. Because of the sharp shortage of teachers in some majors such as English and mathematics, the Ministry of

Education recruits teachers with an academic degree in the subject matter but no prior experience in education. Some of them may have not stepped into a classroom before. For many teachers, like me, the first year is the most difficult. In accordance with the regulations, any teacher who fails to pass the first year as a teacher with less than sixty points out of 100 is not eligible for the teaching profession, and, as a consequence, he is terminated from teaching. Once the decision is taken to terminate his career as a teacher, he has the right to appeal. Sometimes, after an appeal, the teacher does not lose his job, but is transferred to other administrative duties with a much lower salary.

As far as curriculum is concerned, all curriculum and textbooks are created by the Ministry of Education, and all teachers follow that national curriculum. There is a separate department in the Ministry of Education that is responsible for designing textbooks, revising the existing ones, and suggesting any changes. Teachers are not free to create curriculum materials. If teachers have questions about the materials, they are given a fax number to voice their concerns and suggest any changes. However, the process of changing anything is frustratingly slow. Changes must be approved by many committees, and the final decision to alter an existing textbook is normally overshadowed by other persistent issues such as shortage of teachers, the conditions of school buildings, and the like.

Education in Saudi Arabia, as seen by this English teacher, has changed for the better over time. However, there is consensus among most people that much is still needed. King Abdullah's Project for Educational Reform is in full swing nowadays; we hope that reform will come. It is something that is wholeheartedly desired by the people of Saudi Arabia.

Notes

NOTES TO INTRODUCTION

1 Rosetta Marantz Cohen and Samuel Scheer, *Teacher-Centered Schools: Reimagining Education Reform in the Twenty-First Century* (Lanham, MD, and Oxford, UK: Scarecrow Education, 2003).

2 The strongest links between teacher quality and student effectiveness seem to involve verbal ability. This has been known since the Coleman Report of 1966, when teacher scores on verbal tests were the only school input found to have a positive effect on student achievement. See Christopher S. Jencks, "The Coleman Report and the Conventional Wisdom," in *On Equality of Educational Opportunity*, ed. Frederick Mosteller and Daniel Patrick Moynihan (New York: Random House, 1972), 69–115. See also Ronald F. Ferguson, "Can Schools Narrow the Black-White Test Score Gap?," in *The Black-White Score Test Gap*, ed. Christopher Jencks and Meredith Phillips (Washington, DC: Brookings Institution Press, 1998), 318–374. In an analysis of 900 Texas school districts, Ferguson found that teachers' expertise as measured by scores on licensing examinations accounted for about 40 percent of the measured variance in students' reading and mathematics achievement at grades 1–11, more than any of other single factor. He also found that every additional dollar spent on more qualified teachers netted greater increases in student achievement. See also Linda Darling-Hammond, "Teacher Quality and Student Achievement: A Review of State Policy Evidence," *Education Policy Analysis Archives* 8 (January 2000), available at http://epaa.asu.edu/epaa/v8n1/. Darling-Hammond's study concludes: "While student demographic characteristics are strongly related to student outcomes at the state level, they are less influential in predicting achievement levels than variables assessing the quality of the teaching force" (p. 36).

3 John Trumbull, *The Satiric Poems of John Trumbull*, ed. Edwin Bowden (Austen: University of Texas Press, 1962), 74.

4 Nancy Hoffman, *Woman's "True" Profession: Voices from the History of Teaching* (Boston: University of Massachusetts Press, 1981), xv.

5 Catherine Beecher, *The Evils Suffered by American Women and American Children: The Causes and the Remedy* (New York: Harper & Bros., 1846), 10–11.

6 Willard Waller, *A Sociology of Teaching* (New York: John Wiley, 1932), 457–458. Waller wrote the first comprehensive sociology of the teaching profession, built on both qualitative and quantitative methods. The book in some ways is a historical curiosity; in other ways it still resonates.

7 Clifford Geertz, *The Interpretation of Culture* (New York: Basic Books, 1973); John Berger, *Ways of Seeing* (London: Penguin Books, 1972).

8 Sara Lightfoot, *The Good High School: Portraits of Character and Culture* (New York: Basic Books, 1983), 5. See also Sara Lawrence-Lightfoot and J. H. Davis, *The Art and Science of Portraiture* (San Francisco, CA: Jossey-Bass Publishers, 1997); Sara Lawrence-Lightfoot, "Reflections of Portraiture: A Dialogue between Art and Science," *Qualitative Inquiry* 11, no. 1 (2005): 3–15.

9 Berger, *Ways of Seeing, 200.*

10 There are many fine examples of teacher portraits (and self-portraits), starting in the 1970s and continuing through the 1990s. Among them are Jonathan Kozol, *Death at an Early Age* (New York: Plume, 1985); Samuel Freedman, *Small Victories: The Real World of a Teacher, Her Students and Their High School* (New York: Harper Perennial, 1991); and Greg Michie, *Holler If You Hear Me* (New York: Harper Perennial, 1991). My own book, *A Lifetime of Teaching: Portraits of Five Veteran High School Teachers* (New York: Teachers College Press, 1991), grew out of the tradition begun by Kozol and the work of Sara Lightfoot in her portraits of secondary institutions (see Lightfoot, *The Good High School).*

NOTES TO CHAPTER 1: FINLAND

1 Ann Lieberman and Lynne Miller, "A New Look at Some Pieces of Old Puzzles. Learnings from Schools and Teachers," Report No. 9016 (Texas University, Austin: Research and Development Center for Teacher Education, April 1982).

2 P. Sahlberg, *Finnish Lessons: What Can the World Learn from Educational Change in Finland?,* 2nd ed. (New York: Teachers College Press, 2014). Sahlberg's book provides an excellent and comprehensive overview of the Finnish schools, the history of their transformation, and the comprehensive and largely successful ways in which they have created a system that empowers teachers.

3 Ibid. This idea of *prevention instead of repair* pervades Sahlberg's descriptions of Finnish schools in *Finnish Lessons.* He also articulates the philosophy on his website (http://pasisahlberg.com/letter-to-next-education-minister/) in an open letter to "The next minister of education," addressed to any policy-maker in any country. In it, he defends the core principles of Finnish school reform and argues that many of these policies could be implemented anywhere.

NOTES TO CHAPTER 2: TAIWAN

1 Male teachers in Taiwan outnumber female teachers most conspicuously in traditionally male subjects such as math, physical education, and science; women outnumber men in languages, literature, and the arts. See http://english.moe.gov .tw/ct.asp?xItem=14508&CtNode=11431&mp=11.

2 OECD, "Pisa 2012 Results," available at www.oecd.org/pisa/keyfindings/pisa-2012-results.htm.

3 Republic of China, Ministry of Education, "Education in Taiwan, 2013–2014," available at www.studyintaiwan.org/album/v4_publications/5254f4fbf2027.pdf.

4 Two articles on the issue of teacher retention and attrition in Taiwan offer useful summaries of why the teacher job market is so competitive. See Bih-Jen Fwu and Hsiou-Hsiou Wang, "The Social Status of Teachers in Taiwan," *Comparative Education* 45, no. 2 (2002), and Hsiao-Jung Li, "The Oversupply of Teachers in Taiwan: Causes and Consequences," *Education Journal* 41, nos. 1–2, (2013): 107–133.

5 In addition to the Ministry of Education White Paper noted above, see Hao Chen and Hsin-Hsien Fan, "Education in Taiwan: The Vision and Goals of the 12-Year Curriculum," *Taiwan-U.S. Quarterly Analysis* 15 (2004). Chen and Fan outline the key components of the 2014 White Paper, including the strategies for improving teachers' performance and professional standards. The White Paper makes clear that the glut of qualified teachers in Taiwan presents an opportunity to raise standards across the board.

NOTES TO CHAPTER 3: GREECE

1 Alexander Kentikelenis et al., "Greece's Health Crisis: From Austerity to Denial," *The Lancet* 383, no. 9918 (2014): 748–753.

NOTES TO CHAPTER 4: AZERBAIJAN

1 Iveta Silova, Mark S. Johnson, and Stephen P. Heyneman, "Education and the Crisis of Social Cohesion in Azerbaijan and Central Asia," *Comparative Education Review* 51, no. 2 (Feb. 2007): 161. Silova et al. wrote: "One of the most acute questions is whether the degradation of the state-sponsored secular education system is approaching a 'tipping point' ... at which institutional and professional capacity drain away so that the educational systems are no longer capable of regenerating themselves."

2 Ibid., 159–180.

3 Iveta Silova, Virginia Budiene, and Mark Bray, eds., *Education in a Hidden Marketplace: Monitoring of Private Tutoring in the Nine Countries of the Former Socialist Bloc* (New York: Open Society Institute, 2006).

4 Freedom House, *Nations in Transit 2005: Democratization from Central Europe to Eurasia* (Washington, DC: Freedom House, 2005).

NOTES TO CHAPTER 5: FRANCE

1 Ministére de l'Éducation Nationale, Enseignment Supérieur et Recherche, "Taux d'inscription immédiate des bacheliers dans les différentes filières de l'enseignement supérieur," available at www.enseignementsup-recherche.gouv.fr/cid20709/taux-d-inscription-immediate-des-bacheliers-dans-les-filieres-d-enseignement-superieur.html. Acceptance rates into the *classes preparatoires* are low. In 2007, only 7.5 percent of those who applied, nationally, were accepted into these programs.

Entrance is based on grades and on students' scores on the baccalaureate. Of those who succeed in matriculating in the first year of the two-year sequence, even fewer will ultimately pass the arduous exams that come at the end, a series of six-hour written tests, given over the course of two weeks. In 2015, out of 3,629 students nationwide who took the final exams to go to the École Normale Supérieure Lyon Sciences Humaines, the test for which Laurence prepares her students, only 114 passed. See the *École Normale Supérieure de Lyon – Concours d'entrée – Rapport* 2015, p. 23. During the summer, after completing the *classes prépas*, those students who succeed in the written exams then take a further set of exams, usually thirty-minute oral exams, during which they are given texts related to their major to analyze. After one hour of preparation, the candidate presents the document to a jury, who then spars with and challenges the candidate. Afterward, candidates receive a final national ranking, which determines admission to the Grandes Écoles of choice.

2 The recent history of French teachers' unions can be found in Roger Duclaud-Williams, "Teacher Unions and Educational Policy in France," in *The Politics of Teacher Unionism*, ed. M. Lawn (London: CroomHelm, 1985). During my conversation with Alain, he gave me information about a planned strike the following month. The flyers he was distributing called for a unified action among all teachers, regardless of their union affiliations, citing dramatic statistics showing how teachers' salaries had lost ground over the past thirty years in France. The flyer read (translated): "In 1982, a starting teacher was paid 80% above the guaranteed minimum wage. In 2014, new teachers make 12% above the minimum wage. Enough is enough!"

3 Alan Bloom, *Closing of the American Mind* (New York: Simon and Schuster, 1987), 51–55.

NOTES TO CHAPTER 6: CHILE

1 Torture in Chile under the Pinochet regime is well documented. Both the National Commission on Political Imprisonment and Torture and the Commission of Truth and Reconciliation approximate that there were 35,000 victims of physical human rights abuses in Chile, with 28,000 tortured, 2,279 executed, and 1,248 "disappeared." For others who were not physically affected, studies estimate that 200,000 citizens were exposed to situations of extreme terror. See *Report of the Chilean National Commission on Truth and Reconciliation* (Notre Dame, IN: University of Notre Dame Press, 1993), vol. I/II, foreword, xx–xxii, available at www.usip.org/files/resources/collections/truth_commis sions/Chile90-Report/Chile90-Report.pdf. A report from Amnesty International ("The Case against Augusto Pinochet," *Amnesty International*, October 16, 2008, available at www.amnesty.org/en/library/asset/AMR22/004/2008/en/ 310008e6-915b-11dd-88fe-eb153597f981/amr220042008en.htm) outlines not only the human rights violations but the structural tactics put in place (the Amnesty Law of 1978) to guarantee impunity to those responsible for torture and murder.

2 Beatrice Avalos and Jenny Assael, "Moving from Resistence to Agreement: The Case of the Chilean Teacher Performance Evaluation," *International Journal of Educational Research* 45 (2006): 254–266.

3 Raimundo Ladron de Guevara, "Embattled Education Minister Faces Stern Congressional Interrogation," *Santiago Times* blog, entry posted November 27, 2014, available at http://santiagotimes.cl/embattled-education-minister-faces-stern-congressional-interrogation/.

4 A description in English of the events can be found at www.huffingtonpost.com/2014/05/19/francisco-tapia-artist-burns-student-debt-papers_n_5351380.html.

NOTES TO CHAPTER 7: THE UNITED STATES

1 Jonathan Kozol, The Shame of a Nation: The Restoration of Apartheid Schooling in America (New York: Crown, 2005).

NOTES TO CONCLUSION

1 Max Weber, *From Max Weber: Essays in Sociology*, trans. and ed. Hans Gerth and C. Wright Mills (New York: Free Press, 1946).

2 "Top Ten Lists: Lowest Paying Jobs," available at www.myplan.com/careers/top-ten/lowest-paying.php. The website lists the 300 lowest paying jobs in America. Nannies and child care workers rank 22 and 23 on the list, with an average (2012) salary of about $21,000. Fitness/aerobics instructors are ranked 287, earning $37,000.

3 Richard Hofstader, *Anti-intellectualism in American Life* (New York: Vintage, 1966).

4 Alan Bloom, *Closing of the American Mind* (New York: Simon and Schuster, 1987). Bloom introduced the idea that American intellectualism had all but disappeared. His book argues that the consequences of this dumbing-down of the education system would be dire. The book served as one of several national reports and treatises to usher in more teacher "accountability," including high-stakes testing and more formal state curricular standards.

5 Valerie Strauss, "Why Teachers Can't Hotfoot It out of Kansas Fast Enough," *Washington Post*, August 2, 2015, available at www.washingtonpost.com/blogs/answer-sheet/wp/2015/08/02/why-teachers-cant-hotfoot-it-out-of-kansas-fast-enough/. "The average teaching salary in Kansas in 2012–2013 (the latest year for which data were available), was $47,464, lower than the pay in all but seven states ... though not by much in most of them. Last year, job protections were cut by state lawmakers, who have also sought to reduce collective-bargaining rights for public employees. [Additionally,] the severe underfunding for public education by the administration of Republican Gov. Sam Brownback, [forced] some school districts to close early this past school year because they didn't have the cash to keep operating." For conditions in Wisconsin, see Todd D. Milewski, "Blame Attacks on Public Education for Teacher Shortages, Percy Brown and Tim Slekar Say," *The Capital Times*, August 16, 2015, available at http://host.madison.com/news/local/writers/todd-milewski/blame-attacks-on-public-education-for-teacher-shortages-percy-brown/article_07e59142-f8f1-51e0-a797-0532a7b42ebf.html#ixzz3jC4C1NAW.

6 Eric Scroggins, "California Can No Longer Ignore Teacher Shortage," EdSource, May 12, 2015, available at http://edsource.org/2015/california-can-no-longer-ignore-teacher-shortage/78829. In California, enrollment in the state's teacher-preparation programs fell nearly 53 percent from 2008 to 2013, one of the biggest declines in the nation. In Indiana, the number of first-time teacher licenses issued by the state has dropped by 63 percent (*Lafayette Journal and Courier*, July 15, 2015).

7 UNESCO Institute for Statistics, "The Global Demand for Primary Teachers – 2012 Update," available at www.uis.unesco.org/FactSheets/Documents/ib10-2012-teacher-projections.pdf (accessed November 15, 2012).

8 Ibid.

9 "Massachusetts Teacher Certification: How to Become a Licensed Teacher in Massachusetts," Concordia Online Education, available at http://education.cu-portland.edu/blog/teaching-license/massachusetts/.

10 Linda Darling-Hammond, "Constructing Twenty-First Century Teacher Education," *Journal of Teacher Education* 57, no. 10 (2006): 1–5. Darling-Hammond's superb books on teachers and teacher education are all worth reading: *The World Is Flat: How America's Commitment to Equity Will Determine Our Future* (New York: Teachers College Press, 2010), *Getting Teacher Evaluation Right: What Really Matters for Effectiveness and Improvement* (New York: Teachers College Press, 2013), and *Beyond the Bubble Test: How Performance Assessments Support 21st Century Learning* (San Francisco, CA: Jossey-Bass, 2014).

11 U.S. Department of Education, National Center for Education Statistics, Common Core of Data (CCD), "Local Education Agency Universe Survey" (2012–2013). See "Digest of Education Statistics 2014, Table 204.20," available at http://nces.ed.gov/programs/digest/d14/tables/dt14_204.20.asp.

12 Teacher education was criticized as a means for producing nationalist teachers, and the curriculum was criticized for not responding to the fast-changing labor market. For a detailed description of the history of Taiwanese high school, see Q. R. Wang, *The Construction of the Secondary Education Programme in Taiwan* (Taipei: Shida Shuyuan Press, 1997).

13 Bih-Jen Fwu and Hsiou-Huai Wang, "The Social Status of Teachers in Taiwan," *Comparative Education* 38, no. 2 (May 2002): 215. The authors argue that a constellation of cultural characteristics and historical events has allowed the teacher's role to remain fairly stable in terms of prestige and status.

14 An online site discussing the French job placement system included the following post: "My wife is a teacher and tried passing the CAPES but it wasn't to be. Instead she passed the PLP2 which is exactly the same, but you teach in a *'lycée professional'* [a vocational school]. The PLP2 is (or certainly WAS) pretty much looked upon by being a second class CAPES, (by those who had a CAPES) but in fact it does have certain advantages, for example you get more free time as the students are often on work experience. Be aware though, when you do get your CAPES or PLP2 you will be on a points system, and your first post could be in the north or in the suburbs of Paris. You do get extra points if you have kids and if you're married (*rapprochement du conjoint*), but in your area and anywhere down south it is really, really hard to get in. On the other hand, you'll find that the regional *rectorats* are recruiting outside staff because they can't find replacement teachers due to cut backs, and it's cheaper than paying other teachers to do overtime."

15 The details of the rules surrounding the *agrégation* can be found on Legifrance. gouv.fr. The version that is presently available is based on a 2012 revision of a 1986 law, outlining the key components of the examination.

16 "French to Reform Teacher Training," The *Times* Higher Education World University Ranking, April 25, 2003, available at www.timeshighereducation.co.uk/news/french-to-reform-teacher-training/176287.article.

17 W. Randolph Burgess, "Four Censuses of Teachers' Salaries," *American School Board Journal* 61 (September 1920): 27–28; quoted from Susan Carter, "Incentives and Rewards of Teaching," in *American Teachers: Histories of the Profession at Work*, ed. Donald Warren (New York: Macmillan, 1989).

18 Dan C. Lortie, *Schoolteacher: A Sociological Study* (Chicago, IL: University of Chicago Press, 1975). See especially chapter 4, "Career and Work Rewards," 82–108.

19 Sarah Marsh, "How the Job of a Teacher Compares around the World," *The Guardian* Teachers' Blog, September 5, 2014, available at www.theguardian .com/teacher-network/teacher-blog/2014/sep/05/how-the-job-of-a-teacher-com pares-around-the-world. Recent OECD statistics are summarized in this article.

20 There have been many studies that document the factors motivating young people to teach; most conclude that salary is not a primary concern. For a summary of this research, see Sarah Marsh, "Five Top Reasons People Become Teachers – and Why They Quit," *The Guardian* Career Advice Column, January 27, 2015, available at www.theguardian.com/teacher-network/2015/ jan/27/five-top-reasons-teachers-join-and-quit. Marsh concludes that the top three motivations for new teachers, worldwide, include (1) desire to make a difference in the lives of young people, (2) the variability of the work, and (3) love of subject. Salary and compensation were not listed at all.

21 Weber, *From Max Weber.*

22 The list of writers who created popular fictional characters of inept and heartless teachers is a long one. It includes Philip Freneau, Washington Irving, Warren Burton, Edward Eggleston, and many others. Even Walt Whitman, himself a high school teacher, wrote stories of horrible male teachers, bullying their charges. In one, "Death in the School-Room (A FACT)," Whitman describes a teacher beating a boy for failing to respond to a question, only to find out afterward the child was already dead. Images of teachers did not become positive in the popular press until after the feminization of the profession, at which time a new sentimental literature was created to describe these maternal and long-suffering figures. See "A Wreathe for Miss Totten," by Hortense Calisher, for an excellent example of the contrast. All these stories are compiled in R. M. Cohen and Samuel Scheer, *The Work of Teachers in America: A Social History through Stories* (Mahwah, NJ: Lawrence Erlbaum, 1997).

23 Gerald Grant, *The World We Created at Hamilton High* (Cambridge, MA: Harvard University Press, 1988), 122–125. Grant makes a brilliant connection between Weber's categories and the dilemma of teachers in America, in terms of their potential power and authority in the contemporary school. His description of the shift in teacher authority over the course of the twentieth century (using the metaphor of fruit: from avocado to cantaloupe to watermelon) is especially vivid and useful.

24 B. Fwu and Hsiou-Huai Wang, "The Social Status of Teachers in Taiwan," *Comparative Education* 38, no. 2 (May 2002).

25 According to Doris Santoro, "Little controversy is raised by claiming that teaching is a moral profession, but teachers who attempt to raise moral concerns about their work may face conditions similar to Cassandra's. As

public servants teachers are expected to enact the policies that have been handed down by those with more political power. While I do not claim that teachers are prophets, they do have the power of sight regarding the effects of policy in schools and classrooms that might not be known or anticipated by those in power. Teachers' ability to see the harm that comes to students, their communities, faculty and schools may cause them to voice their concerns about policies and practices emotionally and passionately. In this paper, I argue that disregarding teachers' moral concerns about the wellbeing of their school communities and discrediting teachers as moral agents creates the conditions for moral madness." D. A. Santoro, "Cassandra in the Classroom: Teaching and Moral Madness," paper presented at the Philosophy of Education Society Annual Meeting, Memphis, TN, March 2015; D. A. Santoro, "Teachers and Moral Madness: When Increased Responsibility and Diminished Authority Meet," paper presented at the American Educational Research Association Annual Meeting, Chicago, IL, April 2015. See also D. Santoro and L. Morehouse, "Teaching's Conscientious Objectors: Principled Leavers of High-Poverty Schools," *Teachers College Record* 113, no. 12 (2011): 2670–2704.

26 Jonathan Kozol, *Death at an Early Age* (New York: Bantam Books, 1968). Kozol recounts his experiences as a fourth-grade teacher in one of the poorest sections of Boston. Kozol was ultimately fired for deviating from the curriculum by teaching a poem by Langston Hughes, "Ballad of the Landlord," an act that was interpreted by the district as "advocating defiance of authority." Kozol's subsequent career has been devoted to addressing the endemic inequities of the education system.

27 Jordan Catapano, "Back to School Prep Guide: 8 Metaphors for a Teacher," available at www.teachhub.com/8-metaphors-understanding-role-teacher.

28 C. Beecher, *The Evils Suffered by American Women and American Children: The Causes and the Remedy* (New York: Harper and Bros., 1846), quoted from Nancy Hoffman, *Women's "True" Profession: Voices from the History of Teaching* (New York: Feminist Press, 1981), 37.

29 For an excellent selection of letters and journals from pioneer teachers, see Polly Welts Kaufman, *Women Teachers of the Frontier* (New Haven, CT: Yale University Press, 1984); Hoffman, *Woman's "True" Profession.*

30 Charlotte Forten was among a minute number of Northern black women who went South to teach during and after the Civil War. Forten spent two years working in South Carolina, teaching and writing about the experience. Descriptions of her life as a teacher can be found in *The Atlantic Monthly* 13 (May–June 1864), 124–132.

31 Dan C. Lortie, *Schoolteacher: A Sociological Study* (Chicago, IL: University of Chicago Press, 1975). This is one of a small number of comprehensive sociologies of the profession. Lortie writes generally about a wide range of professional characteristics, including career and work rewards, and recruitment, drawing on historical material, national and local (five towns in Florida) surveys, findings from observational studies of other researchers, and content analysis based on intensive, open-ended interviews with teachers.

32 Ibid., 221.

33 "The MetLife Survey of the American Teacher," March 2012, available at www.metlife.com/assets/cao/contributions/foundation/american-teacher/MetLife-Teacher-Survey-2011.pdf. According to this MetLife poll, "Teacher job satisfaction has dropped 15 points in the past two years, the lowest level in more than two decades. Today, 44% of teachers are very satisfied with their jobs as teachers, a drop from 59% in 2009 and reflecting a decline to levels not seen since the 1980's. A similar pattern is seen in teachers' views on leaving the profession. Three in ten (29%) teachers say they are likely to leave the teaching profession to go into some different occupation within the next five years, a 12 point increase since 2009 (17%), and a return to a level comparable to 1986 (27%)."

34 John Dewey, "Democracy in Education," *Elementary School Teacher* 4, no. 4 (December 1903), available at www.journals.uchicago.edu/doi/pdfplus/10.1086/453309. Dewey wrote: "until the public school system is organized in such a way that every teacher has some regular and representative way in which he or she can register judgment upon matters of educational importance, with the assurance that this judgement will somehow affect the school system, the assertion that the present system is not, from the internal standpoint, democratic seems to be justified. Either we come here upon some fixed and inherent limitation of the democratic principle, or else we find in this fact an obvious discrepancy between the conduct of the school and the conduct of social life – discrepancy so great as to demand immediate and persistent effort at reform."

35 John Dewey, *How We Think* (New York: D. C. Heath, 1909). Dewey's views on teaching are best and most thoroughly expressed in his masterwork *Democracy and Education* (1916), a volume that synthesizes many of the principles of rigor (what he terms "the subject") and affect (what he calls "the child"). Richard Hofstader and other twentieth-century critics of Dewey's progressivism seem not to have read this work.

36 Dewey, *How We Think*, 274–275.

37 Nel Noddings, *Caring: A Feminine Approach to Ethics and Moral Education*, 2nd ed. (Los Angeles: University of California Press, 2003).

38 "Research Spotlight on Recruiting and Retaining Highly Qualified Teachers," available at www.nea.org/tools/17054.htm.

39 Valerie Walkerdine and Luis Jimenez, *Gender, Work and Community after De-Industrialization: A Psychosocial Approach to Affect* (Basingstoke: Palgrave Macmillan, 2012). A professor at Cardiff University in England, Walkerdine is best known in the States for her book *Daddy's Girl: Young Girls and Popular Culture*. All her work investigates the impact of stereotypes and cultural expectations on women and work, often reflecting on her own working-class roots.

40 Pasi Sahlberg, "What If Finland's Great Teachers Taught in U.S. Schools?," *Washington Post*, May 15, 2013.

41 Center for Public Education, "High Stakes Testing and Effects on Instruction: Research Review," posted February 10, 2006, available at www.centerforpubliceducation.org/Main-Menu/Instruction/High-stakes-testing-and-effects-on-instruction-At-a-glance/High-stakes-testing-and-effects-on-instruction-Research-review.html#sthash.60ApvRUr.dpu. According to the Center for

Public Education, "Teachers report complicated and sometimes contradictory views of how high-stakes tests affect instruction. While a large majority of teachers believe that testing will have a negative impact on instruction, an equally large majority said that it has not affected their own teaching." Tim Walker, "Nearly Half of Teachers Consider Leaving Profession Due to Standardized Testing," *NEA Today*, posted November 2, 2014, available at http://nea today.org/2014/11/02/nea-survey-nearly-half-of-teachers-consider-leaving-pro fession-due-to-standardized-testing-2/. The NEA reports that nearly half (45 percent) of surveyed member teachers have considered quitting because of standardized testing.

42 Michael Perelman, *The Invisible Handcuffs of Capitalism: How Market Tyranny Stifles the Economy by Stunting Workers* (New York: NYU Press, 2011).

43 Noelle Nelson, *Make More Money by Making Your Employees Happy*, Kindle e-book, www.amazon.com/Make-Money-Making-Employees-Happy-ebook/ dp/B007Y9ZW12. Nelson is a clinical psychologist who has written widely about business issues. Nelson cites a study from the Jackson Organization, which shows that companies that effectively communicate their valuing of employees enjoy a return on equity and assets more than *triple* that experienced by firms that don't. For *Fortune*'s "100 Best Companies to Work For," stock prices rose an average of 14 percent per year from 1998 to 2005, compared with 6 percent for the overall market.

44 George Counts, *Dare the Schools Build a New Social Order?* (New York: John Day Company, 1932). Counts became affiliated with the strand of progressive education that is called Social Reconstructionism, one that posits that schools have the capacity to change culture and that they should work aggressively to do so. In this sense, he is the father of critical pedagogy, as it has been practiced in the United States. An activist throughout his career, Counts served as president of the American Federation of Teachers, was founder of the New York State Liberal Party, and was a candidate for the US Senate.

45 Rob Nixon, *Slow Violence and the Environmentalism of the Poor* (Cambridge, MA: Harvard University Press, 2013). Nixon described this as "a violence of delayed destruction that is dispersed across time and space, an attritional violence that is typically not viewed as violence at all" (p. 13). His book considers this slow violence through the work of writer-activists, approaching environmental justice literature from a transnational perspective.

Index

ability grouping, 148–149, 159–160
    diversity and, 160–161
Abubakar, Fatima Bensali, 188–191
academic performance, diversity and, 142
accountability, 1, 184–186
adult education
    in Greece, 71–72
    in the Philippines, 188–189
Advanced Placement (AP)
    classes, 148–149, 160
    tests, 148–149
agrégation examinations, 171–172, 222
Americanization of international cultures, 6–7, 166
anti-intellectualism, 165
AP. See Advanced Placement
de Araújo, Ana Paula, 191–194
Armenia, Azerbaijan and, 94
art
    in Finland, 34–35
    in Greece, 72–73
    in Taiwan, 43–44
Al Asmary, Abdullah Ali, 212–215
assessment
    PISA, 11–12, 182–183
    student, in Taiwan, 42
    teacher, in Greece, 64–65
Athens, Greece, 57
athletics, in U.S., 155
attrition, 181–182
authority, 174–178
    defining, 175
    derivation of, 178
    in France, 176
    in Greece, 177–178
    loss of, 186
    in Romania, 206
    in South Africa, 202–203
    status of teacher and, 177–178
    in Taiwan, 45, 176
    in U.S., 175

autonomy, in Finland, 18–20
Azerbaijan, 13–14, 75–96
    Armenia and, 94
    bribery in, 77, 88
    civic mindedness in, 88, 93
    corruption in, 85
    critical thinking skills in, 90
    democracy in, 85
    disabilities education in, 83–84, 94
    diversity in, 85–87
    education reform in, 92–93
    English Access Microscholarship Program,
      91–92
    examinations in, 76–78, 89
    foreign language learning in, 82
    fundamentalism in, 85–87
    future of, 84–87
    history of, 75–76
    homophobia in, 85
    "interactive teaching" in, 92–93
    perspectives on, 83–87
    present-day, 85
    prestige of teachers in, 95
    professional development in, 79
    refugees in, 76–77
    renovations in, 85, 87
    respect in, 95
    school classroom in, 80
    school director in, 91
    secularism in, 75, 219
    Soviet influence in schools, 75–78, 92–95
    Soviet rule of, 75–76, 83–85
    struggles of, 76
    student participation in, 81
    students in, 79, 91, 93
    teacher preparation in, 82–83
    teacher salaries in, 78
    teachers' lounge in, 76–77
    teaching profession in, 95–96
    teaching schedule in, 78–79

Azerbaijan (cont.)
  tutoring in, 78, 89
  university entrance and, 77–78

Beecher, Catherine, 4, 178
benefits, 118. *See also* pensions; salaries
best practices, culture and, 15
book-learning, in U.S., 165
Brazil
  dropout rates in, 194
  foreign language learning in, 191–193
  resources in, 192
  socioeconomic class in, 193–194
  teacher preparation in, 191
  technical high schools in, 192–193
bribery
  in Azerbaijan, 77, 88
  in Taiwan, 49–50
budget cuts
  in Chile, 127
  in Finland, 32
  in Greece, 57–58, 60–62
budgets, 15
burnout, teacher, 161, 180–182

camaraderie, teacher, 118–119
CAPES (*certificat d'aptitude au professorat de
  l'enseignement du second degré*) exam,
  171–172, 222
"Cassandra effect," 177–178
*certificat d'aptitude au professorat de
  l'enseignement du second degré* exam. *See*
  CAPES exam
charismatic authority, 175
Charlie Hebdo terrorist attacks, 110
charter schools, 1, 68
child-centered pedagogy, 182
child-centeredness, 180
children, 165
  childcare, in France, 103
  teaching whole child, in Finland, 27–34
Chile, 14, 122–140
  budget cuts in, 127
  class size in, 131–132, 137
  classroom in, 129–130
  curricular materials in, 131–132
  decline in education system of, 132
  education reform in, 126–127, 140
  group discussion in, 137
  Liceo 1 Javiera Carrera, 125, 133–134
  pensions in, 129
  politics in, 122–123, 125–127, 138–139
  prestige of teachers in, 134–135
  private schools in, 125–126, 136
  protests in, 126, 140
  public schools in, 126
  resources in, 133, 135, 139–140

Santiago, 122
school funding in, 123–124, 126–127
socioeconomic class and, 126, 131–132,
  135–136, 139–140
student loan debt in, 140
student strikes in, 136–137, 140
teacher preparation in, 124–125, 170
teacher salaries in, 127, 129, 136, 138, 174
teachers' lounge in, 129
teachers' unions in, 138
teaching schedule in, 128–132
tenure in, 128
violence in, 220
class size
  in Chile, 131–132, 137
  in Finland, 32
  in France, 117
  in Greece, 61
  in Norway, 208
  in South Africa, 203
  in Taiwan, 41–42
classes préparatoires, 99–100
  acceptance rates into, 219–220
  teachers of, 101–102, 121
  in technical high schools, 113–114
classroom
  in Chile, 129–130
  in Greece, 62–63, 65–66
  in Norway, 208
  in Siberia, 196
Communism, 67–68
  common property in, 204–205
  intellectualism and, 205
  in Romania, 204–206
  in Siberia, 196–197
competition, in teaching profession, 22
corruption. *See also* bribery
  in Azerbaijan, 85
  in the Philippines, 191
cost of living
  in Taiwan, 51
  teacher salaries relative to, 172–173
Counts, George, 186
cram schools, 59, 64
critical thinking skills
  in Azerbaijan, 90
  in U.S., 153
culture
  Americanization of international,
    6–7, 166
  best practices and, 15
  prestige and, 164
curricular materials
  in Chile, 131–132
  in Finland, 24–25
  in Taiwan, 49–50, 53–54
  teacher creation of, 24–25, 49–50

curriculums
  in Chile, 131–132
  in Greece, 66–67
  open, 1
  in Saudi Arabia, 215
  in South Africa, 200
  in Taiwan, 53–54
  teacher preparation of, 170–171
  in U.S., 152–153, 184

Darling-Hammond, Linda, 168–170
debate, 109. *See also* group discussion
democracy
  in Azerbaijan, 85
  education and, 111
  intellectualism and, 165
  school governance and, 180
Dewey, John, 180, 225
disabilities education
  in Azerbaijan, 83–84, 94
  in Finland, 28–29
  in U.S., 144
disciplining students. *See also* student behavior
  in South Africa, 202–203
  in Taiwan, 46, 55
diversity, 15
  ability grouping and, 160–161
  academic performance and, 142
  in Azerbaijan, 85–87
  in Finland, 19–20
  in France, 97, 99–100, 110–113
  in Greece, 70–71
  laïcité and, 110–111
  in U.S., 141, 151–152, 160–161
dropout rates, in Brazil, 194

ecological crisis, teacher crisis and, 186–187
education
  democracy and, 111
  globally, 165–166
  reform, 1–2
education policy
  corporate management and, 184–185
  in U.S., 184–185
educational philosophy, 180–182
educational studies, 11
egalitarianism, 119
electives, 1
English Access Microscholarship Program,
    Azerbaijan, 91–92
essential skills, 1
ethnographic portraitures, 9–10. *See also*
    specific countries and teachers
  drawing connections across, 15
ethnography, 9–11
Evjenth, Renate, 208–212
examinations

agrégation, 171–172, 222
AP, 148–149
  in Azerbaijan, 76–78, 89
CAPES exam, 171–172, 222
  in Finland, 30–32, 34
  in France, 97, 113–114, 171–172, 219–220, 222
  for *Grandes Écoles*, 99
  in Greece, 68
  high-stakes testing, 225–226
  matriculation, 30–32
  in Siberia, 197
  in South Africa, 203
  standardized testing, 1, 225–226
  in Taiwan, 53–54
  teacher, 82–83
  teacher preparation, 104–105, 171–172
  university entrance, 77–78, 97
  in U.S., 148–149
experimental schools, 64, 68

failing schools
  answer to, 1
  teacher talent and, 1–2
feminization, of teaching profession, 3–4,
    173–174
Ferry, Luc, 172
Fineman, Bonnie, 14–15, 143–153
  private life of, 156–158
  school administration certification, 152
  teacher preparation for, 150–151
  teaching challenging students, 143–148
  teaching strongest students, 153–155
Finland, 12–13, 17–39, 182–183
  autonomy in, 18–20
  budget cuts in, 32
  class size in, 32
  curricular materials in, 24–25
  disabilities education in, 28–29
  education reform in, 19–21, 32–33
  education system problems in, 32–34
  examinations in, 30–32, 34
  hierarchy in, 19–20
  pensions in, 37
  professional development in, 24–25
  school choice in, 34–35
  school funding in, 33
  school pacing in, 18–19
  school structure in, 18
  Tampere, 25–27
  teacher preparation in, 23–24, 170–171
  teacher success in, 183–184
  teachers in, 18–20, 39
  teaching schedule in, 18
  teaching whole child in, 27–34
  transformation of, 20–27
  unemployment in, 33
firing teachers, 64–65

foreign language learning
in Azerbaijan, 82
in Brazil, 191–193
in Siberia, 194–197
in South Africa, 201
France, 14, 97–121
authority, teacher in, 176
changing education system in, 115–118
childcare system in, 103
class size in, 117
classes préparatoires, 99–100
classroom in, 105
debate in, 109
diversity in, 97, 99–100, 110–113
education standards in, 115–118
egalitarianism in, 119
examinations in, 97, 113–114, 171–172,
219–220, 222
Grandes Écoles, 99
group discussion in, 98–99, 105–108,
112–113
internships in, 105
Islam in, 110–111
laïcité in, 110–113
lycée général, 99
Lycée Jean Jaurès, 97
marriage in, 102
motherhood in, 101–103
Paris, 100
pensions in, 115
post-secondary institutions, 99
prestige of teachers in, 116–118
private *versus* public schools in, 110
school lunch in, 109
socioeconomic class and, 109, 111, 116–117
status of teachers in, 116, 165–166
student participation in, 105–108
teacher benefits in, 118
teacher camaraderie in, 118–119
teacher preparation in, 104–105, 170–172
teacher salaries in, 219–220
teacher strikes in, 120
teacher workload in, 117
teachers' unions in, 115–116, 220
teaching profession in, 119–121
technical high schools, 99, 113–114
U.S. and, 111–112
fundamentalism, 85–87
funding, school
in Chile, 123–124, 126–127
in Finland, 33
in Greece, 57–58, 60

gender of teachers
feminization of teaching profession and, 3–4,
173–174
in Taiwan, 50–51, 218

globalization, 166
Grandes Écoles, 99
Greece, 13, 57–74
adult education in, 71–72
art in, 72
Athens, 57
austerity measures in, 57–58, 60–62
authority, teacher in, 177–178
budget cuts in, 57–58, 60–62
celebrations in, 72–73
class size in, 61
cram schools in, 59, 64
diversity in, 70–71
education reform in, 62, 67–68
examinations in, 68
experimental schools in, 64, 68
government of, 67–69
group discussion in, 62–63, 73
intercultural schools in, 70–71
lesson planning in, 66–67
minorities in, 70–71
motivating students in, 59–60
prestige of teachers in, 63
"project class" in, 66
protests in, 67–69
public schools in, 64
relocation of teachers in, 70–72
resources in, 66
salaries in, 60–61
school funding in, 57–58, 60
secondary school system, 59
socioeconomic class and, 68
strikes in, teacher, 62
teacher preparation in, 64, 70, 170
teacher salaries in, 174
teaching profession in, 61, 63–65,
70–72
tenure in, 64–65
textbooks in, 66–67
unemployment in, 61
group discussion
in Chile, 137
in France, 98–99, 105–108, 112–113
in Greece, 62–63, 73
in Taiwan, 42–43
in U.S., 145

Haciyeva, Gulnaz, 13–14, 76–79, 87–89
civic mindedness of, 88
teaching schedule of, 78–79
teaching style of, 80–81, 89–91
work/life balance for, 81–83
Harker, Jeannette, 197–204
hierarchy, in Finland, 19–20
high-stakes testing, 225–226
homophobia, 85
humanities, 166

IEP. *See* Individualized Education Plan
incentives
    student, 42
    teacher, 173–174, 185–186
individuality, in Finland, 29
Individualized Education Plan (IEP), 94
informality, in Greece, 62–63
intellectualism
    anti-, 165
    Communism and, 205
    democracy and, 165
    in U.S., 221
"interactive teaching," 92–93
intercultural schools, 70–71
international school educators, 135
international teachers
    narratives of, 6–8
    prestige of, 5–8
    status shift and, 6–8
Internet, authority and, 175
internships, teaching
    in Azerbaijan, 82–83
    in Finland, 23
    in France, 105
    in South Africa, 198–199
    in U.S., 150–151
intrinsic rewards, of teaching profession,
    179
Islam, in France, 110–111

Japan, teacher salaries in, 174
journaling, 45, 52–53

Kansas, U.S., teaching in, 221
Kirillin, Viktor, 194–197
Kozol, Johnathan, 177–178, 224
Kuo, Feng-juan, 13, 40–56
    artistic pursuits of, 43–44
    school life and home life balance, 52–53
    teacher preparation, 171

laïcité (secularity), in French schools, 110–113
    diversity and, 110–111
Laslau, Gabriela, 204–207
leadership position, of teacher, 180
lectures, 41–42
legal-rational authority, 175
license, teaching, 150
    in Chile, 124–125
    in the Philippines, 188
Liceo 1 Javiera Carrera, Santiago, Chile, 125,
    133–134
Lieberman, Ann, 19–20
Lortie, Dan, 173–174, 224
lycée général, 99
    classes préparatoires in, 99–100
Lycée Jean Jaurès, Paris, France, 97

Manfrini, Laurence, 14, 100–105
    authority of, 176
    teacher preparation for, 171–172
    teaching style of, 103–104
material authority, 176
matriculation exams, 30–32
metaphors for teachers, 178–179
    change and, 179
    global, 182
    service, 182
    unions and, 179
methodology, 9–11
    subjectivity in, 10–11
Michailodou, Vassiliki, 13, 58
    authority of, 177–178
    private life of, 69–70
    teaching style and philosophy of,
        62–63, 74
minorities
    in Greece, 70–71
    in U.S., 148–149, 169–170
morality, teaching and, 3–4, 223–224
motherhood
    in France, 101–103
    teaching and, 103, 157–158
    in U.S., 157–158
motivation, student, 179
    in Greece, 59–60
    in U.S., 159–160
motivation, teacher, 180–182, 223
multidisciplinary teaching, 116

nepotism, in Greece, 64–65
new teachers
    attracting, 185–186
    in Norway, 210–211
Noddings, Nel, 180–182
Norway, 208–212
    class size in, 208
    classroom in, 208
    new teachers in, 210–211
    teacher preparation in, 208–210

open curriculum, 1

parents, teachers and, 34, 158,
    202–203
Paris, France, 100
participant observation, 9
pedagogy
    child-centered, 182
    progressive, 180
pensions
    in Chile, 129
    in Finland, 37
    in France, 115
    in Taiwan, 51

Index

Pfeffer, Jeffrey, 184–185
the Philippines, 188–191
  adult education in, 188–189
  corruption in, 191
  prestige of teachers in, 188
  student participation in, 190
  teacher education in, 188, 190
  teaching profession in, 188
  teaching schedule in, 190
  violence in, 189–191
PISA (Programme for International Student
    Assessment), 11–12, 182–183
politics
  in Chile, 122–123, 125–127, 138–139
  teachers' unions and, 115–116
prestige of teachers, 1–2
  Americanization of international cultures
    and, 6–7
  aspects impacting, 167
  in Azerbaijan, 95
  in Chile, 134–135
  culture and, 164
  defining, 165
  in France, 116–118
  in Greece, 63
  in the Philippines, 188
  internationally, 5–8
  meanings of, 164–167
  reform and, 164
  in Romania, 207
  in South Africa, 199
  in Taiwan, 50–51
  teacher preparation and, 167–168
  in U.S., 1–2, 165
privacy, in Taiwan, 55–56
private schools
  in Chile, 125–126, 136
  in France, 110
  in Taiwan, 48–50
professional development
  in Azerbaijan, 79
  in Finland, 24–25
Programme for International Student
    Assessment. See PISA
progressive education, 226
"project class," 66
Project Opening Doors, 148–149
protests
  in Chile, 126, 136–140
  in Greece, 67–69
psychic rewards, of teaching profession,
    173–174, 179
public schools
  in Chile, 126
  in France, 110
  in Greece, 64
  in Taiwan, 48

  teacher preparation for, 48, 50
public servants, teachers as, 178
punishment, in Taiwan, 46, 55

racial integration. See also diversity
  global perspective on, 7–8
  in South Africa, 198–201
  in U.S., 148–149
Ramirez, Mauricio, 14, 123–125
  recognition of, 128
  teacher preparation for, 124–125
reform, education, 1–2
  in Azerbaijan, 92–93
  in Chile, 126–127
  in Finland, 19–21, 32–33
  good teachers and, 163–164
  in Greece, 62, 67–68
  prestige and, 164
  protests of, in Greece, 67–68
  in Taiwan, 54–55
  of teacher preparation, 169–170
  teachers and, 1–2, 184
religion, teaching profession and,
    4, 179
resources
  in Brazil, 192
  in Chile, 133, 135, 139–140
  in Greece, 66–67
  in Siberia, 195–196
  in South Africa, 199, 201
respect
  in Azerbaijan, 95
  in Taiwan, 55–56
  in U.S., 184
rewards
  in Taiwan, 46, 55
  of teaching profession, 173–174, 179
rights of teachers, 180
Romania, 204–207
  authority, teacher in, 206
  education in, 206–207
  prestige of teachers in, 207
  Soviet Union and, 204–206

salaries, 172–174
  in Azerbaijan, 78
  in Chile, 127, 129, 136, 138, 174
  cost of living and, 172–173
  in Finland, 37
  in France, 219–220
  globally, 174
  in Greece, 60–61, 174
  metaphors for teachers and, 179
  in Saudi Arabia, 214
  in South Africa, 199
  in Taiwan, 51
  in U.S., 173–174

Santiago, Chile, 122
　Liceo 1 Javiera Carrera, 125, 133–134
　socioeconomic class in, 139
Santoro, Doris, 177–178
Saudi Arabia, 212–215
　curricular materials in, 215
　educational system in, 214
　student-teacher relationship in, 214
　teacher preparation in, 213
　teacher shortages in, 214–215
　teaching schedule in, 213
school administration, 152
school choice, in Finland, 34–35
school governance, 180
school lunch, in France, 109
science, technology, engineering, and
　mathematics (STEM), 166
secularism
　in Azerbaijan, 75, 219
　laïcité, 110–113
self-effacement, 45
self-sacrificing role, of teachers, 180–182
Siberia, 194–197
　classroom in, 196
　examinations in, 197
　foreign language learning in, 194–197
　resources in, 195–196
Singapore, teacher salaries in, 174
single-sex schools, in Chile, 133–134
site-based management, 1
Social Reconstructionism, 226
socioeconomic class
　in Brazil, 193–194
　Chile, 139
　in Chile, 126, 131–132, 135–136, 139–140
　France, 109, 111, 116–117
　in Greece, 68
　in the Philippines, 188–189
　in U.S., 142, 151–152
South Africa, 197–204
　class size in, 203
　curriculum in, 200
　disciplining students in, 202–203
　examinations in, 203
　foreign language learning in, 201
　prestige of teachers in, 199
　race in, 197–198
　racial integration in, 198–201
　resources in, 199, 201
　salaries in, 199
　teacher preparation in, 198
　teacher workload in, 199
　teaching internships in, 198–199
Soviet Union
　Azerbaijan and, 75–76, 83–85
　Azerbaijani education system and influence
　　of, 75–78, 92–95

Romania and, 204–206
Siberia and, 194–197
standardized testing, 1, 225–226
status of teachers, 163. *See also* prestige of
　teachers
　aspects impacting, 167
　authority and, 177–178
　child-centered pedagogy and, 182
　defining, 164–165
　in Finland, 18–20
　in France, 116, 165–166
　internationally, 6–8
　in Taiwan, 45–46
　teacher education and, 167–172
STEM. *See* science, technology, engineering,
　and mathematics
stereotypes, 3, 179, 223, 225
strikes, student, 136–137, 140
strikes, teacher
　in Chile, 136–140
　in France, 120
　in Greece, 62
student behavior
　in Finland, 28
　problems with, 160–161
　in U.S., 144, 160–161
student health, in Finland, 28–29
student loan debt, 140
student participation
　in the Philippines, 190
　in Taiwan, 42
　in U.S., 146–148, 153–154
student teaching, 150–151
students
　demographic complexity of, 169–170
　self-efficacy of, 28
　teaching challenging, 143–148
　teaching strongest, 153–155
　verbal ability of teacher and achievement of,
　　217
student-teacher relationship
　in Norway, 212
　power dynamics in, 62–63
　in Saudi Arabia, 214
subjects, 11–16
　selecting, 11–12
success, teacher, 183–184
Suonio, Annukka, 12–13, 21–25
　Finnish educational system and, 17–39
　home life of, 35–37
　teacher preparation for, 170–171
　teaching style of, 38–39

Taipei, Taiwan, 13, 40
Taiwan, 40–56, 182–183
　authority in, 45, 176
　bribery in, 49–50

Taiwan (cont.)
  class size in, 41–42
  cost of living in, 51
  curricular materials in, 49–50
  education system in, 45–46
  examinations in, 53–54
  gender of teachers in, 218
  group discussion in, 42–43
  humanizing of schools in, 55
  lectures in, 41–42
  pensions in, 51
  prestige of teachers in, 50–51
  privacy in, 55–56
  private schools in, 48–50
  public schools in, 48
  reform in, educational, 54–55
  rewards and punishments in, 46, 55
  school cleaning in, 51–52
  student assessment in, 42
  student participation in, 42
  Taipei, 13, 40
  teacher education in, 222
  teacher meetings in, 53–54
  teacher preparation in, 46–51, 170–171
  teacher salaries in, 51
  teaching profession in, 54–56
  teaching schedule in, 51–54
Tampere, Finland, 25–27
Teach for All movement, 185–186
Teach for America, 182
teacher education
  difficult entry into, 170
  entrance requirements for, 172
  in the Philippines, 188, 190
  reform of, 169–170
  status of, 167–172
  in Taiwan, 222
teacher meetings, in Taiwan, 53–54
teacher preparation
  in Azerbaijan, 82–83
  in Brazil, 191
  in Chile, 124–125, 170
  content and curriculum of, 170–171
  examinations for, 171–172
  in Finland, 23–24, 170–171
  in France, 104–105, 170–172
  in Greece, 64, 70, 170
  low status of, 168–169
  in Norway, 208–210
  prestige of teachers and, 167–168
  for public schools, 48, 50
  rigor of, 168
  in Saudi Arabia, 213
  in South Africa, 198
  in Taiwan, 46–51, 170–171
  in U.S., 150–151, 168
  watering down of, 166

teacher shortages, 166–167
  global, 167
  in Saudi Arabia, 214–215
  in U.S., 166–167, 221
teacher-centered schools, 182–187
teachers. *See also specific topics*
  commonalities, 163
  in community, 2–3
  in comparative perspective,
    163–187
  depiction of, 3
  differences among, 163
  good, 163–164
  importance of talented, 1–2
  verbal ability of, 217
teachers' lounge
  in Azerbaijan, 76–77
  in Chile, 129
  in Finland, 19–20
  in Greece, 58
teaching
  challenging students, 143–148
  conditions for, global, 185–186
  first year of, 210–211, 214–215
  in rural schools, 189–190
  strongest students, 153–155
teaching profession
  attitudes toward, 186–187
  attracting people to, 185–186
  in Azerbaijan, 95–96
  competition in, 22
  complexity of, 168–169
  criticism of, 170
  difficult entry into, 167–172
  feminization of, 3–4, 173–174
  in France, 119–121
  global comparison of, 15
  global perspective on, 5–9
  in Greece, 61, 63–65, 70–72
  in the Philippines, 188
  interest in, 167
  intrinsic rewards of, 179
  morality and, 3–4, 223–224
  prestige of, 1–2
  psychic rewards of, 173–174, 179
  religion and, 4, 179
  service and, 4–5
  in Taiwan, 54–56
  in U.S., 2–5, 158–161
teaching schedule
  in Azerbaijan, 78–79
  in Chile, 128–132
  in Finland, 18
  in France, 117
  in the Philippines, 190
  in Saudi Arabia, 213
  in South Africa, 199, 203

in Taiwan, 51–54
in U.S., 152
technical high schools
in Brazil, 192–193
in France, 99, 113–114
tenure
in Chile, 128
in Finland, 24
in Greece, 64–65
testing. *See* examinations
traditional authority, 175
traditionalism, in Taiwan, 46
tutoring, in Azerbaijan, 78

unemployment
in Finland, 33
in Greece, 61
unions
in Chile, 138
in France, 115–116, 220
metaphors for teachers and, 179
multidisciplinary teaching and, 116
politics and, 115–116
United States (U.S.), 14–15, 141–162
ability grouping in, 148–149, 159–160
AP testing in, 148–149
athletics in, 155
authority in, 175
book-learning in, 165
critical thinking skills in, 153
curriculums in, 152–153, 184
disabilities education in, 144
diversity in, 141, 151–152, 160–161
education policy in, 184–185
education reform in, 1–2
feminization of teaching profession in,
173–174
France and, 111–112
group discussion in, 145
integrated, 148–149
intellectualism in, 221
Kansas, teaching in, 221
low-level classes in, 143–149

minorities in, 148–149, 169–170
motherhood in, 157–158
motivating students in, 159–160
prestige of teachers in, 1–2, 165
reading level in, 143
respect in, 184
school administration in, 152
school announcements in, 159
socioeconomic class in, 142, 151–152
student behavioral problems in, 160–161
student participation in, 146–148, 153–154
student teaching in, 150–151
students in, 143–148, 153–155
teacher preparation in, 150–151, 168
teacher salaries in, 173–174
teacher shortages in, 166–167, 221
teacher success in, 183–184
teaching in, 143–148
teaching internships in, 150–151
teaching profession in, 2–5, 158–161
teaching schedule in, 152
Windsor High School, Connecticut, 141–142
work/life balance in, 156–157
university entrance examinations, 77–78, 97
U.S. *See* United States

veteran teachers, reenergizing, 186
violence
Charlie Hebdo terrorist attacks, 110
in Chile, 220
in the Philippines, 189–191
slow, 226

Walkerdine, Valerie, 182
Waller, Willard, 4–5
whole child, teaching, 27–34
Windsor High School, Connecticut, 141–142
diversity in, 141
work/life balance, 103, 157–158
in Azerbaijan, 81–83
in France, 101–103
in Taiwan, 52–53
in U.S., 156–157